THE BIG CHILL

THE BIG CHILL

EVE PELL

with research assistance by Seth Rosenfeld

How the Reagan administration, corporate America, and religious conservatives are subverting free speech and the public's right to know

BEACON PRESS BOSTON

Beacon Press books are published under the auspices
of the Unitarian Universalist Association of
Congregations in North America,
25 Beacon Street, Boston, Massachusetts 02108
Published simultaneously in Canada by
Fitzhenry and Whiteside Limited, Toronto

Printed in the United States of America

(hardcover) 9 8 7 6 5 4 3 2 1

Library of Congress Cataloging in Publication Data

Pell, Eve.
The big chill.

Bibliography: p.
Includes index.
1. Freedom of speech—United States. 2. Freedom of
the press—United States. I. Title.
JC599.U5P375 1984 323.44'3'0973 83-71942
ISBN 0-8070-6160-3

For my sons—Daniel, Peter, and John

Acknowledgments

The Center for Investigative Reporting took this book under its kindly wing and provided encouragement, coffee, and files from the very beginning. The C S Fund helped with money, as did the J. Roderick MacArthur Foundation, Stanley Sheinbaum, and Carol and W. H. Ferry. Viola Weinberg of C S consistently showed her deep concern and that of the Fund for open government and First Amendment rights. The idea for this book began with MaryAnn Lash, formerly at Beacon Press.

Organizations whose work contributed much to this book include the American Civil Liberties Union, the Campaign for Political Rights, the Center for Constitutional Rights, the Center for National Security Studies, the Data Center, the Fund for Open Information and Accountability, Inc., the National Emergency Civil Liberties Committee, the National Coalition Against Censorship, the National Coalition Against Repressive Legislation, People for the American Way, the Reporters Committee for Freedom of the Press, and the Society of Professional Journalists, Sigma Delta Chi.

I am indebted for ideas and insights to Seth Rosenfeld, associate at the Center for Investigative Reporting, who helped edit and write parts of the government section.

I am indebted to readers and critics who waded through early drafts: Jean Dickinson, Dr. Harold Relyea, and Mary Clemmey.

My gratitude goes to purveyors of moral support and encouragement: Nat Hentoff, Laura Lent, Karen O'Neil, Ann Kyle, David Burnham, Eleanor Bertino, Peter Franck, Nina Serrano, Haven and Simmy Pell, Michael Castleman, David Weir, Matt Rothman, Susan Trott, Margaret Livingston, James Myers, Robert Kennedy, Victor Navasky, Ben Bagdikian, and my editor, Joanne Wyckoff. Jeff Smith and Chiquita Sturgis of Beacon Press took on the painstaking task of the end notes.

People who helped me understand the issues and provided information include Tonda Rush, Dan Noyes, Elaine Elinson, Amitai Schwartz, Susan Jaffe, Margaret Crosby, David Bank, Leanne Katz, Ann Mari Buitrago, Richard Reynolds, Michael Ratner, Diana Hembree, Maggie Roth, James Larson, Dennis Riordan, Robert Wellington, Michael Miller, Barbara Parker, and Marcie Ricken.

Special thanks to George Frazier, Angus Mackenzie, Doug Foster, Zoia Horn, Valerie Miner, Elizabeth Farnsworth, Elinor Blake and Mary Jean Haley who generously helped with all the above and much more.

Contents

THE BIG CHILL

Introduction

Congress shall make no law respecting an establishment of religion, or prohibiting the exercise thereof; or abridging the freedom of speech, or of the press; or the right of the people peaceably to assemble, and to petition the government for a redress of grievances.

—First Amendment to the Constitution

Conflicts over access to information and freedom of expression are hardly new in these United States, but now, in the early 1980s, they are particularly widespread and acute. At issue are major questions like these: Who is allowed to know what about our government? How much is the press allowed to publish, about either public or private matters? How free is the individual to express ideas and to engage in political activity? To what extent is dissent to be tolerated within our society?

All of these issues revolve around the First Amendment. And while they may appear wide ranging and abstract, they are, fundamentally, situations that can affect us all:

• Teachers say they should be able to determine reading lists for their classes without interference. Parents want the right to forbid books of which they disapprove.

• Reporters want the right to learn whether or not nuclear weapons are stored near a particular town. The military wants the right to refuse to disclose that information.

• Unions maintain that workers have the right to know what chemicals they work with and the effects of those chemicals. Companies maintain they have the right to keep that information secret.

• Consumer groups say that a parent should be able to learn from a government agency whether or not infants have had a series of accidents involving a particular toy. Manufacturers want the agencies to restrict the information.

• An environmental group challenges a city council's decision to allow a developer's condominium project. The developer sues the environmental group for libel.

The First Amendment to the U.S. Constitution guarantees certain rights that we believe to be basic to democracy. But these rights must be reexamined and redefined from time to time as conditions change and new issues arise. As information becomes more and more a source of power, First Amendment rights suffer new encroachments. The most apparent and the ultimate life-threatening issue, of course, is the possibility of nuclear war. A secrecy-prone administration could set off a nuclear war through policies never debated in public. How much information must be kept secret in order to maintain our national security? How much openness is required for the democratic process to be meaningful? President Reagan said in an interview with *TV Guide,* "Trust us." His critics feel that is not the answer.

The federal government has become, over the years, a major source of information about all aspects of our lives. The government sucks up data like a huge vacuum cleaner, runs them through various agencies in Washington, and makes them available through reports and publications. From the census to economic indicators to health studies and agricultural techniques, the federal government plays a major role in collecting, interpreting, and disseminating information about almost everything we do. How much of what is collected should be open to the public? These questions arise in the 1980s because a number of powerful forces on the U.S. political scene are pressing for a more closed form of government and for cutbacks in freedom of expression, freedom of the press, and the public's right to know.

Let us turn briefly to the right of the public to know what its government does. Freedom of speech and freedom of the press are guaranteed by the First Amendment to the Constitution, and while people may differ over what these freedoms mean and how far they extend, as a nation we recognize that those are fundamental rights. The "right to know" is not as universally recognized, since it is not spelled out in the Constitution, but it is just as important. For if you cannot know what your government is doing, how can you or the press usefully exercise your rights to speak and to publish? No matter how artfully writers, broadcasters, and speakers may express themselves, without accurate information their views are meaningless or misleading. Justice William O. Douglas took note of this in a 1965 Supreme Court decision recognizing the right to know; Congress recognized the right to know in legislation establishing the Freedom of Information Act in 1966.[1] James Madison, founding father and fourth president, put it this way:

> A popular Government without popular information, or the means of acquiring it, is but a Prologue to a Farce or a Tragedy; or, perhaps both. Knowledge will forever govern ignorance; And a people who mean to

> be their own Governors, must arm themselves with the power, which knowledge gives.[2]

Whatever their reasons, high officials in the Reagan administration have shown themselves ill disposed to openness in government. Jerry Friedheim, a former Pentagon public affairs officer who is now an executive with the American Newspaper Publishers Association, says the Reagan administration "seems deliberately bent on replacing our historic presumption of openness in government with a presumption of closure." [3]

A number of influential congressmen, like Senator Orrin Hatch of Utah, also believe that openness in government can endanger national security. A rationale for their views is expressed in the Heritage Foundation's 1980 agenda for the newly elected president and his appointees. A conservative think tank, the Heritage Foundation recommended weakening the Freedom of Information Act, strengthening the capacity of the Central Intelligence Agency for covert action, and monitoring leftist political organizations, all in the interests of protecting the national security.

The foundation also expressed considerable distrust of politically active citizens and even of ordinary citizens who speak their minds. The report warned that "clergymen, students, businessmen, entertainers, labor officials, journalists, and government workers may engage in subversive activities without being fully aware of the extent, purpose, or control of their activities." [4] It suggested the use of private companies to monitor dissenters, since private companies would be under no obligation to respect an individual's constitutional rights.

The press is the only private industry mentioned in our Constitution. It is the fourth estate of government, charged with the responsibility of keeping the public informed. How much should the press know? What should it be able to say? In an era that has seen intense controversy over the publication of the Pentagon Papers and the *Progressive*'s article on the H-bomb, and government efforts to prevent both from seeing the light of day, more rather than fewer controversies are expected. From many quarters in the federal government—bureaucrats who don't want the public looking over their shoulders, intelligence operatives who wish to work in secret, conservative legislators who believe that government has an inherent right to shut out public scrutiny and participation, former business executives accustomed to privacy who are now running federal agencies—from all these and more there appears a bias against openness in government.

But government isn't the only arena for conflicts over the public's right to know, freedom of the press, and the proper extent of freedom of expression. Reporting about nongovernmental issues is also in question, as libel suits increase in number and the dollar amounts of judgments soar. Those interested in suppressing certain kinds of criticism have found a novel tool in recent years: the libel suit. Utility companies building nuclear power plants sue antinuclear demonstrators for libel and slander. Police officers sue citizens who complain of police brutality. What are critics and protesters allowed to say? Does this use of the courts amount to censorship?

Censorship itself has mushroomed in the early 1980s. The number of reported attempts to censor books has leaped from one hundred annually in the early 1970s to almost one thousand in 1981, with actual bannings taking place in at least thirty-four states. Schoolteachers and librarians face outraged groups of parents and citizens flatly opposed to certain books. Members of the Moral Majority, for instance, share a strong desire to legislate morality—the way people spend their daily lives, and the way they express themselves. Some of this stems from a fear of diversity. How much variety is to be tolerated? Can fundamentalist religious parents force the banning of books they dislike? How about black parents concerned about racial stereotypes in texts?

The question of diversity also applies to political dissenters and critics of the government. Since the Reagan administration came into office, several organizations that gather and publish information and opinion running counter to administration policies have had their nonprofit tax status challenged by the Internal Revenue Service. Though no harassment of those groups may be intended, at the least the IRS audits prompt the people involved to consider very carefully what they should publish, and self-censorship takes hold as the groups fear further unwanted attention. Still the question remains. What is the proper role of the government toward dissenting groups and individuals? Such questions are now increasing in both urgency and frequency as opposing interests choose sides and slug it out in Congress, the courts, and the press.

Corporate America, the most powerful segment of our society, is more aggressive than ever in striking out at critics by means of lawsuits and economic pressure. With the vast resources at their command, the corporations have the means to stifle some critics and to deter others. Certainly, the business community has never lacked power in the United States, but until recently the exercise of that power has been out of fashion. In contrast to the 1960s and early 1970s, there is now less criticism of corporate values; greater importance is placed on efficiency, economic growth, and national security. Civil liberties and diversity seem to have faded in importance.

The confluence of these forces strongly opposed to the free circulation of ideas, information, and opinions bodes ill for our democratic way of life and our pluralistic society. Without free speech, a free press, and enforcement of the public's right to know, the people cannot be truly free.

The great innovation of the American Revolution was the idea that the people rule, not monarchs. In a system of popular sovereignty like ours, those in charge of the White House, the Congress, our state capitals, and local counties work for us, the citizens. And as their bosses, we have the right and the obligation to know what they are doing, particularly since we put them into office and pay their salaries.

Most of us bosses, however, spend our time earning a living, watching television, and worrying about our personal affairs, and we have neither the time nor the energy to become involved in government or to supervise our employees. That's one reason why we have the press. Thomas Jefferson wrote before he was president:

> The basis of our government being the opinion of the people, the very first object should be to keep that right; and were it left to me to decide whether we should have a government without newspapers or newspapers without a government, I should not hesitate a moment to prefer the latter.[5]

Over the years since the Revolution, our freedoms have evolved unevenly. Our nation did not, as history texts might lead one to believe, have its origin in a golden age of liberty. At times, the government has failed to honor the guarantees of the First Amendment. During World War I, for instance, a Minnesota man was convicted for belittling the efforts of patriotic women who were knitting socks for soldiers.

But laws are not the only forces that affect our rights to free speech and press, and to know what our government is doing. Less tangible things —climates of opinion, social movements, the state of the economy, shifts in popular culture—also determine what we feel able to say as well as the way the press functions and the government responds. Our fears of repercussion, of having to suffer for what we say, are as important as the law in determining whether or not we exercise our political freedoms. Yet unless people can and do speak out, full debate of issues cannot take place.

For almost one hundred years after the Civil War, most blacks in the South did not exercise their constitutional rights or protest segregation. Partly they were deterred by laws, partly by fears for their physical safety and that of their families, as well as by fears of losing their jobs and of being socially ostracized. But in the 1960s they mobilized themselves and white supporters to gain the exercise of their rights. Since then, blacks have changed their lives and, in so doing, have changed the actions of the federal government as well.

The so-called chilling effect on the exercise of our freedoms is hard to document while it is taking place, since the same fears that lead people to keep quiet in the first place also keep them from mentioning their silence. These pressures to conform, which have been labeled prevenient restrictions, suffocate free debate. In addition, besides chilling free speech, the process effectively thwarts social change, since the less powerful are intimidated by the more powerful. The process also hampers the interchange of ideas and impedes freedom in universities and scientific investigation. (Galileo, a victim of the same process in an earlier time, was excommunicated for saying that the earth revolved around the sun. He ultimately had to recant, and science had to wait until another age for the acceptance of this more accurate picture of the solar system.) If certain ideas are labeled unpatriotic or subversive by authorities, people will hesitate to advocate them, and the merits of those ideas will never be known. Democracy and diversity suffer.

As we examine the state of free speech, freedom of the press, and the public's right to know, let us bear in mind not only the specified result of any law or order but also the possible chilling effect. While more subtle, it may be the more important.

OF SWINGING PENDULUMS

At a time when the mails, phone lines, airwaves, and even space itself throb with an infinite variety of messages and communications, it may seem odd and inappropriate to call for increased freedom of expression and for a fuller exercise of the public's right to know. Haven't we enough information?

True. We have. But let us look at the swinging pendulum. From the middle 1960s to the middle 1970s, unconventional life styles blossomed, free speech flourished, and the public's belief that it had a right to know what its government did gained strength. There were underground papers, hippies, outpourings of protest against racism in the South, and hundreds of thousands of demonstrators marching in the streets against an unpopular war. Publication of the Pentagon Papers in 1971 unmasked Lyndon Johnson's deception of the American people about the origins of the Vietnam War. Reporting by Bob Woodward and Carl Bernstein, Seymour Hersh, and others exposed the Watergate scandal, My Lai, and the CIA's Operation CHAOS. Women were demanding their rights, as were minorities and gays. Traditional American values like the family, business success, and flag-waving patriotism went out of style, at least among the segments of the population and the press that commanded the most attention.

The Freedom of Information Act, first passed in 1966, was strengthened in 1974 and the changes passed over the veto of President Ford. Journalism schools were flooded with applications as investigative reporting became almost as glamorous a profession as acting. The public's right to know was seen as a weapon against the doers of evil. In large part because of the actions of President Richard Nixon, who resigned rather than face impeachment proceedings, and the actions of his predecessor, Lyndon Johnson, the press and public developed some distrust of their leaders.

But the national mood changed. The full pardon granted Nixon by President Ford wrapped him in full immunity from prosecution. With a new president generally perceived as decent if not very bright, the ending of the Vietnam War, and perhaps an overall weariness after so much upheaval, the nation proceeded into what some call the me generation.

As the seventies waned, protest became less shrill. Women, instead of wanting to overthrow the system, learned to climb the ladder of success. The more flamboyant minority protesters were dead, jailed, engaged in local politics, or involved in something else. Pot smokers took up white wine and gin; marijuana brownies were replaced by croissants. The economy sagged and inflation worsened, and earning a living took priority over reforming the system. Hippies had to raise their children.

The international situation shifted, as the Iranians overthrew the shah and took American hostages, the Russians marched into Afghanistan, and socialist governments took power in Grenada, Nicaragua, and, for a short time, Jamaica. It was time, said many politicians and commentators, for America to pay for its excesses. We were told that our defenses were weak; our military power was second to that of the Russians, and we could not match our competitors abroad. Too many had fattened at the federal trough for too long; belts had to be tightened.

As it turned out, the new leaders of the 1980s believed that certain belts needed tightening more than others, especially the belts of the old, the disabled, the sick, and the young. Those of defense contractors, by contrast, loosened as the military budget grew. The belts of oil and gas company executives could be let out a few notches as utility bills doubled and tripled after the deregulation of energy prices.

The new mood reflected changes throughout the nation. The rise of the right-wing religious fundamentalists, epitomized by the Moral Majority's Jerry Falwell, brought a radically different attitude toward free speech, the press, and the public's right to know. Books were burned; writers were urged to be "positive" about America, to extol its virtues and lay off its sins. The public wanted to hear "good news" and to be able to trust its leaders again.

Even the values of democratic self-government were questioned. James Robison, television evangelist extraordinaire, suggested, "We might raise up a tyrant who might not have the best ethics to protect the freedom interests of the ethical and the godly." [6] The Reverend Jerry Falwell stated that he did not want everybody to vote, because the strength of Christian fundamentalists increased as voting decreased.[7] A few right-wing fundamentalists talked about changing the Constitution so that the godly could take over the country and enact their values into law. Although the political influence of the right-wing Christian fundamentalists in the Reagan administration has, perhaps, declined in the early 1980s, they nonetheless remain active in the censoring of books and in opposing sex education in schools—both free speech issues—and in opposing abortion.

The ethos of these groups runs directly opposite to the values of open government and democracy. Those who assert that the Bible tells citizens how to vote on issues of public policy do not value open discussion, since the correct answer is already written and available to the faithful. The viewpoint of the Moral Majority may reflect only a minority in the country, but it is a vocal, well-funded, well-organized pressure group. It represents the most extreme point to the right of the swinging pendulum, a point at which concern for civil liberties and a well-informed public is negligible.

The fundamentalist preacher, the corporate executive, the right-wing ideologue, and the CIA agent may not have much in common with one another. But in the early 1980s, it is fair to say that all of them are more highly thought of and more influential than they were ten years earlier. And, in general, they do not regard openness in government or society as beneficial.

The various attempts to stifle free speech and other freedoms stem in large part from corporate America's need to silence its critics. If we look at whose speech is being threatened and whose speech is not, we gain an understanding of who tends to benefit from silence. A small example: The nuclear industry finds itself troubled by a vociferous lobby of antinuclear activists. In economic trouble, with its power plants being shut down because of technical breakdowns and its costs skyrocketing, the industry is beleaguered. Meanwhile, the Reagan administration, cutting down on government publications in order to reduce federal expenditures, eliminated numerous publications promoting solar and alternative sources of power; publications promoting nuclear power were not cut back so hard. Budget cutting applies to some information and some points of view, but not to others. Furthermore, the government's steps to increase the amount of information it may hold secret also strengthens the hand of a business-oriented administration at the expense of consumers and less affluent citizens. Without information about the chemical ingredients of products, for instance, buyers cannot learn about possible harmful or adverse effects from those products.

One can argue that there is little connection between wanting to protect the CIA from publicity that could be threatening to the national security and wanting to prevent workers from gaining access to knowledge about the chemicals with which they work, as was recently proposed by the Occupational Safety and Health Administration (OSHA). The theme that unifies those two positions is the right to know as the bedrock of citizen power: the right of the citizen to see that the CIA no longer runs unchecked in the Third World, and the right of workers to know what risks they are running every day in the factory or office.

Who is the opposition to government secrecy? The other side comprises the environmentalists, antinuclear activists, labor unions, civil libertarians, liberals and leftists, pacifists, much of the press, feminists —in short, those who fear abuses from a corporate sector that already holds tremendous power, and from an administration that favors those corporate interests over the interests of others.

These groups, in general, advocate freedom of expression and favor tolerance of diversity in society. Some, like the American Civil Liberties Union (ACLU), even defend unpopular groups like Nazis, communists, and pornographers. Many like the ACLU feel that the public needs to be fully informed about policy issues in order to debate those issues. In general, they have less money than the opposition; they also consider themselves to be the true heirs of the founding fathers, in their advocacy of open government, democracy, and pluralism. These groups question the belief that the unregulated free market always operates to the benefit of society, and they oppose the concentration of power in the corporate sector. They support decentralized power and the public's right to know. They tend to question authority, be skeptical of official press releases, and be concerned about the rights of minorities, women, and the individual.

Any delineation of the two sides runs the risk of oversimplification and of failing to do justice to the variety of groups and individuals involved. That is the danger of linking a variety of issues in which so many different kinds of people are engaged. Certainly there are more than two sides to these issues, as we will see in the chapters to come.

The current conflicts over free speech, a free press, and the right to know strike at the heart of our democracy. Once again, it is time to discover the value and the meaning of our historic First Amendment rights.

1

History

"It is by the goodness of God," wrote Mark Twain, "that in our country we have those three unspeakably precious things: freedom of speech, freedom of conscience, and the prudence never to practice either of them." Any quick study of the history of First Amendment rights shows the basis of Twain's cynicism, for those who fought the battles for freedom of speech, press, assembly, and religion often paid a painful price.

Despite the democratic ideals that inspired the American Revolution and the ringing rhetoric of the founding fathers, free speech arrived late on the American scene.

It was not until 1919 that a series of significant free speech cases reached the U.S. Supreme Court, forcing the justices to define the limits of the First Amendment, despite the uncountable occasions before that time when free speech had been denied. During the infamous Palmer Raids at the opening of the year 1920, for example, more than five thousand people were rounded up in mass arrests—because they were suspected of holding radical political opinions. Peaceful picketing was not given constitutional sanction until 1940. In the 1950s, people lost their jobs because of presumed political associations. The right to assemble peacefully in protest against government policy was not won until the 1960s. And yet, ironically, although one can make a strong case showing how intolerant and hypocritical our nation has been in its treatment of dissenters, our First Amendment is the strongest guarantee of civil and political freedom anywhere on this planet. In addition, a greater number of people in the United States today can exercise those freedoms far more fully than ever was possible in the past.

Most histories of the First Amendment begin by quoting the amendment in full, explaining its preeminent position in the Bill of Rights as the bedrock of our democracy. Then, perhaps after quoting some stirring words declaimed by one of the founding fathers, the author goes on to say that the First Amendment does not mean what it says, and in fact it never has, for there have always been restrictions on free speech. One of the reasons for these restrictions is the way our legal system functions. The Constitution, together with its amendments, is the ultimate authority on what the government and its citizens can and cannot do. When state law says one thing and federal law another, federal law takes precedence. The U.S. Supreme Court is the final arbiter of legal issues.

Let us trace the history of one case. In the late 1950s and 1960s, the civil rights movement was shaking the South. Blacks were organizing to gain equal treatment with whites and to change laws that discriminated against them. Many were arrested for sitting in at lunch counters and restaurants that refused to serve them, charged by local police with disturbing the peace.

In March 1961, a group of black students decided to march to the State House in Columbia, South Carolina, to ask the legislators there to end discrimination. They marched in an orderly line, carrying signs with messages like "I am Proud to be a Negro" and "Down with Segregation." The Columbia city manager, who along with about thirty policemen was watching the demonstration, ordered the crowd to disperse. The crowd stayed on, singing "We Shall Overcome" and "The Star-Spangled Banner." The police arrested 187.

At trial, all were found guilty. The case could have ended at this point, but the demonstrators, aided by the National Association for the Advancement of Colored People (NAACP) Legal Defense and Educational Fund, appealed to the South Carolina Supreme Court. Lawyers for the state said the blacks were guilty of disturbing the peace. Lawyers for the blacks said they had simply exercised their First Amendment right to free expression, to free assembly, and to petition for the redress of grievances. The high court of South Carolina upheld their convictions.

Unwilling to give in, the demonstrators appealed to the U.S. Supreme Court, saying that their federal constitutional rights had been violated. The Supreme Court agreed to hear the case and said that the South Carolina law under which they had been convicted was too vague and broad to be valid. The case, *Edwards v. South Carolina,* took two years from the time of the demonstration to the final decision. It set an important precedent: Any state that prosecuted peaceful demonstrators by using a law like the one the U.S. Supreme Court had ruled unconstitutional would probably not succeed. This decision meant a great deal to the civil rights movement. But it is important to note that even though the demonstrators won this major legal battle in 1963, Southern states did not instantly wipe discriminatory laws off the books or stop arresting peaceful demonstrators. Civil rights activists continued to take part in other demonstrations in other Southern states; many of them also were convicted and appealed those convictions. Thus, other unconstitutional state laws were struck down.

The *Edwards* case illustrates that while the Constitution and the Bill of Rights permit the exercise of democratic rights, those rights must be fought for time and again. The First Amendment does not, as we shall see, assure that the right to free expression and political association and assembly will automatically be protected. *Edwards* also shows how we rely *on* the government to protect us from encroachments on our rights *by* the government: The federal courts were called on to protect the demonstrators from state laws.

Yet historically, the Supreme Court has often failed to protect speakers and activists from governmental violations of their rights. During World War I, for instance, a small band of immigrant anarchist socialists wrote a leaflet to protest the action of the United States in sending troops to Russia. The leaflets called on Americans to unite against capitalism; one called for a general strike so that American bullets would not be used against Russian revolutionaries. Jacob Abrams and four associates distributed the leaflets by flinging them from the window of their third-floor rear apartment in New York City. For this act, three were sentenced to twenty years, one was sentenced to fifteen years, and one received three years. They were convicted of violating the Espionage Act, which Congress had passed in 1917 and strengthened in 1918 as the much-feared Bolshevik Revolution toppled the czar.[1] The Espionage Act made certain criticisms of our government illegal.

Plainly, a flutter of leaflets from a Lower East Side window posed no danger to the security of the United States, particularly since some were written in Yiddish. But that did not matter to the court that convicted them or to the U.S. Supreme Court, which in 1919 upheld their conviction. The act passed by Congress stood; the free speech rights of Jacob Abrams fell.

During wartime and other crises in our history, our government has ignored the limitations placed on its powers by the First Amendment and has effectively extinguished criticism of its policies. At other times, it has upheld the right of the people and press to speak out. Historical circumstances (and even accidents) help to determine how fully we can exercise our First Amendment rights without risking prosecution. Laws and their interpretation do not take place in a vacuum. All the factors that shape human history come into play to influence the expansion and contraction of what the government will permit. For while the law pretends to be abstract and distant from the ebb and flow of emotion and contemporary trends, it is just as open to influence by social, political, or economic trends as any other human institution. The personalities of individuals who sit on lower or higher courts, the peace or peril of international relations, the tenor of the times—all these contribute to the decisions reached.

The history of our rights is by no means just the history of Supreme Court decisions. It also includes those mobs and vigilantes who sacked and burned newspapers (and even sometimes killed editors). It includes congressional committee members who dedicated themselves to rooting out one political heresy or another; the antiimmigrant hysterias that have periodically seized the nation; and the fanatics, visionaries, and dissenters who refused to be silenced and fought tenaciously for their right to think and say what they believed. It also includes individuals and groups who fought to protect their rights and organized to protest abuses of governmental power like Watergate and the Vietnam War. As Edwin S. Newman writes,

> Under the Constitution, the government should not act to quiet an unpopular viewpoint; but there was little to stand in the way of a mob riding a man out of town because he spoke his mind.[2]

Even as the framers drafted the Constitution and the Bill of Rights, people of color, women, and minors could not claim the right of equal protection of the law, and they really could not exercise the freedoms guaranteed by the First Amendment. Large segments of the population do not even appear in traditional histories because they had no rights they could exercise. Apart from a brief time during Reconstruction, blacks had no enforceable rights despite the passage of the Fourteenth Amendment after the Civil War. The rights of aliens and noncitizens suffered many limitations, and for years the government followed the act of Congress passed in 1790 which restricted naturalization to free, white persons.

Only quite recently in our history did Congress remove racial restrictions on citizenship, and until it did so the courts upheld the restrictions. In 1870, Congress allowed persons of African birth or descent to become eligible. In 1924, Congress recognized all native-born Indians as citizens of the U.S. Chinese immigrants were made eligible for citizenship in 1943, Filipinos in 1946. Japanese immigrants, who had been eligible until a Supreme Court decision in 1922, did not become eligible again until 1952.[3] Minorities have thus only recently come under full constitutional protection. As historian Milton Konvitz notes, "These developments remind us that American democracy has had a gradual, and a painfully and embarrassingly slow, evolution."[4]

The First Amendment was not an afterthought tacked onto the Constitution because the framers had been absent-minded after the Revolution; it was a hotly debated issue. Because the Constitution gave only certain powers to the government, argued Alexander Hamilton and others, the government could not at a later time appropriate to itself other powers. According to that argument, the government was not given the specific power to limit speech or the press. Thus no Bill of Rights was needed.

James Madison, on the other hand, observed that the British Constitution failed to mention the right to free expression, and that government had certainly not restrained itself. In fact, as historian Irving Brant noted, "For hundreds of years Englishmen [were] fined, whipped, pilloried, imprisoned and had their ears cut off for speech and writings offensive to government or society." [5] Madison argued that the real danger in the new United States would be the tyranny of the majority over the minority; the government, representing the majority, should be prevented from violating the rights of the minority. Thus, minority rights had to be specifically assured. Madison's arguments carried the day, and the Bill of Rights was adopted in 1791.

Yet the struggle for free expression was just beginning. On the one hand, the adoption of the First Amendment represented an epochal advance in civil and political liberty. A truly revolutionary concept, the amendment meant that the people, as sovereign, had the right to say what they pleased about the government, their servant. It reversed the historic notion that the government, as represented by the king or queen, could punish the people for speaking out. The government could not chop the hands off pamphleteers or draw and quarter printers who offended their betters, as England had done well into the eighteenth century.

On the other hand, the First Amendment meant very little, because, a mere seven years after its adoption, in 1798, Congress violated those democratic guarantees by passing the Alien and Sedition Acts. These laws, written when Europe was reeling from the effects of the French Revolution, promised severe sanctions for writing, printing, or uttering words that would bring the president, Congress, the government, or the military "into contempt or disrepute."

The first prosecution under this act was brought against Congressman Matthew Lyon of Vermont for writing an article attacking President John Adams. Lyon wrote that "every consideration of the public welfare was swallowed up in a continual grasp for power, in an unbounded thirst for ridiculous pomp, foolish adulation and selfish avarice." He also published a letter from an American in France who said that Congress should commit President Adams to the madhouse. Lyon was convicted and sentenced to four months in prison and a $1,000 fine. His constituents responded by reelecting him to Congress while he languished behind bars.[6]

Popular outcry against the Alien and Sedition Acts contributed to the repudiation of Adams's Federalist party in the next election, which brought Thomas Jefferson to the presidency. Jefferson pardoned those who had been convicted under the acts, and Congress even repaid most of their fines. Jefferson endured vigorous criticism, but he abided by his principles and left the press alone.

Throughout the nineteenth century virtually no nationwide legal doctrine concerning the First Amendment was developed. Freedom of expression waxed and waned, but there was no nationwide policy because in one important respect the First Amendment meant exactly what it said: Congress shall make no law abridging the freedom of speech. Unlike the situation now, state and local governments could make whatever laws they wanted to limit free speech, press, assembly, and religion. And they did. In the South, especially, people could not speak freely. Before the Civil War, every Southern state except Kentucky had made it illegal to advocate the abolition of slavery. Even the state universities were bound by these laws.

Mobs acted to silence those with unpopular opinions. Angry crowds attacked the religious journal *The Observer,* an antislavery paper published by the Reverend Elijah Lovejoy of Alton, Illinois. Three separate times his press was torn apart and dumped in the nearby river. Three times he brought in another press, doggedly insisting on his right to publish his views. On one occasion he told a hostile assembly, "The present excitement will soon be over; the voice of conscience will at last be heard. And in some season of honest thought . . . you will be compelled to say, 'He was right; he was right.' " That day never came for Elijah Lovejoy. In November 1837, during yet another mob attack, he was shot and killed.[7]

Free speech did not wither during these years, but it flourished only sporadically, depending on the issues and historical situations. During the Civil War, Lincoln suspended the right of habeas corpus, permitting the arrest of approximately thirty-eight thousand people suspected of disloyalty to the Union. By contrast, criticism of the government escalated during the unpopular war with Mexico and during the Spanish-American War. Abolitionists and suffragettes sometimes spread their messages without difficulty; on other occasions they were arrested or beaten.

In 1868 the United States adopted the Fourteenth Amendment, which expressly forbids the states to abridge the rights of citizens and to deprive any citizen of life, liberty, or property without due process of law.

Much later, these provisions were interpreted in a way that overturned state and local laws limiting free expression, but for the first fifty-seven years after its adoption, such interpretation was expressly repudiated by the courts. In 1873, the U.S. Supreme Court ruled specifically that the federal government could not intervene to protect its citizens against state laws that limited their constitutional rights. As Irving Brant wrote, "If a state systematically violated the privileges and immunities of one class of its citizens, or of all of its citizens, what remedy did the victims have under this clause of the Constitution? They could walk into a federal courthouse and walk out again, enjoying the full protection of the Fourteenth Amendment until they reached the sidewalk." This happened, Brant explains, because "the plain and virtually admitted truth was that five members of the [Supreme] Court were not willing to extend freedom from slavery into equality with white freemen, because it would upset the established political and social order of racial inequality, and produce very serious transitional problems." [8] Free speech rights for all had to wait.

Certain groups of whites also suffered for expressing their ideas: aliens, workers seeking to organize, and political radicals. The assassination of President McKinley in 1901 by an American-born anarchist with a Polish surname further inflamed fear and hatred. The government deported aliens considered undesirable because of their political opinions and cultural heritage. In 1902 New York State forbade the advocacy of "criminal anarchy"—the idea that organized government should be overthrown by force and violence—and membership in any group that advocated that idea. Thus, even if an anarchist were to *do* nothing at all, but merely speak favorably about overthrowing governments, she or he could be prosecuted and imprisoned. Other states followed suit with similar legislation.

With the advent of World War I, prospects for free speech went from bad to dreadful. In 1917, Congress passed the Espionage Act, making it a crime to obstruct recruiting by the military, to attempt to cause insubordination, or to make false statements with the intent to interfere with U.S. military forces. A year later, Congress passed a second act, sometimes called the Sedition Act, to plug any loopholes that might have remained in the first, making it unlawful to express opinions contrary to the policy of the government, especially about the war or conscription. Several states passed similar laws. About two thousand prosecutions took place before the 1918 law was repealed in 1920. (The 1917 Espionage Act is still on the books.)

One case involved a woman named Rose Pastor Stokes, who was sentenced to ten years in prison for writing in a letter, "I am for the people and the government is for the profiteers." The Reverend Clarence Waldron of Windsor, Vermont, received a sentence of fifteen years for handing to five persons a leaflet saying that Christians ought not to take up arms. A former British soldier named D. H. Wallace was sentenced to twenty years for saying that soldiers were giving up their lives for capitalists, and that allied forces were issued defective guns and ammunition because of graft. The conviction of Mrs. Stokes was later overturned, and the Reverend Mr. Waldron subsequently was pardoned, but Wallace went insane in prison and died there.

During this inauspicious period, the U.S. Supreme Court began to formulate a First Amendment doctrine. Supreme Court decisions set precedents; in arriving at decisions, the justices sometimes establish tests, or standards, by which issues are to be judged. These tests then are used by lower courts to determine how the laws within their jurisdiction are to be interpreted to accord with the Supreme Court's decision. The first in a series of free speech cases to come before the justices involved Charles T. Schenck, who appealed his conviction for distributing socialist circulars opposing the draft. In 1919, Justice Oliver Wendell Holmes wrote in *Schenck*:

> The most stringent protection of free speech would not protect a man in falsely shouting fire in a theatre and causing panic . . . . The question in every case is whether the words used are used in such circumstances and are of such a nature as to create a *clear and present danger* that they will bring about the substantive evils that Congress has a right to prevent. It is a question of proximity and degree [emphasis added].

Thus, speech that posed a clear and present danger was not protected by the First Amendment, and people who engaged in it could be prosecuted. It did not matter that Schenck's circulars had absolutely no known effect on conscription. If judges or juries said the speech posed a clear and present danger, the speaker was guilty. Paradoxically, this famous decision developed into a standard for the protection of critical expression. While bad for Schenck, it was an improvement in the law.

Another standard that came to be used about this time was the less protective "bad tendency" test. If speech might have even an indirect bad effect on military recruitment or the war effort, then it could be punished. This standard allowed for less freedom of expression than the "clear and present danger" standard: A poem favorably likening anarchist Emma Goldman to the wind could be censored, and it was. This bad tendency test was also called killing the serpent in the egg, because it stopped the bad idea from spreading. This test flew in the face of the American ideals of tolerance and free expression. It diminished diversity of opinion and punished the expression of certain ideas. It reflected the state of public opinion at the time, a harsh climate indeed for those who held unorthodox political views.

In 1925, the Supreme Court decided another landmark case, and took a significant step forward in the evolution of First Amendment rights. In the case of Benjamin Gitlow, who had written a left-wing manifesto in a socialist newspaper in New York, the justices reversed longstanding precedents and held that the Fourteenth Amendment protected First Amendment freedoms. Unfortunately, Gitlow, like Schenck, went to prison, along with his associates, because the Court found that their exhortations to "revolutionary mass action" incited the readers to overthrow the government. Even though the Court found that Gitlow's writings had no effect on the body politic, it ruled that the government had the right to "suppress the threatened danger in its incipiency." (Or, to use the more colorful phrase, to kill the serpent in the egg.) As Nat Hentoff writes in his excellent history of the First Amendment, "There are times when the reasoning of the High Court is not particularly lucid, and [Gitlow] was one of those instances." For although the manifesto posed no danger to orderly government and although it violated a state law that the Court found unconstitutional, Gitlow's conviction stood anyway because of the manifesto's "bad tendencies." [9]

With the *Gitlow* decision, the Fourteenth Amendment—more than fifty years after it had been adopted—became the instrument that would force state and local governments to respect First Amendment guarantees of free speech and a free press. Any law that denied those rights could be challenged in federal court and ruled unconstitutional.

In 1931, the Supreme Court reversed a Minnesota law that permitted the shutting down of offensive publications (*Near v. Minnesota*). The writings in the *Minneapolis Saturday Press* were far from attractive. In accusing a cabal of Jewish gangsters of running rackets in Minneapolis, the paper said, "Practically every vendor of vile hooch, every owner of a moonshine still, every snake-faced gangster and embryonic egg in the Twin Cities is a JEW. . . . It is Jew, Jew, Jew, as long as one cares to comb over the records." But even though blatantly racist, the writings were protected from prior restraint. The judges ruled that even a scandal sheet whose accusations were not necessarily accurate could publish. Quoting James Madison, the opinion said, "Some degree of abuse is inseparable from the proper use of everything, and in no instance is this more true than that of the press. . . . It is better to leave a few of its noxious branches to their luxuriant growth, than, by pruning them away, to injure the vigour of those yielding the proper fruits." [10]

The Supreme Court, of course, cannot simply declare laws invalid. It has to wait until a case makes its way through the lower courts, decide to hear it, then reach a decision. In this case, the Minnesota regulation of newspapers was deemed incompatible with a free press.

Another 1931 decision, *Stromberg v. California,* overturned a California law forbidding display of red flags. Fears of political radicals, besides restricting spoken and written speech, had also resulted in state laws forbidding symbolic speech—the display of colors, buttons, emblems, and so forth. By 1920, thirty-two states carried such laws on their books. West Virginia forbade any display "indicating sympathy or support of ideals, institutions or forms of government hostile, inimical, or antagonistic to the form or spirit of the Constitution, laws, ideals and institutions of this state or of the United States." (A Massachusetts law prohibiting red or black flags was repealed, not because a particular concern for free expression suddenly arose in that state, but because the law inadvertently prohibited the brandishing of the Harvard crimson.) The 1931 decision served to expand the rights of dissenters to express their feelings; for instance, people could hang from a window an American flag with a peace symbol superimposed on it to indicate opposition to the Vietnam War, or wave red and black flags to show support for the United Farm Workers, or even wear swastikas in a Nazi parade in Skokie, Illinois.

A 1937 decision stemmed from the case of Angelo Herndon, a black Communist party organizer active in Georgia. He was convicted of inciting insurrection under a state law that allowed the death penalty for such actions. During his trial the prosecution focused on the pamphlets in his possession, which called for Negro self-determination, the establishment of a Black Belt in the South, and the right of the Negro majority there to rule the white minority. The Supreme Court threw out his conviction, calling the Georgia law too vague in its sweeping prohibitions.[11]

It is instructive to consider that less than fifty years ago, a state law carried the death penalty for the kind of political organizing Herndon was engaged in. In fact, First Amendment rights suffered as the 1930s began. When the Depression struck, millions of Americans were out of work and in bread lines, and the national self-confidence reached a low point. These conditions breed intolerance and repression. Jerold S. Auerbach, a specialist in the history of civil liberties, describes the period this way:

> The most immediate impact of hard times on the Bill of Rights was a rapid acceleration of civil liberties infractions. Fear of unrest and disorder amid economic catastrophe produced more civil liberties cases in the early months of 1930 than in any single year since World War I. The number of free speech prosecutions jumped from 228 in 1929 to

1,630 in 1930; the number of meetings prohibited or disbanded increased from 52 to 121; incidents of mob violence more than quintupled; and lynchings nearly tripled. Indeed, for the first half of the Depression decade, there was a dismaying uniformity to the pattern of civil liberties violations. Radicals, especially Communists, were the primary victims of suppression for their unionizing efforts, hunger marches, public demonstrations, picket lines, and advocacy of social change.[12]

Landmark decisions of the later thirties, however, gave constitutional protection for the right to protest and agitate peacefully. During the thirties and early forties, the Wagner Act of 1935 and court decisions recognized the right of labor to organize. Employers were not to interfere with workers' rights to free speech and assembly. In 1940 the Supreme Court recognized the right to picket. This right, even though it was later subject to restrictions, marked a clear advance in First Amendment rights. The legal foundations for the right to nonviolent dissent were gradually being laid.

But as World War II broke out in Europe, another grim period for civil liberties set in with the passage of the Alien Registration Act, in 1940, more commonly known as the Smith Act. Another spasm of anti-alien hysteria gripped the United States, at least partly in response to gains made by the Communist party during the Depression. Among the reasons cited for the passage of the Smith Act were the advent of war, a resurgence of the identification of the term *radical* with *alien,* and testimony by military leaders to Congress that soldiers and sailors might be subverted by Communist party propaganda. The mood of that era in Congress was summed up by a California congressman who said, "If you brought in the Ten Commandments today and asked for their repeal and attached to that request an alien law, you could get it." [13] The Alien Registration Act had little to do with registration of aliens. It forbade advocacy of the overthrow or destruction of any government in the United States by force and violence, advocacy of insubordination or disloyalty in the military, joining with others to advocate overthrow, and knowingly joining a group that called for the overthrow of the government.

With the passage of the Smith Act, speech itself—without any action—became criminal once again, as it had been under the Alien and Sedition and the Espionage Acts. The phrase "advocacy of the overthrow of the government by force and violence" might bring to mind the raving of armed terrorists and seem like a legitimate thing to prohibit. But what that phrase actually targeted was criticism of our government, urging fundamental change in government, or advocating communism or anarchy.[14] "Intemperate political and economic controversy" became punishable under this act, according to historian Zechariah Chafee, who called it a return to the state sedition laws overturned by the *Gitlow* decision in 1925.

The Smith Act was used to prosecute unpopular dissenters, like Communists. Pages of Lenin and Marx were read into court records to show the advocacy of force and violence inherent in party doctrine. The first case based on the Smith Act was decided by the Supreme Court in 1951. *Dennis v. United States* involved eleven prominent American Communists convicted of conspiring to organize the Communist party and of teaching and advocating the overthrow of the government by force and violence. The Supreme Court upheld the convictions, the majority ruling that the conspiracy indeed posed a clear and present danger to the government. Justice Felix Frankfurter, who agreed that the Communists were guilty, used a different test. He weighed the Communists' First Amendment rights against the threat to national security and decided that the threat was more important than the First Amendment. Frankfurter conceded that the Court's decision violated the First Amendment by restricting the interchange of ideas and that the decision "inevitably will also silence critics who do *not* advocate overthrow." [15] But he held that the threat to national security was more important. The "balancing" test, as this was called, became (and still is) extremely important in First Amendment case law. Justices Hugo Black and William O. Douglas, strong adherents of free speech, dissented from the opinion of their colleagues, calling the benefits of free discussion well worth the risk. They opposed weighing constitutional rights against other considerations. In their view, constitutional rights were paramount.

More than one hundred Communists were prosecuted under the Smith Act until 1957, when another Supreme Court decision—in a case very similar to *Dennis*—resulted in a different decision. In *Yates v. United States,* the Court found that it was legal for the Communists to advocate an *abstract* doctrine of forcible overthrow of the government. The subtleties differentiating *Yates* from *Dennis* have puzzled legal scholars. Professor Franklyn S. Haiman of Northwestern University finds it impossible to distinguish between them.[16] In both situations, Communist party members were going about their normal business of organizing and speaking; no charges of violence of any kind were brought. But historical circumstances may explain the change: *Dennis* was decided in 1951, when the Korean War was raging and World War III appeared imminent. By 1957 times were calmer, and the Court had some new members.

In general, free speech suffered grievous setbacks during the 1940s and 1950s. The depredations of congressional and state un-American activities committees, Senator Joseph McCarthy, and agents of government, from the president to local school boards, wreaked havoc on people's lives. The right of political association suffered as Congress passed laws to prohibit the Communist party from functioning. Several states excluded Communists from the ballot.[17] By 1953, thirty-two states required loyalty oaths from teachers.[18] Government employees had to be "loyal" and were subjected to close scrutiny, harassment, and firing. Union officials could not belong to the Communist party or even believe in its tenets, or their unions would be excluded from the services of the National Labor Relations Board. The Supreme Court used the balancing test to justify this restriction on belief, saying that union leaders with the wrong beliefs might resort to strikes, and therefore Congress could make laws excluding them from office. According to several legal historians, the balancing test is usually used to defeat free expression.

The Supreme Court also used the balancing test in another arena: determining what limits, if any, applied to congressional committees. During the 1950s especially, groups like the House Un-American Activities Committee interrogated witnesses about past associations with the Communist party. The witnesses were publicly excoriated and risked prison terms for contempt if they refused to answer questions put by committee members. But while the courts were unfriendly to the First Amendment rights of publicly despised left-wingers, they strengthened the First Amendment rights of another unpopular group, the Jehovah's Witnesses.

This religious sect forbids its members to bow down before graven images of any kind, including the flag of the United States. The sect believes in spreading the Christian gospel by word of mouth and by distributing tracts, periodicals, and phonograph records. In precedent-setting opinions the Supreme Court affirmed the right of Jehovah's Witnesses and others *not* to communicate. By 1939, seventeen states had enacted laws requiring people to salute the flag. Schoolchildren have risked expulsion if they refused. Jehovah's Witnesses argued that their religion forbade such obeisance. In 1943, the Supreme Court held that the First Amendment protects the individual from coerced communication; the Witnesses did not have to salute the flag anymore. The decision, in favor of a West Virginia family named Barnette, said that authority in the United States "is to be controlled by public opinion, not public opinion by authority. . . . Freedom to differ is not limited to things that do not matter much. That would be a mere shadow of freedom. The best of its substance is the right to differ as to things that touch the heart of the existing order." [19] Communists, however, did not seem to warrant the right to differ.

In the same year, the Court struck down a city ordinance that banned the Witnesses from going door to door to distribute their tracts. The Court held that there is a "right to receive" information. This right ought to be protected, said the Court, so that enlightenment can prevail over ignorance. The fullest spread of information, it said, promoted the fullest democracy and the best society. Two years later, the Court continued this trend by recognizing a "right to hear" in upholding the right of workers to listen to a labor organizer.

These rights—to receive and to hear information—are important both in themselves and as they contribute to the concept of a "right to know," which was more explicitly recognized in 1965 in a Supreme Court decision and by congressional legislation in 1966 establishing the Freedom of Information Act. Plainly, the law had come a long way from the era when a minister opposed to World War I could be convicted for handing out pacifist pamphlets on a street corner.

But there was still a long way to go, notably in the protection of dissent and assembly. States and cities, particularly in the South, had drafted laws to stop unionizing and to frustrate organizations active in civil rights. Some of these laws were overturned because they infringed on First Amendment freedoms; from the late 1950s through the 1960s, these were prominent cases before the Supreme Court.

As the civil rights movement gained momentum, several states tried legal stratagems to prevent social change. Alabama tried to force the NAACP to reveal its membership lists and accused it of acting in ways injurious to the property and civil rights of the citizens of the state. Virginia accused the NAACP of breaking a state law that forbade stirring up legal business for the enrichment of lawyers. In ruling on that case in 1963, the U.S. Supreme Court held that litigation is a form of political expression and hence must be protected. The Court struck down the Alabama actions, as well.

The right to demonstrate peacefully, as we saw at the beginning of this chapter, was upheld in 1963, when the Court overturned a South Carolina law under which a nonviolent assembly had been labeled a breach of the peace. The lower-court convictions of the demonstrators, said the Court, were "repugnant to the guarantee of liberty contained in the Fourteenth Amendment," and were therefore overturned. If that amendment had not been held applicable to First Amendment freedoms, the South Carolina convictions would have stood, and the entire civil rights movement might have been severely hampered, if not stifled altogether.

One can readily see as we follow the expansion and contraction of First Amendment rights that the social conflicts of any era are reflected in court decisions. Members of a group seeking to exercise their rights and improve their position in society can seek relief in the courts if other methods are blocked, or if they feel harassed by laws they believe to be unconstitutional. For example, in 1963 New Orleans police arrested three white members of an organization called the Southern Conference Educational Fund, which worked against segregation. Their alleged offense: failing to register as members of an organization designated as communist-linked, as required by Louisiana law. (The chairman of the Louisiana Un-American Activities Committee said they had been arrested for "racial agitation.")[20] But even before the state began to prosecute them, the three went straight to federal court, claiming that their rights to free expression and free association had been violated. Louisiana argued that the criminal prosecution had to take place first, and the normal order of things had to be followed before the federal courts could intervene.

While the legal process went forward, the Southern Conference Educational Fund had to curtail its activities; police had seized its membership lists, records, and equipment. Donations fell off. The federal district court ruled against their claim, and they appealed to the U.S. Supreme Court, which decided in *Dombrowski v. Pfister* that any "criminal prosecution under a statute regulating expression" may "inhibit the full exercise of First Amendment freedoms." The Court recognized that "the chilling effect upon the exercise of First Amendment rights may derive from the fact of the prosecution, unaffected by the prospect of its success or failure." The Louisiana laws were held unconstitutional.

This concept called a chilling effect has been used effectively in constitutional law ever since. A law may not stop free expression from taking place and, an important step farther, it may not inhibit expression. In addition, the success of the accused in going immediately to federal court for relief encouraged others to use the same tactic.

In 1965, the Supreme Court rendered another landmark decision. In *Griswold v. Connecticut* the Court overturned a Connecticut law that forbade the distribution of information about birth control. While this was vitally important for the advancement of reproductive freedom, the decision also had major repercussions for First Amendment rights. Justice William O. Douglas wrote the opinion, in which he said that there is a "right to know" included "within the penumbra" of the First Amendment. Douglas seemed to be saying that the right to know is at least partly protected by the First Amendment. He continued:

> The state may not, consistently with the spirit of the First Amendment, contract the spectrum of available knowledge. The right of freedom of speech and press includes not only the right to utter or to print, but the right to distribute, the right to receive, the right to read . . . and freedom of inquiry, freedom of thought, and freedom to teach.[21]

This decision strengthened the constitutional foundation of the individual's right to know, a corollary to the right to free expression and an essential component of democracy. Four years later, in a case requiring broadcasters to allow time for presentation of both sides of a controversial issue, the Court said:

> It is the purpose of the First Amendment to preserve an uninhibited marketplace of ideas in which truth will ultimately prevail. . . . The right of the public to receive suitable access to social political, esthetic, moral and other ideas and experience is crucial here.[22]

Other free speech rights were affected by cases decided during the turbulent 1960s. Protest against the Vietnam War took varied forms, some of which were declared legal—like wearing a jacket that said, "Fuck the draft"—in *Cohen v. California.* In 1969 the Supreme Court said that school officials could not prevent students from wearing black armbands in protest against the war. Thus the First Amendment was extended to protect free expression by students in school, a precedent that has permitted school newspapers to claim constitutional rights to print stories that school officials dislike.

Different forms of protest, like burning draft cards, posed more complicated issues. In 1965, in *United States v. O'Brien,* a man appealed his conviction for burning his draft card; the Court rejected his argument that he was engaging in symbolic speech that ought to be protected by the First Amendment. It said he had engaged not only in protected speech but also in unprotected conduct. By burning the card, he had broken the law requiring men of his age to keep draft cards on their persons.

During the same period, the Court went further in widening the bounds of permissible speech. In *Brandenburg v. Ohio* (1969) the Court struck down the conviction of a Ku Klux Klansman who demanded "revengance" against blacks. According to that decision, "constitutional guarantees of free speech and free press do not permit a state to forbid . . . advocacy of the use of force or of law violation except where such advocacy is directed to inciting or producing imminent lawless action and is likely to produce such action." In this case, the clear and present danger test as well as the balancing test went by the boards. Urging illegal conduct in the future or saying things that might have bad effects were allowed, said the Court. Sacrificing First Amendment rights in favor of other interests was not. For speech to be illegal, according to the *Brandenburg* decision, it has to be at the point of producing lawless action. Advocacy of communism or anarchy is protected so long as speech is not about to produce a violation of law. The *Brandenburg* decision, which overturned an Ohio law against criminal syndicalism, is now the law of the land, according to law professor

Franklyn S. Haiman.[23] Such things as protesting a foreign war, preaching an unpopular religion, or advocating socialism are now protected by the First Amendment.

In 1969, Chief Justice Warren Burger was appointed by President Nixon to head the Supreme Court. Since then, the Court has been considered less friendly to civil liberties. In some instances, like the publication of the White House tapes, the Court upheld the public's right to know against strong attempts by the Nixon administration to weaken it. But during the 1970s, in general, First Amendment freedoms, along with other civil liberties, suffered rather than advanced. The Nixon administration, especially through Attorney General John Mitchell, pursued "law and order," which did not mean vigorous enforcement of the Bill of Rights. Rather, government agencies sought to infiltrate and disrupt legitimate political protest through illegal policies. But because of previous advances in First Amendment rights, people who opposed government policies had and used the legal freedom to agitate for change; there was no legitimate way for government to silence them. Edwin S. Newman, writing in 1979, likened Nixon's policies to the Palmer Raids under President Wilson:

> The Administration . . . asserting its representation of the "silent majority," interprets its policies in terms of tempering the traditional scope for freedom of expression for the majority of the citizenry against the tyranny of the militant minorities. In general it can be said that the Administration's tone has encouraged local law enforcement officers to crack down on dissent.[24]

Tracing the history of First Amendment rights reveals how fluid our system of government is, how subject to current trends. It is hardly accidental that some of the greatest advances in First Amendment rights occurred during the New Deal years of the 1930s and during the 1960s, when large numbers of people organized to achieve what they perceived as a more just society, and held fiercely to their rights to express themselves. In the same way, First Amendment rights suffered greatly when people were less politically active, as in the 1920s and 1950s, and when the threat of foreign domination was used by those in power to silence criticism. Similar trends, unfortunately, are reappearing in the early 1980s.

Much of the history of the First Amendment remains to be written. Legal scholars have characterized the current state of the First Amendment as chaotic. Logical inconsistencies abound in court decisions and in the law, making it difficult to discern the boundary between protected free speech and activity for which one might face prosecution. As we have seen, the tenor of the times and the vigor with which people fight for their rights influence the evolution of the law.

The remainder of this book examines the state of free speech, free press, and the public's right to know during the presidency of Ronald Reagan. We will see the effects that current federal policy has been having on these freedoms, as well as what is happening at the state and local levels and in the private sector. The First Amendment became law in 1791, but the protections it promises have been a long time in coming.

2

The Federal Government as Censor

At the same time that the federal government guards our constitutional rights and liberties, it is often the very entity that threatens to usurp them. Although our Constitution states that the people are sovereign, the government commands the means of power and the apparatus of the state. Under the Reagan administration, the federal government has clamped down hard on the flow of information that informs the press and public about its policies. The government collects fewer data than it used to, publishes less and charges higher prices, and has become more closed to the citizen and to the press. While none of these trends began under Reagan—every president since Washington has wanted to restrict some information—censorship imposed by the federal government has increased markedly since he took office.

The executive branch of government controls many of the outlets from which information flows. It alone has the authority and resources to study and report on almost every phase of daily life, whether it be census data on how many American homes lack indoor plumbing or weather forecasting by satellite systems. The information produced by federal agencies not only gives us a multitude of facts but also shows us how we as a people relate to one another.

The executive branch, with its manifold departments and agencies, generates information about our nation and public policy that we as citizens need to know if we are to oversee what the government is doing. By claiming that national security requires the classification of more documents, by asserting that a tight budget requires reduced data collection and publication, by issuing executive orders and supporting legislation that expands governmental power to keep secrets, and by placing political policy before scientific fact, the Reagan administration cut back sharply on the access of the press and the public to information both about the government's policies and about situations that may or may not trigger government action. For example, the administration maintained that the Environmental Protection Agency was properly carrying out its mission to clean up sites where industries had abandoned toxic wastes. As congressional committees and reporters discovered, however, very little was being done, and administration appointees were maintaining close relationships with the industries they were supposed to police. President Reagan tried to keep secret government documents describing those problems. His administration also prevented reporters from accompanying American troops invading Grenada, thus assuring a media blackout of the controversial operation.

More ominously, the president and his top advisers warned often that information is dangerous. While some information should indeed remain secret, particularly about nuclear weapons, the Reagan administration extended the definition of dangerous information far beyond previous limits and then established a network of rules and penalties to police the new limits.

The president's information policies clearly reflect the belief that government has been too open in the past, the conviction that First Amendment rights are not sacrosanct, and the suspicion that political opponents may be harming U.S. interests. Open government and civil liberties, in this view, become expendable. In explaining his support of the Intelligence Identities Protection Act, legislation designed to penalize the release of any information that might lead to the naming of an intelligence agent, Senator Richard Lugar (R-Ind.) told the *New York Times,* "I am willing to take risks with regard to all the [constitutional] protections we have set up. . . . I don't think on a continuum we are going to be able to have both an ongoing intelligence capability and a totality of civil rights protection." [1]

Protecting national security is the predominant rationale given by the government for keeping information from the public. Unfortunately, governments stretch the definition of the term *national security* to mean what they want it to mean. Egil Krogh, chief of the White House plumbers in the Nixon administration, made this statement just before he was sentenced for perjury:

> I see now . . . the effect that the term "national security" had on my judgment. The very words served to block critical analysis. It seemed to me presumptuous if not unpatriotic to inquire into just what the significance of national security was. . . . Freedom of the president to pursue his planned objective was the ultimate national security objective.[2]

Throughout the federal government today, officials are censoring information. From the Oval Office to the public information assistant, from the State Department to the customs office, information is being blocked, hidden, shredded, and classified. The government is building a barrier of secrecy for the good of the American public.

THE PRESIDENT AND OPEN GOVERNMENT

Ronald Reagan began to block the flow of government information to the public at his very first press conference, just nine days after he took office. With the charm that has become his trademark, he flashed a broad smile and winked at reporters before announcing he would block two Carter administration rules from taking effect: one broadening patient access to nursing home records, and another requiring the National Highway Traffic Safety Administration to inform car buyers how their vehicles had performed in crash tests.

At his third press conference, held on June 16, 1981, the president began to get into trouble with the media. He made an error that his Press Office staff had to correct later, and on other issues he was vague. He seemed unfamiliar with the details of major foreign affairs issues, like whether a war in Europe could be contained or would mushroom into a nuclear conflagration. The press criticized him. Eventually, United Press International and Associated Press began to issue stories listing Reagan's errors and their corrections after every major presidential address. The president and his staff seemed to resent the criticism. They fired back at the media, especially at what they called unfair reports on the economy, emphasizing the woes of the poor. But even then the president made gaffes. "Is it news that some fellow out in South Succotash some place who has just been laid off should be interviewed nationwide?" an irritated Reagan complained to an Oklahoma City audience on March 16, 1982.

As the administration progressed, the White House explained its views on the proper role of the press and the harm caused by dissemination of information. On September 30, 1982, Reagan told a Las Vegas meeting of the Radio-TV News Directors Association in a videotaped message that he was concerned about a lack of balance "between the media's right to know and the government's right to confidentiality in running the affairs of state, not to mention the national security." Reagan said he doubted whether "hot light" coverage had "aided the public understanding of our nation's problems or whether in some instances it actually had hindered government's functioning and, thus, slowed the solution of our problems."

Not long afterward, Reagan press aide Larry Speakes called on the television network anchormen to report more "upbeat" news. Presidential adviser Edwin Meese III charged that the press was ignoring

Reagan's successes and indulging in "a period of questioning" and "undue scrutiny" of presidential policy. Reagan himself expressed the view that the fourth estate should function less independently and more as an adjunct of the administration. In an exclusive interview with a publication that seemed uniquely appropriate, *TV Guide,* Reagan complained that news leaks had interfered with the government's foreign policy objectives. Reagan implied that media bias had caused us to lose the war in Vietnam and was now interfering with the U.S. mission in El Salvador. He told *TV Guide* interviewer John Weisman that he preferred that journalists "would trust us and put themselves in our hands, and call and say, 'I have this story.' . . . But they just go with the story —and we read it." [3]

In taking on the media, the president rejected some advice given by a contributor to *Politics and the Oval Office,* a book published by the Institute for Contemporary Studies, a conservative think tank in San Francisco, right after the 1980 election. Writer Charles Peters advised the new head of state to rise above the fear of media criticism and to encourage the free expression of differing opinions. According to this author, Reagan should "challenge the press to do constructive reporting, to use its wit and guile not only to find out what is wrong but also to figure out why it's wrong and to determine what needs to be done." [4] Instead, the president followed more closely the recommendations of another contributor to the volume, Duke University professor Robert M. Entman, who advised cutting back on reporters' access to officials, discouraging coverage of political motivations and strategies, disseminating dry data to discourage reporters, and restricting personal contacts between press officers and journalists.

The press reacted sharply to the president's policies and accused the administration of giving government officials a blank check to hide mistakes and manage the news. "President Reagan seems relentlessly determined to control the flow of information to the American people," wrote syndicated columnist Jack Anderson. "He speaks of 'security'; the correct word is 'censorship.' . . . The truth is, of course, that he hopes to use the security issue to manage the news." [5]

Whether or not that was the president's objective, he took strong action to increase the ability of the government to keep secrets. The administration's efforts to stem the flow of information ran the gamut from passive methods like cutting down on press releases and reports and withholding requested data, to active methods like threatening and punishing employees who dared to speak out. As Reagan's first term wore on, the executive agencies moved increasingly from passive methods of information control to more aggressive means.

Agencies sharply curtailed the information routinely released to the media. The CIA abolished its Office of Public Affairs and appointed an assistant to the director to deal with the press in what was called inverse public relations. The agency also sharply curtailed its publication of unclassified reports and analyses. Among those discontinued, *U.S.-Soviet Military Dollar-Cost Comparisons* and *Communist Aid Activities in Non-Communist Less Developed Countries.*

The National Security Council staff in the White House, which included many specialists who often provided background to reporters, was declared off-limits to the press. And, according to the *Washington Post,* the regular briefings at the Departments of State and Defense reached "their least productive point in many years in the information they yield or the opportunities to extract more than what amounts to a daily government press release." [6] One veteran Capitol Hill reporter observed that during a regular forty-five-minute briefing at State, the spokesperson responded more than thirty times with "Don't know," "Can't say," "No comment," or "I've got nothing for you on that."

At the Pentagon, reporters were told that there would no longer be any detailed accounting of United States and Soviet naval power in the Mediterranean; such information was routinely provided under previous administrations. Deputy Secretary of Defense Frank C. Carlucci III also used lie detectors in efforts to track down the source of leaks. Besides the threat leaks pose to national security, Carlucci wrote in a memo to Pentagon bureaucrats, they tend to "make our work more difficult by stimulating inquiries about the subject matters revealed. I am particularly concerned that there be no wounds of this type inflicted by members of this office." [7]

Over the months, press offices throughout the executive branch experimented with various methods of holding reporters at bay. In January 1983, the White House asked its staff members to get clearance before discussing certain matters with journalists. David R. Gergen, then Assistant to the President for Communications, was to designate a small number of aides who would handle questions. The day after this policy was announced, a reporter with a question about the budget inquired about whom to see. Gergen replied that no official had yet been named for that. Later in the day, given the name of the proper official, the reporter tried again. The official, when contacted, said he could supply no information.

The problems of access to information, of course, applied not only to the press; public interest groups and Congress itself had tremendous difficulty prying documents from the tight grip of the executive branch.

THE EXECUTIVE ORDER ON CLASSIFICATION

Since George Washington, presidents have kept information secret, particularly in wartime. Franklin Roosevelt established the first comprehensive system for classifying security information in 1940 by issuing an executive order. The material to be kept secret included maps, designs, and specifications under the authority of the War and Navy Departments. FDR apparently derived his authority for this order from a 1938 statute concerning the security of armed forces installations and "information relative thereto."

Although the presidential power to make information secret has been questioned, presidents have long used executive orders for that purpose. Presidents typically cite a relevant statute and the vague "inherent powers" of the office as the basis for their authority. Unlike ordinary legislation, executive orders require no congressional or judicial approval. The president simply issues them.

Since Roosevelt, most presidents have issued executive orders on classifying security information. Truman's order, written at the time of the Korean War, extended classification authority for the first time to all agencies and to all information "the safeguarding of which is necessary in the interest of national security." As World War II shaded into the cold war, the United States entered a limbo between war and peace. As a world power engaged in global struggle, the United States pursued an interventionist foreign policy; one important effect of this policy was the lessening of congressional power and the concomitant increase in power of the executive. As the leader of a nation involved in a continuing state of emergency, the president assumed increasing powers to classify information secret in order to keep it from the enemy and to preserve national security.

The amount of secret information mushroomed, as did the number of executive-branch paper stampers. Recommendations by congressional committees that Congress set up a classification system by statute were not acted upon; presidents clung to their authority to control information, however insubstantial the source of their authority may have been. Even when Congress finally passed the Freedom of Information Act in 1966 to expand the access to government information, properly classified information remained exempt from the act. Until the Reagan administration, the general trend in recent decades had been to reduce the amount of information that could be classified and the number of civilians with the power to classify.

President Carter ordered a survey of the classification system. The executive order he subsequently issued in 1978 specified that information could be classified only if its release would cause identifiable damage to the nation's security. The order required that the public interest in access to the information be weighed against the need to keep that information secret. If there was any doubt about the proper category, information was to be classified at the least restrictive level. The order also required that declassification be emphasized as much as classification; documents were to be declassified as early as national security considerations would permit, and a justification had to be provided for classification lasting longer than six years.

One might have thought, with his campaign promises to "get government off the backs of the people" and to cut expenses, that Ronald Reagan would cut back on the paper stampers and file keepers required to staff the elaborate classification system he inherited. But the opposite happened. In an executive order developed and issued in secrecy, Reagan reversed the trend toward more open government. In the fall of 1981, the Reagan administration circulated drafts of an executive order on classification that would drastically increase the amount of information the government could keep secret.

The planned order would make several important changes in the rules governing the classification of information. Where the Carter order had *permitted* officials to keep documents secret when they met certain standards, the Reagan order *required* them to keep documents secret when there was only "reasonable doubt" about the need for classification. If there was doubt about the proper level of secrecy, the higher classification was mandated. Reagan's draft order added three new categories of information that could be classified: material about "vulnerabilities or capabilities of systems, installations, projects or plans relating to the national security"; cryptographic data (information about codes and code breaking); and information gained from "confidential sources." A *confidential source* was defined as any individual or organization that provides information to the government about "national security," and expects the information to be kept secret.

The Reagan secrecy order was itself shrouded in secrecy. Administration officials refused to testify before congressional oversight committees concerned with the subject before the order was issued, and the views of interested private organizations were not solicited. The administration's refusal to cooperate with the lawmakers blocked participation by Congress and the public in the development of the order.

Even as the White House was drafting the executive order on classification behind closed curtains, the administration was taking other steps to stem the flow of information to the public. While the ostensible reason was to protect national security, in many cases they seemed designed to protect the president's political security. In May 1981, Attorney General William French Smith wrote a letter to all agency heads, encouraging them to withhold information requested under the Freedom of Information Act (FOIA). Smith, like FBI Director William Webster and CIA Chief William Casey, is a harsh critic of the FOIA. He claimed that because of information released pursuant to the act's provisions, "informants are more reluctant to share information . . . foreign intelligence services are more reluctant to provide information . . . and other impediments to effective government are created." [8] Smith also said he favored surprise raids on news rooms to discover the source of leaked information. Such opinions on the part of the administration's top lawyer sparked fears of a return to the Nixon era, when government secrecy cloaked illegal actions by the CIA, the FBI, and the president himself.

In March 1982, Democratic Senator Joseph Biden of Delaware, a member of the Senate Select Intelligence Committee, complained that the administration was keeping information even from the Congress. "Everything is just closing down," he said. "In 1979, when the agency [CIA] came up here, I would ask the following question: 'Tell us what's happening in El Salvador.' They would give us a detailed account, including the blemishes. Now, all I'll get is what they want to tell me." [9]

Curiously enough, it seemed the only dissenting voice in the administration's push toward secrecy was that of Edwin Meese. In a March speech to the National Newspaper Association (NNA), he appeared to disavow the draft order on classification, saying that while the administration really wanted to decrease the number of classified documents, the "bureaucracy" was trying to expand classification. Perhaps trying to escape responsibility for the order, a draft of which had been sent out over his signature, Meese implied that the "zealous bureaucrats" had taken the initiative, but the administration was now getting control over them, and would in fact reduce unnecessary secrecy. "We are trying as an administration . . . to decrease the number of classified documents to those that are actually vital to the national security and then do a better job of safeguarding those," he said. "But I've got to admit that early on, as they always do, the bureaucracy tested us and they tried to expand classification. And I do think you'll find that that is being corrected in the current drafts of the classification executive order that is now being studied by us." [10]

Despite Meese's speech, the president signed Executive Order 12356 on April 2, 1982, giving those "bureaucrats" vastly increased power to classify. The president's signing made Meese's words to the NNA sound like double speak, but gave the ring of truth to earlier speculation by the *Washington Post* that Meese's role in the controversy over secrecy was similar to a role he had played in the president's executive order on intelligence. On that issue, Meese had assured newspaper editors that there was "absolutely nothing" in the intelligence order that would "expand the ability of the CIA to engage in domestic spying." Nonetheless, the order for the first time authorized the CIA to mount covert operations in the United States and to spy on Americans in other ways that had never before been permissible.

The new executive order on classification was praised by some Republican members of Congress as an escape hatch from the Freedom of Information Act. But Democrats, other Republicans, and the press criticized it for the very same reason. They charged it would cheapen the meaning of "classified" because it made so much more information secret. Newspapers across the country released a barrage of editorial criticism. In an op ed piece in the *New York Times* attorneys James Goodale and Lawrence Martin said:

> Vital national secrets are of course stamped, but so are politically embarrassing documents (such as the Pentagon Papers) or any piece of paper that seems vaguely sensitive. With so much technically secret, no one knows what is truly secret. Officials come to see the stamp as a political tool that allows them to keep secret what would hurt them and to leak what they want publicized.[11]

The *Washington Post* declared that the new order "represented the flowering of an unwarranted and unbecoming spirit of distrust of the public." Noting that no court has overruled a government classification of information labeled secret on national security grounds, the *Post* continued, "It seems that the intelligence agencies wanted more solid ground on which to claim exemptions from making disclosures under the FOIA." The order, it concluded, "might give the wrong ideas to the folks with the rubber stamps. That's where the loss to the public lies."[12]

Many of the new order's measures were designed to maintain secrecy in government, but one of its unique provisions actually allowed officials to quash information already in the public domain. The order permitted the government to reclassify information that "can reasonably be recovered." Reclassification under any circumstances had been expressly forbidden under the Carter order. Some intelligence agencies seemed so eager to use this new power of recovery that they exercised it even before Reagan's order was signed into law. One case occurred amid a controversy over a book written by former CIA agent Ralph McGehee. McGehee served twenty-five years with the agency. He won a Career Intelligence Medal in 1977, but eventually quit in disgust and disillusionment. After initially telling McGehee his book was cleared, the CIA informed him that some of the material in his manuscript was being reclassified. "Oh, we're operating under a new order," McGehee said the agency lawyer told him in March, weeks before the Reagan order went into effect. McGehee fought the attempted reclassification and won.

Such reclassification may infringe upon First Amendment rights to free speech. When McGehee joined the CIA, for example, he signed the standard secrecy agreement. This allows the CIA to review prior to publication all writing of present and former employees to ensure that no classified information is revealed. The provision seems a logical measure to protect national security. But McGehee found that the agreement was used for other purposes. He reported in his book *Deadly Deceits*:

> The CIA uses the agreement not so much to protect national security but to protect revelations and criticisms of its immoral, illegal and ineffective operations. Had I not been represented by my attorney, Mark Lynch of the American Civil Liberties Union, and had I not developed a massive catalogue of information already cleared by the Agency's Publications Review Board, this book could not have been published.[13]

The agency excised from McGehee's book information that it had allowed to be printed in works by authors favorable to the CIA. McGehee concluded his book with a warning:

> As the CIA becomes more adept at applying the law under President Reagan's Executive Order on Classification, all critical information about the agency will probably be forbidden. . . . Once the Agency is unleashed and the iron curtain of disclosure falls, we all suffer its consequences.[14]

A report issued by the Subcommittee on Government Information and Individual Rights of the House Committee on Government Operations, written after extensive hearings on the executive order on classification, severely criticized the president's action. The report noted that, administration claims to the countrary notwithstanding, "all of the changes appear to expand the authority of government officials to classify information" and that it "establishes no new controls that would be necessary to prevent abuse of classification authority in the future."[15] The subcommittee also found that the order's language was intentionally broad, and the explanation that administration officials provided to the committee of that language did not fully reflect the purpose of the changes. Congressman Glenn English (D-Okla.) said he thought the order reflected a "mania for secrecy" that went all the way to the top of the administration.

With the new executive order on classification in place, the government proceeded to classify more information than ever. The Information Security Oversight Office (ISOO), a joint office of the General Services Administration and the National Security Council, charged with monitoring classification throughout the government, reported that in 1980 sixteen million pieces of information were stamped secret. ISOO predicted that in 1983 the figure would grow to twenty-one million.

Between October 1, 1981, and July 31, 1982, the Department of Defense alone classified 11,691,876 bits of data—more than a million facts and thoughts each month.[16] ISOO also reported gross abuses of secrecy within the classification system. Based on random checks, the office estimated that six hundred thousand documents had been classified without proper authority; another eight hundred thousand had been classified without need.

Staggering as those figures are, with the Reagan order in place, they will only climb higher. Even though the order subjected more information to classification, however, it did not block one time-honored channel for the flow of information—the leak.

ANTILEAK DIRECTIVE NSDD 84

President after president has bitterly complained about unauthorized disclosures of information to the media. George Washington became enraged in 1795 when Senator Stevens Thomson Mason of Virginia leaked a secret copy of a treaty with France to the Philadelphia *Aurora.* Franklin Delano Roosevelt was incensed over a leak of Henry Morgenthau's plan to stop German industry after World War II. Richard Nixon approved unconstitutional wiretaps in his efforts to plug leaks. And in January 1983, Ronald Reagan angrily commented, "I've had it up to my keister with these leaks."

Like other presidents before him, Reagan charged that unauthorized disclosures of classified information hurt the national security. Like other presidents, he ignored a fact that experienced politicians and journalists are quick to point out: Leaks are a vital component of government communications, what *New York Times* reporter Richard Halloran has called "oil in the machinery of government." "Contrary to the widely held perception," he wrote, " 'leaking' is not solely or even largely the province of the dissident. Rather, it is a political instrument wielded almost daily by senior officials within the administration to influence a decision, to promote policy, to persuade Congress, and to signal foreign governments." Leaks are one way the government communicates with itself, according to Halloran. "A presidential aide, afraid to confront the president directly with bad news, gets his message across through the press. A Cabinet officer, unable to get past the White House palace guard, leaks a memo that will land on the president's desk in the morning newspaper."[17]

Rarely do leaks of information harm the national security, observers claim; frequently, they help inform politicians and voters alike; sometimes they embarrass the party in power. Presidents strive to plug leaks because they wish to retain control of the information spigot. Indeed, the president is America's most notable leaker, divulging classified information when it best suits his policy goals. In order to bolster his argument that the Soviets were arming rebels in El Salvador, for example, Reagan overrode the advice of some of his advisers and displayed on television classified reconnaissance photographs of that country.

"Conceivably," writes historian Arthur Schlesinger, Jr., "we might have been spared one or two disasters—the Bay of Pigs, for example—had our recent history been marked by more rather than fewer leaks."[18] Yet under the Reagan administration, complaints about unauthorized disclosures of information reached a new pitch—what Schlesinger termed "the current hysteria over leaks."

During February and March 1982, at the request of national security adviser William P. Clark, Attorney General William French Smith convened a group of high-level attorneys and security officials from the CIA, and the Departments of Defense, State, Treasury, and Energy. Named the Interdepartmental Group on Unauthorized Disclosures of Classified Information, they met at the same time the administration was drafting its executive order on classification. The group's mission was to halt leaks of classified information from government officials to the media. The group's seven-part report, dated March 31, 1982, formed the basis for the subsequent National Security Decision Directive Number 84 (NSDD 84), an unprecedented governmentwide system of censorship designed to halt leaks to the press corps.

The Interdepartmental Group's report depicted a ship of state leaking from every office, on the verge of being capsized by the media. "The continuing large number of unauthorized disclosures has damaged the national security interests of the U.S. and has raised serious questions about the government's ability to protect its most sensitive secrets from disclosure in the media," it stated. "Today the unauthorized publication of classified information is a routine daily occurrence in the U.S." The report neglected to note that among the most frequent offenders in this regard are highly placed White House staff members and cabinet officers trying to advance administration policies.

According to the report, leaks provide our enemies with "valuable intelligence" about our plans for national defense and foreign relations; endanger the lives of intelligence agents and the viability of clandestine programs; make foreign governments reluctant to share sensitive information with us; and interfere with the government's ability to carry out its policies. "This 'veto by leak' phenomenon," the report said, "permits a single bureaucrat to thwart the ability of our democratic system of government to function properly."

The report acknowledged that unauthorized disclosures of classified data to the media are not new. But, it claimed, the "severity" of the problem has "increased greatly" since the *New York Times* published the purloined Pentagon Papers in 1971 and "ushered in an era of heightened media interest in the exposure of classified information." According to the report, the reporting of leaked information has degenerated into a game in which bureaucrats advancing their own political goals peel off secret documents like tickets at a carnival, and thrill-seeking journalists rush into print any classified data they can get their hands on, no matter what its import. Despite the alleged "daily occurrence" of leaks, the report included not a single example.

Leaking takes place in spite of a formidable variety of federal criminal and civil statutes, executive orders, regulations, and general standards of conduct that expressly prohibit improper release of classified information and provide for the investigation and punishment of those who do. President Carter's administration used one statute to obtain an injunction against a story on construction of the H-bomb that was scheduled to be published in the *Progressive.* Leakers may also be disciplined or fired under executive orders and other civil laws and regulations. Like Carter's directive, Reagan's executive order on classification expressly forbids leaks.

Despite all the legal and investigatory antileak artillery already at the government's command, it has been unable to stop leaks, the report claimed. The government has not attempted a single criminal prosecution for leaked information since it indicted Daniel Ellsberg and Anthony Russo for leaking the Pentagon Papers in 1971. That prosecution was dropped because of government misconduct during the investigation.

Summing up the problems behind the current "dismal" antileak situation, the report concluded, "Such investigations frequently involve high-ranking government officials, who may be uncooperative. Sometimes a time-consuming investigation is undertaken only to reveal that the source of the leak was a White House or Cabinet official who was authorized to disclose the information."

The authors proposed to fight leaks by requiring all government employees who handle classified information to sign secrecy oaths, broadening the government's power to investigate and identify leakers, and imposing severe penalties on violators, including administrative sanctions such as firing and even three-year prison terms. They also suggested reviving some of the internal security apparatus used in the fifties to ferret out alleged subversives in government.

The core of the proposal expanded the Supreme Court's 1980 decision in *United States v. Snepp.* The high court ruled that former CIA agent Frank Snepp violated his contractual obligations to the government in publishing his CIA memoirs without prior clearance from the agency, and that the government was therefore entitled to all profits from his book. The report suggested extending such nondisclosure agreements from the intelligence agencies to all agencies that handle classified information and to all government employees with access to a highly classified category of information called Sensitive Compartmented Information (SCI). These employees would have to submit any sensitive writings to a review board before publication, not just while in the government, but for their lifetimes. The report also recommended that each agency be required to develop new rules to control contracts between officials with access to classified information and the media.

With the employee's signed secrecy agreement in one hand and the new rules limiting media contacts in the other, agency heads could take a more aggressive role in investigating leaks and punishing leakers within their agencies. To do this, the report suggested that the agencies develop tougher leak investigation policies, which would also clear the way for a larger FBI role in agencies' internal administrative affairs. The report suggested changing personnel policy to give agency heads the power not only to require employees to take lie detector tests during a leak investigation but also to take "adverse consequences" against employees who refuse to do so, including adverse evidentiary inferences, revocation of security clearances, and possibly firing.

To help fight the war on leaks, the report continued, the FBI should be given back some of its power under the federal personnel security program to collect data on "subversive" groups. "Revisions of Executive Order 10450 would be helpful in streamlining the authority of agencies to revoke security clearances and take other personnel actions in the interest of national security," it said. Signed into law by President Truman in 1953, Executive Order 10450 required the FBI to conduct background checks of government employees, and the attorney general to compile a list of "subversive" organizations. This order fell into disuse, but should it be revived, a governmentwide security apparatus reminiscent of the McCarthy era could be put in place, with persons who once belonged to organizations on the FBI list, whether in fact subversive or not, barred from federal employment.[19]

The report of the Interdepartmental Group on Unauthorized Disclosures and a draft of a directive implementing its recommendations were sent to the White House, crossing the president's desk within days of his signing the executive order on classification. Reagan was urged to sign the new directive. But perhaps because the White House was sensitive to mounting criticism of the new classification order and the administration's efforts in Congress to weaken the Freedom of Information Act, the directive sat on the shelf for months, gathering dust.

On March 11, 1983, less than a year after he placed the presidential imprimatur on the executive order on classification, Reagan finally signed National Security Decision Directive Number 84 into law. The secrecy agreement to be signed by all those with access to classified information is estimated by Stephen Garfinkel of the Information Security Oversight Office to apply to nearly one million workers; other estimates reach 2.5 million. A second agreement, requiring those with access to information in the highly classified SCI category to submit their writings to prepublication review boards even after they leave government service, was estimated to apply to more than one hundred thousand senior employees.

The directive was signed on a Friday, the worst news day of the week. At 3:00 P.M. the Justice Department held its press briefing on NSDD 84. According to the department's "fact sheet," the directive represented a "new approach" to investigating leaks. While NSDD 84 was not expected to dry up all leaks, a press release stated, it was expected to reduce their number. The release assured reporters that the new directive did not make them the target of leak investigations. It did not mention that the group report on which NSDD 84 was based recommended considering a new law that did. The handful of reporters struggled that afternoon to get a grip on the directive. Ironically, the Justice Department spokesperson who briefed them did so only on the condition he not be named, and was often vague in response to their questions.

Whether or not as a result of strategic timing by the administration, the directive initially received scant attention in the press. Subsequent coverage was highly critical. The *Wall Street Journal, Washington Post,* and *New York Times* all ran pointed editorials or op-ed pieces. *New York Times* columnist William Safire criticized the Department of Justice's use of the "obscene euphemism" in the Justice Department fact sheet to describe what he called "this plunge into Big Brotherism." "March 11, the day of President Regan's directive to submit to the polygraph or be fired, is a day that will live in constitutional infamy," Safire wrote. "Until this rape of principle is rescinded, conservatives will bear the shame brought on us by the 'pragmatic' Attorney General and his anything-goes lust to crack down the source of public disclosure of wrong-doing." [20]

The sharp media coverage piqued congressional interest. At the first hearings held jointly before the House Subcommittee on Civil and Constitutional Rights and the Subcommittee on Civil Service on April 21, 1983, critics made their concerns known. Kenneth Blaylock, national president of the American Federation of Government Employees, testified that the directive's wording was "designed to suppress Federal employee disclosure of governmental corruption, waste, inefficiency, and fraud." He claimed that the directive would have "a chilling effect on

Federal employee whistle-blowing and the right of Federal taxpayers to know what their government is doing." Blaylock also charged that the provision that employees may be fired for refusing to cooperate with "harassing, humiliating, unreliable and unscientific" lie detector tests contradicted existing civil service regulations barring mandatory polygraph examinations and set up "a whole new system for firing Federal employees."

In October 1983, the Justice Department announced that it would be "appropriate" for federal agencies to require random polygraph tests to selected employees, and those who refused could be dismissed.

The directive's prepublication review requirements cover every senior official in agencies like the Departments of State and Defense, all members of the National Security Council staff, many senior White House officials, and all senior military and foreign service officers. Said ACLU attorney Mark Lynch, "The Reagan secrecy order will make it extremely difficult for any former official to function as a newspaper columnist, radio or TV commentator, or to participate in political debate, since many of their writings will be subject to a time delay while being cleared." For example, Lynch testified, if the directive had been in effect in the past, the speeches and writings of Richard Allen, Alexander Haig, and Eugene Rostow would now be subject to censorship by their successors. Political candidates like Walter Mondale would have to have their speeches cleared by the very administration they were running against. Reporters like Leslie Gelb would have to submit many of their articles to the government for prior clearance; professors like Anthony Lake would have to clear their lectures in advance, and consultants like Cyrus Vance could not submit reports to their clients before they were cleared. In each case, Lynch explained, the government could censor former officials whom it considered hostile by claiming the information they wished to present was classified. He concluded that the new order would do less to stop leaks than to clamp down on informed debate.[21]

"It is as if the Administration weighed censorship as a positive good instead of evil" when writing the order, testified Professor Lucas A. Powe, Jr., of the University of Texas Law School before the House Subcommittee on Legislation and National Security. *New York Times* columnist Anthony Lewis wrote, "The promoters of the secrecy system are fanatics who do not share the traditional American belief that open debate makes this country stronger." [22] If the administration's concern really was the safeguarding of classified information, suggested Senator David Durenberger (R-Minn.), "Some strong administrative action against the next senior official who leaks classified information that supports administration policy would do more than a thousand lie detectors."[23] In November 1983, Congress voted to postpone for six months the implementation of the prepublication agreement.

Despite the congressional act intended to postpone prepublication review, the administration appeared to have the capability to achieve the same objective without requiring officials with access to SCI to sign the controversial prepublication agreement. By requiring only the signing of the secrecy agreement applicable to the larger group of government employees and then invoking court precedents like the *Snepp* decision, the administration had the power to obtain injunctions to prevent publication of information. As ISOO official Stephen Garfinkel explained to reporter Angus Mackenzie, the government can obtain injunctions "to prevent publication even when the agreements signed do not call for prepublication review."[24] Thus the Reagan administration could achieve the desired censorship despite apparent congressional prohibition.

WEAKENING THE FREEDOM OF INFORMATION ACT

For advocates of the public's right to oversee government, no law is as important as the Freedom of Information Act (FOIA). This provides clear statutory recognition of the public's right to know and acts like a lever to pry loose information from the file cabinets of the executive branch of government. (The act does not apply to either the judiciary or Congress.)

Before passage of the act in 1966, seekers of government information had to prove a "need to know." There were no clear laws to guide them, no courtroom where a judge could order the release of information that had been wrongfully withheld. In effect, executive branch officials held all the cards; individuals could not prevail against any agency or department that arbitrarily decided something was secret. Of course, there has always been some flow of information from government departments and agencies. But before the FOIA, citizens had far less control over what that information was. Now the citizen could request and receive information as part of the citizen's right to know. This is a recent idea in American history: As late as the New Deal, an authoritative book on government said, "As a general rule the executive records of the Federal Government are not open to inspection either by the public or by the Press."[25]

During the period after World War II, the executive branch of the government mushroomed and so, too, did the need of Congress for greater access to executive data in order to carry out its legislative duties. Yet under Presidents Truman and Eisenhower, denial of access to information became a serious problem. They held that no law of Congress could require executive officers and employees to disclose executive files; all congressional demands and subpoenas for information would simply be denied by the agencies and then referred to the president.

In withholding information, executive officers often cited the 1789 act known as the Housekeeping Statute.[26] Enacted at George Washington's request, it allowed department heads to regulate the storage and use of government records. While the act was not intended to provide a rationale for withholding information, it nonetheless was misused to serve that purpose. In 1958, for example, Congress claimed that it wasn't getting enough information from the Pentagon to conduct its legislative business. With California Congressman John Moss leading the way, the legislators began the push to amend the act that would ultimately result in the modern FOIA.

Moss, chair of the newly formed Subcommittee on Government Information, held extensive hearings into the executive's withholding of information. All ten cabinet members opposed Moss's proposal to halt use of the 169-year-old Housekeeping Act "as an instrument of censorship." But Moss maintained that "all manner of people and interests"—scientists, historians, lawyers, reporters, and businessmen—were having trouble getting information they needed from their government. Moss declared that his amendment to the Housekeeping Act was "designed to prevent censorship." Adopted in 1958, it remains one of the briefest bills ever passed. It reads, "This section [of the Housekeeping Act] does not authorize the withholding of information from the public or limit the availability of records to the public." Said Moss to the *New York Times,* "Passage of the amendment is merely a first, timid step toward eradicating unnecessary government secrecy."

Little changed after passage of the bill. Most agencies simply withheld information under another law, section 3 of the Administrative Procedure Act of 1946, which allowed agency heads to withhold information if they decided that secrecy was "in the public interest," or if records related "solely to the internal management of an agency." According to Dr. Harold Relyea of the Congressional Research Service at the Library of Congress, "These refusals were effective not only because the bureaucracy had physical possession of the records, but also because there was no legal recourse available to the public to force review by a higher authority." [27]

Pressure from the media and from Congress grew, and in 1966 the Freedom of Information Act, to give the public greater access to government files, was passed. The bill granted "any person" the right of access to government records, with only a few key exceptions. Under exemptions to the act, classified information about national defense and foreign policy secrets, trade secrets, and personal information could not be released. The most important part of this measure would allow anyone denied access to request that a court review the denial. After initially opposing the measure, President Lyndon B. Johnson signed the bill with ringing rhetoric, if not sincere conviction, on July 4, 1966. Said Johnson, "This legislation springs from one of our most essential principles. Democracy works best when the people have all the information that the security of the nation permits. No one should be able to pull a curtain of secrecy around decisions which can be revealed without injury to the public interest." The president added that the act "in no way impairs the President's power under the Constitution to provide for confidentiality when the national interest so requires."

With the implementation of the act in 1967, the government now had to justify attempts at secrecy. "Right to know" replaced "need to know." Standard procedures were set up for the inspection of records, and judicial remedy was available to those improperly denied access. The Freedom of Information Act of 1966 was milestone legislation, reversing government information practices nearly two hundred years old. According to some experts, the act recognized for the first time that the First Amendment includes not only the right to communicate but also the right to receive information. "In principle, it opened up the entire vast body of documentation in the keeping of the federal authorities to the scrutiny of the public," Rutgers University law professor John Anthony Scott told the American Historical Association.[28]

Yet despite the new law, information did not flow freely from the executive offices of government. The weaknesses of the new law became all too apparent as agencies sought to define exemptions in overbroad terms, tried to withhold information by imposing excessive fees and long delays, and claimed that they could not find requested documents. The law provided no deadlines for government compliance with requests, and no penalties for violations of the law. Some critics labeled it the Freedom from Information Act. In 1972 the House Foreign Operations and Government Information Subcommittee held the first oversight hearings on the act's effectiveness. The subcommittee concluded, "Efficient operation of the FOIA has been hindered by five years of foot-dragging by the federal bureaucracy."

In the wake of the hearings the subcommittee began to draft amendments to strengthen the 1966 act. As Congress struggled to resolve the problems of the act, Watergate began to explode onto front pages across the country; public sentiment against government secrecy grew with each revelation of misconduct, and undoubtedly influenced the efforts of committee members to strengthen the act. The House subcommittee proposed seventeen amendments. One key change would bolster the section on judicial review by allowing judges not only to review the government's withholding of information but also for the first time to review the basis of the withholding: Judges would now be able to inspect the requested information itself to see whether or not it was properly classified as the government claimed.

Through this particular amendment, Congress was taking action to overturn a decision that the Supreme Court under Chief Justice Warren Burger had issued one year earlier, badly crippling the FOIA. In that decision, the Court held that a federal district judge in Alaska did not have the power to review requested documents about an underground nuclear test in Alaska in order to determine whether or not they had been properly classified. Concerned about possible health effects of the blast in their states, Congresswoman Patsy Mink and several other representatives requested information about the test. The Environmental Protection Agency said no. The Burger court's decision in 1973 held that there was "no means for Congress to question any Executive decision to stamp a document 'secret' however cynical, myopic, or even corrupt that decision might have been." The decision effectively removed from the reach of the FOIA and the public all documents having to do with national security.

Other proposed amendments to the act were intended to put more legal power in the hands of those requesting information, and to set specific procedures for the agencies to follow so they could no longer delay or avoid releasing unclassified information. Among the provisions were the following: (1) The government must meet deadlines for responding to requests, under threat of disciplinary action. (2) The government cannot charge requesters for the cost of excising documents, which was said to have made up a large portion of the high fees that discouraged requests under the 1966 act. (3) The government must disclose investigatory files, unless their release would cause one of six specific harms. (4) The national security exemption was changed to prevent the government from using it merely to withhold information. (5) Unclassified parts of a document must be released even though classified parts of the same document cannot.

The procedure for obtaining information under the amended Freedom of Information Act remained much the same. The requester must write a letter to the agency thought to have the information, reasonably describing the documents sought, stating specifically that the request is being made under the FOIA. The agency has ten days under usual circumstances, ten more under "unusual circumstances," in which to reply. Should the agency fail to reply, or deny release of the documents, the requester may then write a letter of appeal to the Department of Justice, which has twenty days in which to reply, and an extra ten days in unusual circumstances. If the government did not make a full disclosure, the requester can sue in federal court, where a judge can review the requested information to determine whether or not it is properly protected and withheld. If it is not, and if the requester's argument prevailed, then the court could order the agency to release the documents and pay the requester's attorney fees as well.

Even with the amendments, certain types of sensitive information were protected under the FOIA and exempt from disclosure. The act provides that agencies may (they are not required to) withhold information in nine categories: properly classified defense and foreign policy information; internal personnel matters; matters specifically exempted by statutes that permit no discretion on withholding; trade secrets; interagency or intraagency memoranda circulated as part of a decision-making process; information whose release would be a "clearly unwarranted invasion of personal privacy"; some types of law enforcement data; bank examination records; and information about oil wells.

President Nixon, predictably, opposed the amendments, as did all other agencies, particularly the CIA, the Justice Department, and the Department of Defense. But before Nixon could veto the measure, he resigned rather than face impeachment proceedings. While the House and Senate were conferring on the amendments, Gerald Ford became president. The man who would later pardon Nixon vetoed the amendments. In his veto message, Ford said he objected to federal judges making what he said amounted to decisions about classification in "sensitive and complex areas where they have no expertise." He conceded that the bill had "laudable goals," but called it "unworkable and unconstitutional."

The veto touched off an intense battle over the act, with Congress and the press on one side and the White House and executive branch agencies on the other. The administration maintained that the amendments to strengthen public access would be too costly and burdensome for government. But even before the Democrats swept the congressional elections in the wake of Watergate, one news survey showed "overwhelming bi-partisan congressional sentiment in favor of overriding the veto." Senator Edward M. Kennedy, who led the Senate fight to override the veto, said the amendments were an attempt to see that "the public's business was carried out in public."

On November 21, 1974, the House voted 371 to 31 to override Ford's veto. No representative spoke in favor of the president's position. One representative shouted from the well of the House, "Hasn't the White House learned that government secrecy is the real enemy of democracy?" The next day the Senate followed suit. Perhaps also in reaction to the executive branch's abuses of power in the Watergate scandal,

Congress simultaneously passed the Privacy Act, which limits the types of information that the government can collect on citizens, as well as how it is used. House Republican leader John Rhodes and Republican Senator Howard Baker joined the bipartisan majority in support of the FOIA. "Two recent tragedies, the war in Vietnam and Watergate, might not have occurred if executive branch officials had not been able to mask their acts in secrecy," Baker observed.

Despite the "teeth" put into the FOIA by the amendments, many agencies failed to comply with its provisions. According to a 1976 *Washington Post* series, the FBI was taking nine months to comply with requests; the CIA had a twenty-four-hundred-case backlog; and the government faced five hundred pending suits for failure to comply with the act. One of the *Post*'s articles, entitled "A Penchant for Secrecy Still Remains," reported that some federal agencies were "still inventing their own excuses to duck the FOIA." One popular excuse involved an abuse of exemption (b)(3) of the act. This exemption allowed agencies to withhold information if that information was "specifically exempted from disclosure by [another] statute." Agencies had been citing any obscure statute, or slipping new ones in with other legislation, as a way to avoid releasing information. When the Supreme Court in 1975 broadly ruled that the act's language allowed agencies to use such loopholes "regardless of how unwise, self protective, or inadvertent" their enactment was, Congress was moved the next year to amend the act in an effort to prevent such abuse.

In 1977 the FOIA was given another boost, this time from the head of the Justice Department under Carter, Attorney General Griffin Bell. It is the Justice Department's job to advise all executive branch departments and agencies how best to comply with the FOIA and to defend them in court when requesters file lawsuits. Bell sent a policy memo to every department and agency head, stating that even if there was technically a legal basis for withholding documents under the FOIA, the documents should still be released if that would cause no harm to the public interest. Bell further stated that Justice would be reluctant to defend any agency withholding records for purely technical legal reasons.

In the same year, the House Committee on Government Operations lauded the act's accomplishments in its Thirteenth Report: "The Freedom of Information Act is based upon the presumption that the government and the information of the government belong to the people. Consistent with this view is the notion that the proper function of the state with respect to government information is that of custodian in service to society. . . . Above all, the statute made it clear that federal agencies were hereinafter to provide the fullest possible disclosure to the public."[29] The report also acknowledged that hundreds of major news stories, magazine articles, and books had been based on documents released under FOIA provisions.

But the FOIA has always had powerful opponents. Despite President Carter's campaign promises of "sunshine" and "minimum secrecy" in government and despite the policies of Attorney General Bell, recent efforts to weaken the information law began under the Carter administration in 1975, the same year the 1974 amendments strengthening the act went into effect. According to historian John Anthony Scott, those amendments ran counter to "deeply rooted traditions of bureaucratic secrecy in Washington. They generated a powerful backlash among federal officials who indeed fear public accountability, desire to go on operating without embarrassment of public scrutiny, and commit errors and even crimes they would prefer to hide." Rather than comply with the newly strengthened act, Scott told the American Historical Association, "they redoubled their efforts to nullify the Act and to bring about its repeal."[30] Benjamin Civiletti, who succeeded Griffin Bell as Carter's attorney general, even explored the possibility of introducing a package of amendments to narrow the scope of the FOIA. Some of them, such as a three- to five-year moratorium on the release of criminal files (as requested by the FBI) and exemptions for CIA documents, went even further than the amendments later proposed by the Reagan administration. Perhaps because the public was then highly critical of government secrecy, the Civiletti proposals were not submitted to Congress.

Also in 1977, the FBI began unauthorized shredding of its files, an action that, if it continued and became widespread among government agencies, would make the FOIA a dead letter. According to Scott, the federal Bureau of Prisons also began destroying files a few years later. (In 1979, a group of historians and the American Friends Service Committee filed suit to stop the destruction, and in 1980 a District of Columbia federal judge ordered the FBI to stop shredding.) The destruction of records is testimony to the agencies' attitudes toward open government and public accountability.

The Reagan administration lost no time taking aim at the FOIA. On May 4, 1981, Attorney General William French Smith sent a memo to all government agencies, instructing them that the Justice Department would defend all denials of FOIA requests based on legal technicalities. Smith's letter reversed the Carter policy, which had stressed compliance with the spirit of the law. Under the Smith guidelines, requesters of information faced the likelihood of long, expensive litigation against Justice Department lawyers in order to obtain records they formerly needed only to request. Several months later, in October, the administration submitted a package of proposals that, in its words, would "fine tune" the FOIA. Smith said changes were necessary because "certain requirements of the Act have interfered unduly with proper law enforcement activities and jeopardized national security functions. In addition, compliance with provisions of the Act has resulted in unnecessary burden and expense to the government." [31]

Proponents of the act countered that the administration plan was not fine tuning at all, but rather a frontal assault. Among the proposed changes were the following: (1) The attorney general could keep secret selected information about terrorism, organized crime, and foreign counterintelligence operations. Under the current version of the act, this information can be kept secret only if its release would interfere with an investigation. (2) Agencies could provide less information about their internal operations. (3) Only citizens and resident aliens could make requests. Current law allows anyone to make a request. (4) The government for the first time could charge extra for documents of commercial value and impose charges for processing and censoring released documents, in addition to previously authorized fees for search and copying. (5) Businesses would be notified of requests for information they had submitted and be given a greater opportunity to contest release. (6) Perhaps most importantly, judges' power to review material related to national security would be severely narrowed. Judges could only determine whether an agency had been "arbitrary or capricious" in its classification, and not whether the documents had been properly classified. Several members of Congress submitted similar proposals to amend the FOIA; the most threatening of these came from Senator Orrin Hatch (R-Utah). Senators Chafee and D'Amato also sought to weaken the act.

The proposed changes precipitated a flurry of controversy and prompted the formation of a coalition to save the Freedom of Information Act. The lineup was familiar: The press, labor unions, liberals, civil libertarians, and academics came to the Capitol throughout the summer, fall, and winter of 1982 to lobby against those who supported the amendments, mostly conservatives, the intelligence agencies, law enforcement groups, and big business. The testimony before Senator Hatch's Subcommittee on the Constitution was hot and heavy.

Two of the leading advocates of "fine tuning" the act headed agencies that had been repeatedly embarrassed by public revelations, through the FOIA, of their misdeeds. CIA Director William Casey, coordinator of all U.S. intelligence efforts, wanted nothing less than a complete exemption from the FOIA for the CIA, National Security Agency, and Defense Intelligence Agency. Casey's testimony struck at the heart of the battle over open government. Casey said, "There are inherent contradictions in applying a statute designed to assure openness in government to agencies whose work is necessarily secret." [32] He amplified his point in an address to the American Legion on August 24: "I question very seriously whether a secret intelligence agency and the Freedom of Information Act can coexist for very long." Casey labeled the act "a self-inflicted wound which gives foreign intelligence agencies and anyone else a right to poke into our files." The CIA chief claimed that the information law had caused "serious compromises of classified information," but he refused to publicly cite examples.

In secret testimony later declassified (the text shows that few of his remarks were sanitized), Casey presented what has been referred to as the perception argument. According to this argument, foreign intelligence agents are refusing to cooperate with the CIA because they believe their identities will be revealed under the FOIA. As Senator Hatch put it, "the perception or fear of possible disclosure could result and has resulted in an awful lot of silence." But Casey was not able to come up with specifics, as excerpts from the hearing show:

> SENATOR HATCH: How many [agents have quit the CIA because of fear of disclosure], Mr. Director?
>
> MR. CASEY: I don't know .We certainly don't have them all. . . .
>
> SENATOR DECONCINI: Can you tell us how many? Six? A dozen? Three dozen?
>
> MR. CASEY: I really can't tell you. I would be guessing. I would be guessing.
>
> SENATOR DECONCINI: But you know firsthand having talked to some?
>
> MR. CASEY: No, no. I get this as hearsay in the organization. . . .
>
> SENATOR LEAHY: Are there any employees?
>
> MR. CASEY: I don't know.[33]

Casey was trying to make the point that his service was losing sources of information because of a *perception* that such identities might be revealed, even though the FOIA exempts from disclosure the identities of CIA operatives. According to a congressional aide, Casey did not give a convincing presentation to the senators even during the classified part of his testimony.

FBI Director William Webster also presented secret testimony to Hatch's subcommittee. He claimed the FBI lost many informants because they feared that through routine disclosures under the FOIA, their identities would be made known. The FBI director cited examples of incidents in which organized crime figures had confronted FBI informants with FBI documents released under the FOIA, which, Webster said, caused the informers to lose interest in informing.

The senators found Webster a convincing witness in his arguments for change in the act, according to one congressional source. But Webster's allegations that the FOIA caused the FBI to lose informants was contradicted by NBC correspondent Carl Stern. In a *New York Times* op-ed piece on February 10, 1982, Stern reported on the contents of FBI files on the FOIA, which he obtained using the act. Webster, Stern noted, had claimed repeatedly that the act cost his agency hundreds of sources, and made informants into "an endangered species." But the FBI's own files revealed that for nineteen months in 1979 and 1980, the FBI tried and failed to collect data to support Webster's claims. After monthly checks of all fifty-nine FBI field offices, the FBI "impact study" revealed that only nineteen out of thousands of informants furnished no information or less information for fear of disclosure under the FOIA. Agents described forty-two instances in which, they believed, the general public refused to cooperate because they feared they would be identified. No harm ever came to an informant as a result of the act, said Stern, and there was only one case in which agents thought an informant was endangered because of released documents.

Stern also wrote that while Webster frequently claimed the act harmed informants, the FBI chief did not report the findings of his "impact study" to Congress. "The reason may be," Stern concluded, "that his frequent statements that the Freedom of Information Act is seriously injuring the Federal Bureau of Investigation are contradicted by his own study." Nevertheless, Department of Justice officials disputed Stern's findings, as did later studies by law enforcement agencies. For example, a Drug Enforcement Administration study indicated that 14 percent of its investigations were adversely affected by the act.

Representatives of law enforcement and intelligence organizations testified that the FOIA imperiled their ability to protect the public against criminals. Among them was Robert Nesoff of the Federal Criminal Investigators Association, whose remarks contained Freudian overtones: "After placing severe restrictions on intelligence agencies, former President Carter complained publicly that they had not provided him with proper information," said Nesoff. "His comments and actions are tantamount to castrating a stud bull and then complaining that it is not doing its job." [34] In general, though, the law enforcement spokesmen focused their criticisms on alleged disclosure of agents' and informants' names, something the act had never allowed.

Press representatives testifying in support of the act claimed that the FBI was crying wolf. They urged the Hatch subcommittee not to fall for the "perception" argument and to leave the act alone. James Wieghard of the American Society of Newspaper Editors challenged Webster's and Casey's arguments about the loss of informants. Wieghard suggested several reasons the intelligence officials wanted their agencies exempted from the FOIA. He told the subcommittee:

> We learned from Freedom of Information disclosures of the vast FBI 15-year investigation, called Cointelpro, in which the National Council of Churches, the Socialist Workers Party, the Southern Christian Leadership Conference, members of the Republican and Democratic parties, and officeholders in the Republican and Democratic parties were routinely subjected to investigation. . . .
>
> Many of the CIA abuses during the period when the Congress of the U.S. itself conducted a very thorough investigation of abuses of power . . . were made available to the public for the first time through the Freedom of Information Act. The testing program that the CIA conducted in the 1950s and 1960s with drugs—hallucinogenic drugs—on subjects who did not know they were being tested—that information was developed through the Freedom of Information Act. . . .
>
> I am not at all surprised that the FBI's list of informants has dwindled over the last decade. . . . Do we really need informants from the Southern Christian Leadership Conference? Do we need informants from the National Council of Churches? . . . This is a large percentage of the informants the FBI has lost. . . .
>
> I am not surprised that local law enforcement agencies are refusing to cooperate with Federal agencies if that is indeed the case—not because the Freedom of Information Act has turned up the names of confidential agents and thereby endangered their lives. . . but because the head of the Secret Service of the United States, the head of the Central Intelligence Agency of the United States, and the head of the FBI of the United States are going around and making public speeches and saying that they cannot protect confidential informants. . . . I have yet to find the name of an underworld informant who cooperated with Federal officials whose names were disclosed to the public through the Freedom of Information Act.[35]

Wieghard went on to say that the vast number of improper disclosures of law enforcement and national security information came, not from the FOIA, but from high-level officials using leaks. He noted that in the Abscam investigation, a Justice Department official leaked information about the investigation even before indictments had been handed up.

Steven R. Dornfeld of Knight-Ridder Newspapers argued that the FOIA benefits the whole of society. "The FOIA does simply not threaten national security," he claimed. "It enhances it by building a well-informed electorate. The FOIA does not endanger the CIA's intelligence-gathering operations. Apparently, it is an annoyance for the CIA at times, but public servants often find public accountability annoying just as retailers sometimes find customers annoying . . . or spouses find each other annoying. . . . Even the agency concedes that not a single word of classified information has even been released by a judge under the FOIA over its objection."[36]

Hatch seemed troubled when officials complained that the FOIA allows anyone to file for government information, even Soviets, felons, and drug dealers. Hatch appeared equally distraught that various law-abiding public interest groups used the act. He described these groups as "non-profit entities of extreme concern to the intelligence experts in this country who are willing to interfere with National Government secrets, intelligence, and top-secret information." Although Hatch did not specifically identify the groups, his reference was widely understood to include the Institute for Policy Studies, a left-wing think tank in Washington, D.C., the Center for National Security Studies, the Center for Defense Information, and other groups critical of U.S. foreign and national security policies.

The harshest opposition to the FOIA, aside from the intelligence and law enforcement communities, came from representatives of big business, who argued that public access under the FOIA should be restricted because their competitors used the act to learn trade secrets. Spokespersons for many industries, as well as lobbying groups like the National Association of Manufacturers, pressed for greater confidentiality of business information, even though trade secrets were already protected under the act.

Of course, not every company must divulge information to the federal government. But many must do so either as a precondition for winning government contracts (such as defense contractors), or because their products affect the health and safety of the public and are federally regulated (such as makers of drugs and medical devices). Thus, the number of businesses affected by the FOIA is substantial. And the volume of paper involved is staggering. One application for a new drug license submitted by Eli Lilly contained more than two hundred thousand pages and weighed more than a ton.

According to one Securities and Exchange Commission lawyer, private businesses account for 60 percent of all FOIA requests filed.[37] Many companies regularly file requests to learn what their competitors are doing. In fact, this has generated an entire cottage industry that does nothing but use the FOIA to gather industrial information for its clients. This is one use of the act that advocates of open government probably did not envision when the law was first passed. On the other hand, public interest groups and reporters have used business information obtained under the act to expose dangerous products and corporate irresponsibility.

During the Hatch hearings, business's arguments against the FOIA often paralleled those of the intelligence agencies. In a variation on the theme "What's good for business is good for America," corporate representatives argued that the FOIA hurt businesses, and this in turn harmed the nation's interests. The act, they claimed, had become a tool of industrial espionage. And like the intelligence agencies, one business study contended that the mere perception that vital business data were being compromised through the act caused major marketplace losses. On the surface these arguments seemed reasonable. Whenever an FOIA request was filed, an official somewhere in the government had the responsibility of sifting through detailed, often scientific documents and determining what information would harm the company if released and what would not. Any official who did not know the ins and outs of that particular market conceivably might not be in a position to judge accurately. This made the business executives anxious.

The executives wanted to narrow the scope of the business data that could be released under the FOIA. They wanted the act amended to include a new procedure under which they would be notified whenever information they had submitted was requested, giving them an opportunity to argue against releasing any material they felt should be off-limits to the public. Despite the claims of other business executives and authorities who had studied the effect of the FOIA on business and claimed that the act in fact stimulated free enterprise and benefited small businesses, such an amendment was proposed.

The final argument presented against the FOIA was financial. Several government officials told the Hatch subcommittee that it is too costly and burdensome to process FOIA requests. The *New York Times* reported on October 5, 1981, that the government says it spends $50 million annually on the act. That does seem like a lot. But proponents of the FOIA pointed out that the United States spends $100 million a year on military bands. In an annual government budget of $700 billion, they argued, the $50 million spent on the FOIA was a sound investment in an informed public.

Even though journalists make only about 5 to 10 percent of all FOIA requests, the most vociferous arguments for preserving the act came from this quarter. Pressure on Congress by journalists (whom, after all, politicians usually prefer not to antagonize) forced the Hatch subcommittee to hold more hearings than it had originally planned. Still, things looked grim. Just before Christmas 1981, the Hatch and Reagan bills were merged. The composite bill featured the more restrictive measures of the Hatch and administration bills. After a long, heated battle, the subcommittee reported out the composite Reagan-Hatch bill, modified through the efforts of Senator Patrick Leahy of Vermont. But even this bill did not pass; it died before the full Senate could act on it.

Though the legislative battle to weaken the Freedom of Information Act in the 97th Congress failed in the fall of 1982, by early 1983 similar amendments had been introduced into the 98th. Those who wished to remove more information from the act's reach had not changed their minds.

INTELLIGENCE IDENTITIES PROTECTION ACT

On June 23, 1982, with much pomp and circumstance, President Reagan journeyed to CIA headquarters in Langley, Virginia, to sign the Intelligence Identities Protection Act. The legislation, first introduced under the Carter administration, was intended to protect intelligence agents working abroad from attack by anti-American groups. But the law had another thrust as well. Some members of the press, constitutional lawyers, and civil liberties groups regarded it as perhaps the most dangerous of all measures of information control the government had taken to date. For the first time in two hundred years of American history, it became potentially illegal for a private citizen to repeat unclassified information already in the public record.

The Intelligence Identities Protection Act itself was straightforward: Anyone not authorized to handle classified documents who divulges any information revealing the identity of a covert agent could be subject to three years in federal prison and a $15,000 fine. Anyone with access to classified information who learns and discloses an agent's identity faces a maximum fine of $25,000 and up to five years in jail; anyone with access to classified documents identifying a covert agent who divulges that information can be fined up to $50,000 and imprisoned for up to ten years.

During the mid-1970s, congressional hearings and journalists exposed an astonishing array of illegal and unconstitutional operations carried out clandestinely by the CIA and other U.S. intelligence agencies. Abroad, the CIA plotted to overthrow or assassinate leaders of foreign governments; at home the FBI and CIA spied on and disrupted lawful political activists.

In the wake of these disclosures, opponents of covert action published journals exposing and criticizing the U.S. intelligence network and identifying its secret agents. Chief among these were *Counterspy* and the subsequent *Covert Action Information Bulletin* (*CAIB*). Several former CIA agents also authored articles and books exposing illegal and unethical covert operations and named former colleagues. Philip Agee, author of *Inside the Company* and an adviser to *CAIB,* was the most prominent. These critics believed it was not only immoral but also hypocritical for the U.S. government, which purports to be a democracy in support of other democracies, to use such totalitarian means as murder, manipulating elections, spreading misinformation, and propping up hated dictatorships to gain political advantage. Only by tearing away the cloak of national security and focusing public light on each individual responsible, they reasoned, could the agencies be made accountable. They believed that naming those involved would help stop the agency's depredations.

Government officials and others thought the activists against covert action were disloyal and should be silenced. In 1981, the Reagan administration took action to stop them by supporting a bill formally entitled the Intelligence Identities Protection Act. Identical to a bill introduced under the Carter administration, this measure was introduced on January 5 by House Permanent Select Intelligence Committee chairman Edward P. Boland. The measure would make it a crime to identify covert operatives of the CIA, FBI, and military intelligence agencies "for the purpose of impairing or impeding the foreign intelligence activities of the United States." Boland said the bill was aimed at "the miscreants who have taken it upon themselves to systematically destroy our intelligence community," and he specifically targeted Philip Agee and his magazine *CAIB*. Normal, "responsible" reporting, Boland said, would not be affected.

Others disagreed. Among them was Congressman Don Edwards, a staunch advocate of civil liberties and a former FBI agent. Said Edwards, "The bill allows no exceptions where disclosures are aimed at revealing illegal activity. The door is open to level this provision at a broad class of individuals, many acting within the Constitution."[38] Without identifying those responsible, argued the critics of CIA covert actions, reporters could not expose agency wrongdoing.

The intense controversy over this bill centered on its possible effect on the press, its curtailment of what the public may know and discuss, and the risk to agents. On one side were the ready defenders of national security and the intelligence community; on the other were the press and civil liberties groups, who were wary of the shadier side of the agency's past record. Supporters of the bill cited the death of the CIA's station chief in Athens, Richard Welch, killed in 1975 after he was identified in a *Counterspy* article. They claimed the magazine was directly responsible for his assassination. Opponents of the law pointed out, however, that Welch had been identified earlier in an East German publication. Moreover, Welch had insisted on living in the home of the previous Athens CIA chief despite repeated warnings that to do so was dangerous. Further, of over two thousand agents whom the "miscreants" had identified, Welch was the only one to be killed. But in 1980, just as the bill came up for consideration in Congress, the home of an agent in Jamaica was attacked two days after his identity was revealed by an editor of *CAIB*. No one was injured.

The risk to agents, on the one hand, and the threat to freedom of the press, on the other, were not the only troubling aspects of this far-reaching measure. To fully appreciate the ramifications of the Intelligence Identities Protection Act, it is necessary to consider two executive orders that preceded it. On December 4, 1981, Reagan signed the first of these, Executive Order 12333, on intelligence, expanding the range of activities in which the intelligence community could engage. Critics charged that the order "unleashed" these agencies, lifting the restrictions imposed on them following the exposure of their illegal acts and permitting, for the first time, CIA counterintelligence activities inside the United States (see chapter 5 for further discussion). The intelligence order tied in neatly with the names of agents bill and was later complemented by Executive Order 12356, on security classification.

These three acts formed a legal structure that could conceal and legalize, in the name of national security, the same kinds of illegal intelligence activities that characterized Watergate, the COINTELPRO operations against lawful political groups, and Operation CHAOS, in which the CIA infiltrated the antiwar movement. Whether designed to or not, the legal structure could function like this: First, the executive order on intelligence allows intelligence agents to infiltrate activist groups; next, the executive order on classification ensures the secrecy of their operations; then, the names of agents bill makes it a crime for journalists to name agents. If the agencies had not had such extensive records of violating the law at home and abroad, perhaps there would be no cause for concern. As it is, the odds for recidivism seem high.

The controversy over the law revealed its dangers. As first introduced, the legislation was aimed at stopping people who reveal agent identities with "the intent to harm" intelligence operations—specifically, the editors of *CAIB* and Philip Agee. But as the bill wended its way through Congress, it was broadened to include anyone who divulged any information identifying an agent, and who had "reason to believe" that such identification would harm U.S. foreign intelligence. A reporter, for instance, would not need to name names to qualify for prosecution; any information that identifies an agent to somebody else is sufficient.

Even though there was intense debate over the "reason to believe" standard and its replacement of the narrower "intent to harm" standard, the bill sailed through Congress. But despite protracted discussion and overwhelming approval, it remains impossible to know exactly what the law means and how it will be used. As this book goes to press, no prosecutions have taken place.

When the House and Senate passed different versions of the bill, a conference committee met to resolve the differences. The conference committee report on the bill filed by the House and Senate members blunted the thrust of the law to some degree by specifying certain kinds of acts that Congress did *not* intend to punish. The acts included reports by an organization to determine whether or not its employees are informants for the CIA, and investigations of illegal activities and controversial government programs where the primary objective of the investigation is not the identification of intelligence agents. Since the legislative history of a law is often instrumental in interpreting congressional intent, the conference committee report could be important in determining which activities merit prosecution and which do not. In a confusing twist, however, some members of Congress rejected the report and stated that the bill meant exactly what it said; no softening was intended.

If the report's recommendations are not binding, some frightening scenarios could take place. James Ridgeway and Alexander Cockburn described some of these in the *Village Voice*:

> You have joined your colleagues in a conference room at the Riverside Church to review progress in organizing a nuclear freeze march. Everybody is taking notes. You leave the room, and walk down Broadway for a cup of coffee. You pass a police car, and by chance notice one of your colleagues inside, reading the notes you have just seen him taking to two people, one of whom is known to you to be an undercover FBI agent. Startled, you hasten back to the room to tell your associates that there is an informer in your midst. As you leave the room, you are arrested and charged under the Intelligence Identities Protection Act with revealing the name of an intelligence operative. You face up to three years in prison and a fine of $15,000.
>
> Discussing the internal politics of Argentina in the wake of the Falkland Islands crisis, you suggest in print, on the basis of sources, that General Galtieri has been a CIA informant. You face the same penalties.
>
> After a couple of drinks at a cocktail party, you speculate that a well-known philanthropist might at some time have worked for the FBI or perhaps military intelligence at Harvard in the late 1960s. Again, you face the same penalties.[39]

While it remains to be seen which, if any, of these scenarios will come to pass, the law has prevented information from reaching the public. With its substantial penalties, it has a chilling effect on reporters, editors, and publishers, who now are forced to consider its provisions and weigh the odds before going ahead with stories on intelligence. Elizabeth Farnsworth, an author and television commentator who is an expert on Latin American policy, said after the law passed, "I'll never name any agent again. I've done it many times in the course of stories on American policy, but I don't even dare come close now." [40]

Even if a journalist should decide in the course of routine work to risk reporting information that might identify an agent, the journalist will have to consider the possibility of jail in order to protect the name of the sources—who have themselves become liable to a long prison term for informing the reporter. Thus the chilling effect is tripled. Reporters may face penalties first for revealing agents and second for protecting sources; finally, the sources themselves face penalties if they are discovered. Reporters on the intelligence beat in Washington have found previously open doors closed in their faces because of the act's penalties.

Some senators deeply involved with the bill described to the *New York Times* their concerns over the new law. Senator John Chafee (R-R.I.), who introduced the bill in the Senate and later added the "reason to believe" clause, reflected the administration's view when he explained how he weighed America's need for a free press against the need for effective intelligence. "They say my bill will inhibit the press, and that's true," he said. "But the press accepts prohibitions in wartime. . . . I don't want to equate this situation with war, but intelligence is a dangerous business."

The implications of Chafee's view were not lost on Senators Joseph Biden (D-Del.) or Patrick Leahy (D-Vt.). Biden expressed the belief that cold war attitudes accounted for the measure's easy passage. "I really do think," he said, "that there is a whole attitude out there that says 'In order to compete with the Soviet Union and protect our interests, we have to write off civil liberties.' " Leahy expressed similar sentiments. "This Administration seems to start from the premise 'How much can we hide?' I start from the premise 'How can we protect the First Amendment?' " [41]

Several law professors were troubled by the passage of the bill. A respected conservative scholar, Professor Philip Kurland of the University of Chicago, wrote, "I cannot see how a law that inhibits the publication, without malicious intent, of information that is in the public domain and previously published can be valid." More than 140 law professors signed a statement in support of his opinion. Kurland called the measure "the clearest violation of the First Amendment attempted by Congress in this era." [42] Law professor Herman Schwartz of American University warned that the law is a "legislative mess and a constitutional catastrophe. The combination of pervasive ambiguities and heavy penalties will give it the chilling effect of a Russian winter." [43]

With the new law aimed so specifically at certain individuals, the obvious question was, Just whom does the First Amendment protect? In debates and on editorial pages of newspapers around the country, most commentators condemned Agee and *CAIB,* and hoped that the law would not harm the "responsible" press like the *New York Times* and the *Washington Post.* Only a few voices called clearly for an absolute interpretation of the First Amendment. Among them was *The Nation,* the oldest weekly in the United States. In a pointed editorial, it said, "The view that the First Amendment protects only respectable criticism based on approved motives is discouraging enough coming from Congress, the White House and the courts. Coming from the press itself, it is downright disgraceful." [44] As authors James Ridgeway and Alexander Cockburn wrote in an article blasting the legislation, "Either you can assail and expose the actions of your government, or you can't."

John Stockwell, a CIA agent for thirteen years who turned against his former employer because of its "long and continuing record of arrogance, incompetence, cruelty and irresponsible activities," testified before the Senate Select Intelligence Committee that "the objective of this bill is clearly not to protect the safety of secret agents, as its proponents claim, because the CIA itself is flagrantly careless of the identities of its own agents." The real purpose of the bill, he continued, is "to gain an important weapon for the CIA to use in silencing its critics." He explained what he meant. "I was a clandestine case officer. . . . I lived under cover. I think it is fair to say that I know how cover functions." He said his first chief of station told him to forget what he had been taught about cover, and to let people know he was a CIA agent so that they would come to him with information. He said he used his true CIA identity in his function as an agent. But the senators dismissed Stockwell as "unpatriotic." After the bill passed, he wrote mournfully that it "inaugurated a new era in which the rights of our secret police supersede those of the people." [45]

Indeed, few wanted to hear that it was a CIA operative who first began naming the names of its agents. In 1969, an informant who had infiltrated underground newspapers and antiwar groups gave the *Quicksilver Times,* a Washington, D.C., underground paper, a list of agents' names. The paper published the names; the operative went on to take part in Operation CHAOS, the CIA program to disrupt the underground and dissident press.[46]

Reporter Angus Mackenzie, who described the government's campaign of sabotage against the underground press in the *Columbia Journalism Review,* called the law "a gun directed at me." [47] In a panel debate with Mackenzie and other reporters in San Francisco, U.S. Attorney Joseph Russoniello called the act "a balance" between the public's right to know and the protection of agents. "If that's a balance," retorted a Stanford law professor also on the panel, "someone's fat thumb is on the scale."

Russoniello reflected the views of his ultimate chief, President Reagan, as he discussed the press's proper role in reporting on intelligence matters. He contended that when reporters wrote about the intelligence agencies, there was no need to use people's names. He also suggested that any reporter with information about agency wrongdoing ought to take it first to the appropriate congressional oversight committee. There was no need to publish it. The need to keep secrets, Russoniello claimed, was far more important than a reporter's story or the public's right to know.

THE COURTS

Frank Snepp was one of the last Americans to struggle into an evacuation helicopter from the roof of the American embassy in Saigon in April 1975. As the Americans left, Vietnamese fought one another in their desperation not to be left behind; crowds surged through the streets toward the embassy, hoping their American allies would not abandon them. It was an ugly scene. Snepp, who joined the CIA in 1968, was the agency's principal analyst for North Vietnamese political affairs, serving two tours of duty with the CIA in Saigon. He left disillusioned with what he regarded as the agency's bungling of its mission in Southeast Asia.

A year later, Snepp resigned from the agency. In 1977 he violated the contract he signed upon joining the CIA by publishing *Decent Interval,* a book criticizing the agency's performance in Vietnam. Although all CIA employees must agree to submit any writings based on information learned through the agency to officials for prepublication clearance, Snepp did not clear his book. He claimed that since it contained no classified information, it was, according to the terms of his contract, not subject to agency scrutiny. The CIA disagreed, and at the agency's request, the Justice Department under President Carter charged Snepp with breaching his prepublication agreement and took him to court. How did Snepp's right to express his opinions about the intelligence agency weigh against the government's claim of a broken contract?

In the past, the courts usually leaned toward the side of the free press. In 1931, the Supreme Court held in *Near v. Minnesota* that the government cannot prevent the press from publishing information except, during wartime, such details as the "sailing dates of transports or the number and location of troops." But by the midseventies, the Court had considerably broadened the rationale for stopping the presses. While the Court's decision to permit publication of the Pentagon Papers was widely heralded as a golden moment in the history of the First Amendment, the ruling had a dark side as well. The judges said that the government had the right to block publication if disclosure would "surely result in direct, immediate and irreparable damage to the nation"—a standard far laxer than the sailing dates of ships in wartime. The Court also held that if Congress should pass a law allowing prior restraint, the standard for quashing publication could be even lower.

After the Pentagon Papers decision, the Court during the Carter administration leaned toward the government's side in First Amendment controversies. In 1976, for example, it ruled that military officials at Fort Dix had the right to ban speeches, the distribution of leaflets, or demonstrations by civilians on parts of the base open to the general public. In 1980, the Court upheld Defense Department regulations requiring servicemen to obtain the written approval of a base commander before distributing written materials, such as petitions to Congress, on a military base or troopship. Following the reasoning in the Fort Dix opinion, the Court said that First Amendment rights of free speech were outweighed by the need for "morale, discipline, and readiness" in the armed forces. But the Court's harshest attack on free speech and the public's right to know were reserved for Frank Snepp.

The first court to hear the case, the Federal District Court for Eastern Virginia, ruled that Snepp had willfully, deliberately, and surreptitiously violated the CIA's trust in him and his agreement. The court ordered Snepp to give all the earnings from his book to the government. Snepp appealed. The appeals court ruled in his favor—somewhat. Even though he had violated the contract, it said, there was no claim that he divulged classified information, and therefore the punishment was too extreme. The government appealed. Without even hearing oral arguments, the U.S. Supreme Court ruled that the first court had been correct. Its decision said that an intelligence agency has the right to demand review of its employees' writings and that the employment contract obliged Snepp to waive permanently his First Amendment rights to speak and publish without prior restraint. The Court was unimpressed with Snepp's claim that nothing classified had been published. It said:

> The government has a compelling interest in protecting both the secrecy and the appearance of confidentiality so essential to the effective operation of our foreign intelligence service.[48]

According to the Court's decision, all government employees with access to classified information automatically have established a fiduciary obligation—a duty that, if not honored, can expose them to lawsuits—

and so the agency employing them can impose a review of their writings without ever having so stipulated in an agreement. The agency, said the Court, can impose "reasonable restrictions on employees' activities that in other contexts might be protected by the First Amendment." Without prepublication review of writings, said the decision, no agency could take measures to prevent employees with access to secret data from concluding on their own "innocently or otherwise—that it should be disclosed to the world." The Court's language made clear its deference to the executive branch's national security arguments. "The CIA is an agency thought by every President since Franklin Roosevelt to be essential to the security of the United States and—in a sense—the free world," the court said.

There were many who saw the other side of the issue. According to John Shattuck of the ACLU, "National security is what protects us from our adversaries, but the Constitution and the Bill of Rights are what distinguish us from them." [49] Congressman Les Aspin, a member of the Armed Services Committee, argued that the *Snepp* decision went too far. "The law ought to set limits on the power of the intelligence agencies to excise, for that is the power to restrict the first amendment rights of all present and former employees," he told Congress.[50]

Aspin cited inconsistent application of rules governing publication by the intelligence agencies. He noted that agency critics like Snepp and John Stockwell found themselves in trouble for their writings, while former agents who wrote favorably about the agency went unscathed, like Howard Hunt, Cord Meyer, and Tom Braden. (After Aspin's speech, former CIA Director William Colby was fined $10,000 for publishing a book about the CIA without first obtaining clearance; compared to what happened to Snepp, that was a mere slap on the wrist.) Aspin also cited differing treatment of categories of publications: books, which the agency reviews carefully; articles, which are reviewed rarely; and speeches, which he said are never reviewed. The logic of this, he said, was questionable. He urged Congress to pass legislation making the prepublication review process more equitable, saying, "We should not set up a process to protect key officials of the intelligence community from embarrassment." [51]

Following the high court's decision, the CIA obtained a court order forbidding Snepp from publishing information about the agency without prior approval from agency officials. Snepp, who had to pay the government $170,000, became impoverished. He began work on two other books, one of which he finished and submitted for the CIA's approval. When the agency wanted something deleted that he felt should stay in, he found himself without the means to pursue an appeal. "I'm forced to think twice every time I put down a word," he told the *New York Times,* "which means they win." [52]

Snepp was not the only former CIA agent to feel the chilling effect of the Court's decision. CIA Director Stansfield Turner forced a number of CIA officials to retire in 1977: "You don't run a good, strong paramilitary or covert action program with a bunch of 55-year-olds," Turner said. "What I've done is cut out high-grade superstructure and doubled the input into the clandestine services, so that we have a group of young tigers."[53]

Many of these embittered "55-year-olds" had considered writing books about their careers and their opinions about the agency, but after what happened to Snepp and the enactment of the Intelligence Identities Protection Act, they had to keep their stories and their resentments to themselves.

Acknowledging that the *Snepp* decision went beyond what it had asked for, the Carter administration issued guidelines limiting the extent to which it would impose prior censorship. The Reagan administration abandoned those guidelines and returned to the letter of the high court's decision. Moreover, the Reagan administration used the *Snepp* decision as the basis for the Presidential Directive on Safeguarding National Security Information, issued on March 11, 1983.

Besides amplifying the power of the executive to quash publication, the Supreme Court has also strengthened its power to withhold information sought under the FOIA. Only rarely has the Supreme Court forced the government to disclose information sought under the FOIA. Since 1973, the Court has allowed the government to suppress underground nuclear test information (on the basis of the *Mink* decision), former Secretary of State Kissinger's telephone transcripts, government contractors' records, Federal Open Market Committee decisions to buy government securities, safety information on exploding television sets, and statements made before an unfair labor hearing.[54] Not since 1976 has the Court ordered disclosure of information in a FOIA case: Before that, it ordered disclosure of National Labor Relations Board legal memoranda and summaries of Air Force Academy ethics hearings. The Court has never allowed the budgets of the intelligence agencies to be revealed, despite laws that mandate public disclosure of all expenditures. Although journalists have tried many times to obtain them, courts have kept the figures secret.

One case in particular emphasizes the way courts weigh conflicting claims of government secrecy against the public's right to know. On October 4, 1982, the Supreme Court denied an FOIA request by Victor S. Navasky, editor of *The Nation,* for a list of books published by the CIA. Navasky had noticed that according to the 1976 report of the Select Committee to Study Government Operations with Respect to Intelligence Activities, led by Senator Frank Church, well over one thousand books had been "produced, subsidized or sponsored" by the agency prior to 1967. Navasky wanted the list for several reasons: Had the CIA been violating its mandate not to operate within the United States? Who wrote for the CIA? What kinds of books had the agency published? Perhaps an interesting *Nation* article on the CIA as publisher could result from the information.

Navasky filed his request in 1976. After what he termed "exquisite procedural, technical and legalistic obstacles" and excruciating delays, he obtained eighty-five documents, but not the list he sought. He learned that the files he wanted varied in size from two to two hundred linear feet (about two thousand pages equal a linear foot), and that CIA publishing, apparently, was a substantial business. He also learned just how important the CIA considers books, which may account somewhat for the ferocity with which the agency went after Frank Snepp. The head of the CIA's covert action staff wrote in 1961, the year the clandestine publishing program began:

> Books differ from all other propaganda media, primarily because one single book can significantly change the readers' attitude and action to an extent unmatched by the impact of any other single medium. . . . Some books have marked changes in history—Marx's *Kapital,* Hitler's *Mein Kampf,* etc., and quite a few others brought about changes in people's thinking on key subjects.[55]

The CIA gave Navasky three reasons for keeping its list of books secret. First, the list was exempt under the FOIA provision keeping information about its "intelligence sources and methods" from disclosure. Second, if it revealed even a single title, that would reveal the "blueprint" by which the publishing operation was accomplished. (A few titles from the CIA's list had already been published in the Church committee's report.) Finally, disclosure of the list would constitute official acknowledgment of the agency's involvement in foreign clandestine book-publishing activities and would have serious foreign relations consequences that could damage our national security. Every court that heard the case accepted the last reason without even asking to hear evidence confirming the agency's claim. The magic words *national security,* like abracadabra, rendered the FOIA powerless.

Navasky concluded a *New York Times* article about his suit by wondering why CIA Director Casey would even bother to try to exempt the CIA from the FOIA, since the act "has yet to be seriously enforced in any practical way against his agency." If the Supreme Court will not force the CIA to release a list of books it published fifteen or twenty years ago, what kind of disclosure *would* the court order?

With each decision increasing the government's control over the flow of information, the Supreme Court does double damage to the First Amendment. For it not only reduces the public's right to know but also decreases government accountability to the people. A recent case involving the National Security Agency illustrates the helpless position of citizens trying to carry out their business free from government surveillance.

In 1980, former *New York Times* reporter Harrison Salisbury filed suit against the government after learning from an FOIA request that the NSA had intercepted and recorded his private overseas communications in the 1960s and 1970s while he was a correspondent. Salisbury asked $10,000 in damages for violations of his First and Fourth Amendment rights. He claimed that the agency, without judicial authorization, had monitored and disseminated conversations by U.S. citizens who had been placed on "watch lists" by the NSA and other intelligence agencies. The United States Court of Appeals discarded Salisbury's lawsuit in *Salisbury v. NSA* because the NSA, in order to defend itself, would have had to reveal information about the way it operated. The agency refused to confirm or deny whether the telegrams of any particular individual had been intercepted. Thus, the NSA was free from any possible damage claims, and its activities could not be exposed. Since Salisbury did not know at the time that his communications were being monitored, he could not have felt inhibited. But he must wonder whether any NSA officials, knowing the content of his communications, might have been in touch with the *New York Times* in attempts to influence its coverage during that period.

Journalists and others now relying on overseas communications, knowing the ruling in Salisbury's case and later lawsuits, must also wonder if their private communications are in fact private. "The courts have been extremely reluctant to play any role in reducing secrecy," wrote Morton Halperin of the Center for National Security Studies in Washington, D.C. "Judges are likely to be even more deferential than they have been in the past to executive branch assertions of what must be kept secret and what powers the executive must have to protect the national security."[56]

ENCROACHMENTS ON SCIENCE AND TECHNOLOGY

Like political opinions and artistic expression, scientific discourse enjoys the protections of the First Amendment. In theory, the government cannot stop the free communication of the results of experiments, plans for a factory, chemical formulas, or articles about electronic circuitry any more than it can stop plays from being produced or socialists from speaking on soapboxes. But as advances in science and technology spread through our society, from video games to the latest in rocketry communications systems, the likelihood grows that private scientific and technical information will touch upon procedures or devices of use to military or intelligence agencies. In science and technology, as in politics and the media, the constitutional right of free expression now conflicts with government claims of national security. The government now claims that some information is "dangerous" and must be suppressed. As a result of recent government actions, many scientists today do not know what they can publish, teach, or discuss.

Until World War II the federal government rarely interfered with scientists and inventors. During the war, of course, it mobilized much of the nation's technical and scientific expertise in the service of the military. "Loose lips sink ships" warned posters and radio stations; information could possibly help the enemy. The president was given powers to censor all communications with foreign countries; the Office of Censorship monitored the press and broadcasting; the atom bomb was developed in secrecy. Information about aspects of science and technology with military applications was strictly controlled.

At the end of the war, Dr. Vannevar Bush, science adviser to the president and director of the Office of Scientific Research and Development, issued a report touching on the future relationships of the federal government to science. Commenting that "without scientific progress, no amount of achievement in other directions can insure our health, prosperity, and security as a nation in the modern world," Bush warned:

> We must proceed with caution in carrying over the methods which work in wartime to the very different conditions of peace. We must remove the rigid controls which we have had to impose, and recover freedom of inquiry and that healthy competitive spirit so necessary for expansion of the frontiers of scientific knowledge.[57]

Instead of genuine peace, though, the world got the cold war. In this state of perpetual tension, where the nation exists neither at peace nor at war, the federal government has had a continuing license to expand its control over information. It has asserted the exclusive authority, in the name of national security, to limit the flow of information about intelligence, defense, foreign relations, and covert action, and, increasingly, to narrow the scope of scientific and technical dialogue. There is, of course, some information, particularly about nuclear weapons, that ought to be controlled. But where is the line separating scientific information legitimately under the control of the government from that which is not? Who draws this line, and how?

With science and technology we have a situation unlike foreign relations, for example, where the information the government seeks to control originates in government agencies. Technical data may have originated in a company laboratory, in a university chemistry experiment, in a research library, in a student's brain. One might expect such material not to be subject to government control unless it was government financed. But given the intense and sometimes deadly rivalry between the United States and its foreign adversaries, the government argues that some nonclassified knowledge must be controlled so that it does not fall into enemy hands.

For many years, government experts charge, the Soviets have been mining U.S. industry and academia for scientific and technological advances they could use at home. According to Assistant Secretary of Commerce Lawrence J. Brady, their spy network "operates like a gigantic vacuum cleaner, sucking up formulas, patents, blueprints and know-how with frightening precision." [58] Using this knowledge, the Soviets have been able to develop their own industries, technologies, and defense systems far more rapidly than if they had had to start building and theorizing from scratch. The U.S. government, particularly the Defense, State, and Commerce Departments and the intelligence agencies, finds this a dangerous situation that must be corrected immediately, since it has presumably contributed to Soviet military progress and development and thus to the threat against the United States. Thus, the government has set in motion attempts to control the spread of scientific and technical knowledge that hitherto was considered purely in the private domain.

Throughout most of our history, scientists and inventors in private industry and universities not connected with the government have been free to communicate their findings in whatever way they chose. But those days may be gone forever. The government's attitude as of the early 1980s was expressed by Assistant Commerce Secretary Brady, who condemned what he called "a strong belief in the academic community that they have an inherent right to . . . conduct research free of government review or oversight." [59] With these words, Brady directly challenged the single most significant difference between the scientific community in the United States and that in other countries like the Soviet Union, where a totalitarian state stifles intellectual inquiry. If the government of the United States were permitted to control the content and dissemination of research, academic freedom as we know it would wither.

In general, there are at present two ways of handling private scientific and technical data. There is the university way, which employs general openness through such means as peer review of experiments and inventions, conferences, symposiums, and publication of results. Private industry is more secretive. As one company seeks to gain competitive advantage over another, it hoards the latest technological advance and swears employees to secrecy. Even corporations, however, communicate freely between their various divisions, including those in foreign countries, and with others in the industry with whom they choose to share the information. Both the university way and the private industry way have been generally free of government intervention until relatively recently, when the government asserted that much new technology had vital national security applications.

One of the major conflicts to erupt involved privately produced cryptography, or research on codes. Toward the end of the Carter administration, in 1978, a set of computer scientists and mathematicians accused the National Security Agency (NSA) of threatening them with sanctions or prosecution for publishing the results of their research. Dr. George Davida, of the University of Wisconsin at Milwaukee, invented a cipher device based on advanced mathematical techniques. After filing for a patent, he received an order from the Patent and Trademark Office telling him not to discuss his device with anyone except agents of the U.S. government or he would face a penalty of up to two years in prison and a $10,000 fine. The order did not specify why national security was involved or say how long the order would be in effect. Davida was given no court hearing or other requirements of due process. The government's order silencing Davida received some criticism in the media, after which the order was withdrawn.

In testimony before Congress, Frank A. Cassell, then assistant chancellor of Davida's university, voiced many scientists' concerns over the issues raised in cases like Davida's:

> Should the executive branch of Government be able to prevent a citizen from speaking or publishing without some involvement by the courts? Should the executive branch of Government be able to invoke the claim of "national security" without demonstrating that our national security was genuinely threatened? Should defense or intelligence agencies be able to interfere with or inhibit academic research through the patent process? Is censorship an appropriate function of the Patent and Trademark Office? Who will prevent abuses of the secrecy order concept that could frighten professors and stifle research in areas someone in a defense or intelligence agency opposes? [60]

The government's rationale for control over private ideas like Davida's encoding system was expressed in an article by patent examiner and attorney Peter D. Rosenberg. He said:

> Access to confidential information belonging to private citizens . . . represents a reasonable exercise of the police power to protect the national security and the proprietary rights of the government. In the interest of self-preservation, a government must assume power to protect itself against, as by the suppression of, the disclosure of potentially destructive weapons and other instruments of warfare.[61]

The law covering these incidents is uncertain. A 1978 Justice Department memo on the issue of government control over private information noted a dearth of First Amendment tests of government action in this area. The Atomic Energy Act, under which the government controls communication of information about atomic energy through injunctions or heavy criminal penalties, has not been challenged conclusively in court on First Amendment grounds.

In an interview with *Science* magazine, Admiral Bobby Ray Inman, then deputy director of the CIA and former chief of the NSA, suggested that the NSA should have authority like that of the Atomic Energy Act to classify the work of any Americans working on cryptography. The Atomic Energy Act provides automatic classification of what it calls restricted data—material about atomic energy. Such material is "born classified"—no matter from what source the idea originates, public or private, it cannot be disseminated. The rules were relaxed to permit private industry to construct nuclear power plants, but the concept "born classified" still applies. Admiral Inman did not get all the authority he wanted, but as a result of his suggestions a study group composed of academic scientists and the NSA was set up to discuss the problem. A Public Cryptography Study Group was formed in 1980; it later recommended that researchers voluntarily submit papers on cryptography to the NSA for review before publishing them, a procedure that was adopted. This marked the first time, except during World War II, that nongovernmental researchers had agreed to the possibility of censorship outside the area of atomic energy and nuclear weapons.

So far the government seems to find this arrangement satisfactory, but not all academics agree. It is a highly unusual situation, some scholars claim, that the government may eventually extend to other areas of research, and may make mandatory rather than voluntary. Some academics charge that they have never even been told why publishing the results of certain cryptography projects would endanger the national security. Admiral Inman dismissed those complaints, saying that their logic was "circular and unreasonable." Yet his own logic seemed somewhat circular. "The specific details of why information must be protected are often even more damaging than the information itself," he said.[62]

The procedure adopted by the Public Cryptography Study Group is just one method available to the government for controlling scientific information originating with private sources. Another means was used to silence Dr. Davida: the Invention Secrecy Act. He had given the rights to his invention to the Wisconsin Alumni Research Association, which then applied for a patent. The invention was found to have implications for the national security. Upon receipt of an application like this, the Patent and Trademark Office, at the request of a government agency, issues a secrecy order. From that point on, the inventor cannot communicate anything about his device without risking heavy penalties. In effect, a private inventor must choose between not patenting his device (in which case anyone can exploit it) and risking confiscation of his ideas by the government. Enacted following World War II, the act supposedly provides for compensation to inventors whose work has been declared secret. But according to a 1980 congressional committee report, that right is more apparent than actual. A government secrecy order may last for years. The law provides no judicial review of either the appropriateness of the secrecy order or related First Amendment issues. The act asserts a government right of eminent domain over the realm of ideas.

President Reagan's executive order on classification also serves to restrict the free flow of private scientific ideas. It requires that scientific, technical, or economic matters relating to national security be considered for classification, including information "under the control of" the United States government. Arguably, private information that is subject to export licensing by the government would qualify as under the government's control. In addition, the executive order classified a whole new category of data: information relating to "vulnerabilities or capabilities of systems, installations, projects or plans relating to the national security." This category is both vague and broad, according to Congressman Glenn English, and conceivably could be stretched to include data about U.S. highway systems. It may also include many kinds of nongovernmental technical and scientific data.

Besides the information the executive branch claims to control under the executive order, there is also the scientific information developed at universities and laboratories under contract to the government, and thus automatically subject to classification. Discussions about that material are foreclosed to all but those who are properly approved to receive protected information and have a need to know about the research in question, whether it is in fact vital to the national security or not.

There are also several acts of Congress that are less well known to the general public but quietly effective in controlling the development of research. Amendments to the Atomic Energy Act passed in 1981 allow the secretary of energy to prohibit unauthorized dissemination of certain *unclassified* information if disclosure could increase the spread of nuclear weapons or lead to the illegal use of nuclear materials; a $100,000 fine may be imposed for violating such an order. The Export Administration Act of 1979 applies to information as well as goods. It covers technical data, which includes basic scientific research as well as information that can be used to produce goods. According to the Commerce Department, which administers the act, the term *export* can encompass communicating information to someone who is going to take it to a foreign country, or even simply publishing the information. There are civil and criminal penalties for violations.

When the Commerce Department and Customs Service began stepped-up enforcement of export control of scientific information in the early 1980s, scientists complained that their academic freedom was being eroded. The law expired in 1983 but was extended by executive order. At this writing, no one knows what form its replacement will take, yet there is no doubt that it will remain a powerful tool for the control of scientific and technical information.

Another means of control, this one under the purview of the State Department, is the Arms Export Control Act of 1976. This covers unclassified information that could be used to produce or maintain a weapon or implement of war. Its implementational rules are known as the ITAR, the International Traffic in Arms Regulations. The scope of the act is wide: The terms *technical data* and *export* are broadly defined. For example, "disclosure through visits abroad by American citizens (including participation in briefings and symposia) and . . . to foreign nationals in the United States (including plant visits and participation in briefings and symposia)" qualify as "export." Civil penalties for violations are the same as for violations of the Export Administration Act; criminal penalties also may be imposed. Nevertheless, at least one court has handed down a decision narrowing this law in order to avoid constitutional problems—violations of First Amendment rights. The court held:

> An expansive interpretation of technical data . . . could seriously impede scientific research and publishing and the international scientific exchange.[63]

According to the court, technical data had to be directly related to specific articles on the government's Munitions List in order to fall under the law.

While some revisions of the ITAR have been proposed in recent years, they would not solve the First Amendment problems raised by the current law, according to a 1981 Justice Department memo to the director of the Office of Munitions Control at the State Department. The regulations could be applied, for example, "to communications of unclassified information by a technical lecturer at a university or to the conversation of a U.S. engineer who meets with foreign friends at home to discuss matters of theoretical interest." The memo concluded that unless there were "special circumstances" posing a grave threat to national security, this law could not be enforced as written.[64]

In addition to specific laws, the government has taken numerous actions that have upset the scientific community. The government has disrupted conferences by pressuring scientists to cancel presentations of papers; forced the withdrawal of conference invitations to participants from communist and socialist nations; seized the papers and books of foreign students; and asked universities to exclude foreign students from certain areas of study. At the same time, a barrage of government statements, speeches, and reports has emphasized the dangers of technology transfer from the United States to the Soviet Union.

The government has also found a new tool in financial threats. The Reagan administration's 1982 budget called for $316 million in Defense Department support of basic research in universities, about triple the 1976 amount. Because of the financial problems facing universities today, there is little likelihood that the academic community will take strong stands against the government's attempts to restrict the free flow of information and thereby jeopardize government funds. During the Vietnam War, universities were better able financially to refuse military-related contracts and to criticize government policies. But times have changed, and so has the economy. According to a *Science* magazine study of the problem, "The universities . . . seem more willing today to do science for the sake of the economy or national security. And, as some higher education officials concede, the universities need the money." [65]

An abbreviated chronology of events related to the conflict between the federal government and scientists over freedom of information gives an idea of the many fronts on which this battle is being waged.

In February 1980, the Commerce Department informed the organizers of an American Vacuum Society conference on computer components called "magnetic bubble memories" that since foreigners from Warsaw Pact nations would be present, the proceedings of the conference would be subject to compliance with export control requirements. In order to avoid possible fines or imprisonment for failure to comply with those wide-ranging regulations, the society had to cancel the invitations sent to people from Hungary, Poland, and the Soviet Union. Participants from the People's Republic of China, who had already left for the conference, were allowed to attend, but had to sign promises that they would not communicate what they learned there to people from eighteen named countries, including their own. Also in that month, the Department of State blocked nine citizens of the Soviet Union from attending a conference organized by the Optical Society of America and the Institute of Electrical and Electronics Engineers on lasers and electro-optical systems.

In early 1981, the State Department imposed so many conditions on the visit of a Hungarian engineer to Cornell University that the visit was canceled. At about the same time, the State Department imposed restrictions under the ITAR on universities doing research on the VHSIC (Very High Speed Integrated Circuit) program, even though the government admitted that information about this general technological and commercial program could not be classified. In addition to the ITAR restrictions, the government asked that foreign students be excluded from the work. Later in 1981, the Defense Department issued a glossy booklet called *Soviet Military Power* describing the might of the Soviet armed forces. Exchanges of scholars, conferences, and symposiums and the openness of American professional and technical literature were blamed for providing the Soviets with the information required to develop a strong technological base.

William D. Carey of the American Association for the Advancement of Science firmly believes, as do many other scientists, that good science depends as much on the free exchange of information as on the empirical process. In a letter to Frank Carlucci, deputy secretary of defense, Carey criticized the booklet. "In particular, that position [blaming unfettered scientific exchanges and openness for harming U.S. military interests] strikes in a deadly way at the dependence of scientific progress on open communication and shared information. Our own military power will be diminished, not enhanced, if the wellheads of scientific communication are sealed and new knowledge confined in silos of secrecy and prior restraint." [66] Carlucci responded with a long, detailed list of incidents in which he claimed the Soviets had abused scientific and technical exchanges with the United States in a "highly orchestrated, centrally directed effort aimed at gathering the technical information required to enhance their military posture." Carlucci closed his reply by saying that he felt it possible to inhibit the flow of militarily critical technology from the United States to the Soviet Union "without infringing on legitimate scientific discourse." [67] Carlucci did not, however, define "infringements" and "legitimate scientific discourse"—the issues that lie at the heart of the controversy.

In December 1981, Attorney General William French Smith raised the pitch, if not the level, of the debate in a speech in Los Angeles, when he accused the Soviets of "trying to remedy their shortcomings by illegal acquisition of Western strategic technology." He blamed the Freedom of Information Act and thousands of Soviet "technology collection officers" throughout the free world for contributing to the Soviet Union's military-related technology. He vowed to thwart the Soviet attempts to steal U.S. technical knowledge.[68]

Continuing the government's attacks, Admiral Bobby Ray Inman, then deputy director of the CIA, warned those attending the annual conference of the American Association for the Advancement of Science (AAAS), in January 1982, that if the scientists did not voluntarily agree to prepublication review of their research, "a tidal wave" of public outrage at the "hemorrhage of the country's technology" would force legal sanctions on them. When asked where this outrage would come from, he said, in effect, that the CIA would create it. Inman went on to suggest a number of subjects that should be covered by prepublication review procedures, including computer hardware and software, crop projections, and manufacturing techniques. In his analysis of Inman's warning, science writer Christopher Paine noted several important omissions made by the admiral. By far the largest "tech transfers" in recent years took place under government-approved contracts for sales by large American corporations to the Soviet Union, such as the 1972 sale of 164 Bryant Centalign B grinders, which make precision ball bearings used in Soviet ICBM guidance platforms. Paine named IBM, Rockwell International, and others as the major deliverers of technology to the Soviet Union, not the individual scientists and researchers whom Inman had lectured in Washington.[69] In addition, according to *Science* magazine, the Defense Science Board, in a 1979 study entitled *Critical Technologies for Export Control,* concluded that sales of factories, license agreements, and other commercial transactions were the principal elements of technology control. Perhaps, said Paine, Inman needed reminding that "it was not individual researchers, but the corporate managers of such defense and intelligence community contractors as Sperry-Univac and Control Data who pushed for less restrictive controls during the 1970s." Inman also failed to mention such former intelligence agents as Edwin Wilson and Frank Terpil, who illegally peddled technological information and arms to other nations.[70]

Inman was rebutted at the AAAS meeting by Peter Denning, of the Purdue University Department of Computer Science. Denning said that the system required to police information in the manner Inman desired "is clearly more compatible with a dictatorship than a democracy." He observed, "It is no accident that the computing field has been free of government regulation and has an impressive record of accomplishment. . . . If you want to win the Indy 500 race, you build the fastest car. You don't throw nails on the track." [71]

In the same month as the AAAS meeting, January 1982, the government hurled more warnings at the scientific community. Both Defense Secretary Caspar Weinberger and the Defense Science Board Task Force on University Responsiveness to National Security Requirements stressed the dangers of the Soviet effort to acquire American technical knowledge. Both promised increased efforts at blocking the transfer of technology.

In February 1982, Senator Henry Jackson addressed the Senate on the same problem and suggested methods of control. FBI agents reportedly monitored the activities of four Polish exchange students at the University of Iowa. One month later, President Reagan sent a message to Congress, noting that he had curtailed exchanges under eleven bilateral agreements with the Soviet Union, because the Soviets had kept their scientific establishments off-limits to foreigners and restricted the communications and travel of their own scientists.

The intelligence community released a report in April 1982 called *Soviet Acquisition of Western Technology.* It described the Russian plan to learn U.S. technology and attributed the success of that plan in large measure to Soviet spies, illegal purchases of controlled equipment, and scientific and technological agreements with the West. The report emphasized the danger to the United States.

In May 1982, the luggage of ten Chinese nationals was seized and searched as they were leaving the Michigan universities where they had been studying. Textbooks, notes, and photocopied material were removed; nothing classified was found. The search was initiated by the FBI.

In August 1982, the Defense Department blocked the presentation of about one hundred technical papers just before they were to be delivered at an international convention on optical engineering in San Diego. A Pentagon official claimed that the presence of Soviet engineers at the conference would enable the Russians to "develop early countermeasures to American military advances." Since most, if not all, of the affected scientists were Defense Department contractors at the conference to discuss contract-project research, the government arguably had the right to block the presentation of the papers. Established preclearance procedures were not followed or broke down. Scientists at the conference, already angry at the cancellation of papers they had traveled long distances to hear, were further upset at not knowing what they could and could not present. One said, "After this incident, I'm not going to publish any more. Eighty percent of my work is in military labs."

The conflicts between freedom of scientific disclosure and government censorship of unclassified information are extremely serious. Dr. Harold

Relyea of the Library of Congress Research Service, an expert in government information policy who belongs to the AAAS Committee on Scientific Freedom and Responsibility, criticizes the government's policies as inconsistent and confusing, more ideological than practical. Relyea points out, for example, that the government has paid little attention to national security as an *economic* concept, concentrating almost exclusively on military rivalry with the Soviet Union and its allies. Said Relyea, "If there are one or two people from the Eastern block in the audience, a person cannot give a paper. Yet the people from Japan and Germany, who are very close competitors with us in a lot of electronic areas, are let in." The level of concern about Japanese industrial spying has not approached the level of concern about industrial spying by socialist or communist nationals.

Admiral Inman, however, adverted to the problem of technological competitors in his warning to the AAAS conference in January 1982. He said, "Unless I'm far wrong, I think in the latter half of the decade, we're going to be defining [strategically important technology] in economic competition terms, not just military."

One can argue that economic strength is every bit as important to the security of the United States as military strength, and that, as Inman suggested, unclassified information deemed vital to economic strength ought also to be subject to government controls. If, as seems likely, government agencies propose additional limitations on the spread of scientific and technological information in the interests of maintaining economic preeminence in the world, the current controversies are bound to intensify.

Meanwhile, new government policies restricting communication are in conflict with old policies, giving the impression of federal schizophrenia. "While you have the Carluccis and the Weinbergers being very hard-nosed on the issue, the Department of State is not taking a very strong line. They have the authority to veto Soviet citizens coming here and they are not doing that," Relyea explains. "Even the Department of Commerce is split: They promote trade with the Soviet Union and trade fairs, but another arm of the Department says we have to have export controls."

Thus, Relyea continues, current government policy creates a lot of uncertainty for U.S. scientists. "Whatever one's image is of the average scientist or engineer," he says, "most of them don't know what to do about this problem. They don't know where to look up the law, they don't know what their obligations are, they are confused about what they can teach." [72]

Ironically, the government's efforts to dam the free flow of scientific exchange in the name of national security may actually harm the nation's welfare. According to several leading scientists, the United States would suffer if the government closed our open scientific system, for this system has been central to American superiority over the Soviets, who have a tightly controlled scientific community. Without a free exchange of ideas and discussion among peers, and without the cross-checking of facts and testing of theories, they argue, science, progress, and America would all suffer.

CUTBACKS IN FEDERAL DEPARTMENTS AND AGENCIES

The Reagan administration cannot claim that national security is endangered when it seeks to block information about occupational health or consumer goods from reaching the public. But in those and other purely domestic arenas, the president's penchant for secrecy trickles down through the layers of federal bureaucracy. Nowhere was this more evident than in the Environmental Protection Agency (EPA).

Since 1970, when the EPA was first established, Hugh B. Kaufman has been the government's chief investigator for hazardous waste pollution cases. When the Reagan administration began to cut back EPA's enforcement projects, especially the Superfund program designed to clean up the nation's most toxic dump sites, he became a vocal critic of agency policy. Kaufman, who had worked on the Love Canal site, appeared before Congress and the California legislature, and on network TV, openly criticizing the agency. "EPA is not about to protect you if your state or local government won't," he asserted on "60 Minutes."

Kaufman knew the EPA would resent his remarks. But he was shocked to learn that agency investigators were secretly photographing him as he checked into a Meadville, Pennsylvania, motel in June 1982, when, on his own time, he made a speech to a citizen's group. For more than three weeks, EPA inspectors followed him and tapped his phone. They later reported that Kaufman entered the motel with a "brunette," [73] and they also tipped off *Newsweek* and the *New York Times*. It turned out that the "brunette" was his wife. Later, documents released under the Freedom of Information Act revealed that Rita Lavelle, director of the EPA's Superfund program, apparently ordered the investigation in hopes of silencing him. Lavelle "wants to fire him," one investigator had written in his notes. Kaufman took his case to the Department of Labor. In a succinct report, the department concluded that the investigation was "an apparent attempt to discredit" Hugh Kaufman and "silence the communication of his ideas."

At first, Kaufman's ordeal seemed like another instance of an administration trying to chill a critical employee. But his case was only the tip of an iceberg, for Kaufman was not the only critic of EPA policy. Environmentalists contended that agency programs, especially Superfund, a $1.6 billion congressional program financed largely by industry for a five-year cleanup of the nation's four hundred worst dump sites, was nothing less than a superflop. Under the Superfund law, EPA could force companies to clean up the dumps they had created; if the company refused, EPA could use the fund to pay for the job and then sue for up to three times the cost. Rita Lavelle was the Reagan appointee in charge of Superfund. Before that she had worked for several chemical companies, and in 1969 was a press assistant for California governor Ronald Reagan. It was then that she became friends with Edwin Meese, now a key Reagan aide. Meese held the Bible when Lavelle was sworn in.

Lavelle said she was committed to cleaning up toxic waste. But Superfund was largely stagnant. By November 1982, only 4 out of 160 dumps on the Superfund priority list had been completely cleaned up. Only one Superfund lawsuit had been filed. EPA spent just $74 million of the $265 million that Congress had made available. The agency had spent no money at all on three toxic waste sites in California and Michigan either owned or partially created by subsidiaries of Aerojet-General, Lavelle's former employer. Critics charged that the Reagan administration was politically manipulating Superfund, and that EPA had a record of cozy relationships with the firms it was supposed to regulate. No fewer than six congressional committees were soon investigating EPA.

In September 1982, committee investigators asked EPA officials for documents on three sites. But the administration refused to turn over key documents. In late October, the House Subcommittee on Oversight and Investigations sent a subpoena for the materials to EPA Director Anne Gorsuch. In early December, the White House directed Gorsuch to ignore the subpoena. The administration argued that the materials were sensitive law enforcement documents about ongoing investigations, and were therefore protected under the doctrine of executive privilege. In response, members of Congress charged that the administration was obstructing a legitimate congressional investigation and the people's right to know in order to cover up "misconduct and unethical behavior by agency officials." An aide to House Speaker Tip O'Neill pointed out that the administration by asserting executive privilege was attempting to extend a very narrow legal doctrine covering limited presidential papers to nonpresidential materials in another agency.

The White House stood firm. Gorsuch withheld the subpoenaed materials contrary to her own advice to the president. On December 16, the House took action. In a historic vote, Gorsuch became the first agency head to be cited for contempt of Congress. Although other presidents claiming executive privilege had fiercely battled with Congress, a compromise had always been reached before a contempt vote. Instead of following the House's order to begin prosecution of Gorsuch, the Justice Department asked a federal judge to declare the contempt citation unconstitutional. The judge took forty-eight hours to throw out the Justice Department case. The scandal at EPA continued to grow.

No sooner had Gorsuch fired Lavelle than the newspapers reported that two "mistakenly ordered" shredders, one of them installed adjacent to the outgoing Lavelle's office, had been operating twenty-four hours a day for several days. The shredding began just after the contempt vote, and no records were kept of what was destroyed. Congressman James Scheuer reported that Lavelle's appointment calendar had "disappeared." The date book was of great interest to several committees looking into possible conflicts of interest involving Aerojet and Lavelle, as well as Lavelle's alleged harassment of Kaufman. Other materials were reportedly removed from Lavelle's office. A congressional investigator charged that EPA aides attempted to remove fifteen boxes of files, though EPA officials said the files and the shredded documents were only surplus copies. When Lavelle was dismissed, Scheuer dropped plans to pursue charges against her for perjuring herself when she testified that she did not try to fire Kaufman; at the request of Congress, the FBI began to investigate the shredding. Lavelle was subsequently convicted of lying to congressional committees investigating the Superfund and in January 1984 was fined and sentenced to six months in jail. Finally, on March 9, 1983, Anne Gorsuch Burford (in February she had married Robert Burford, head of the Bureau of Land Management) resigned. Immediately thereafter, Reagan agreed to turn over to Congress all the documents he had adamantly withheld.

Throughout the ordeal, repeated allegations of improper administration of Superfund, conflicts of interest, and cover-ups seeped from the White House like a stream of toxic waste. The administration had attempted to withhold information on an important public issue, it was charged, through the intimidation and firing of employees, the shredding of files, the erasing of computer data, and overly broad claims of executive privilege. The president responded by simply blaming the EPA critics for "environmental extremism." "I don't think they'll be happy until the White House looks like a bird's nest," said Reagan.

The Superfund controversy displayed a variety of government techniques for withholding information from the public, and a variety of reasons for doing so. Often agencies and officials withhold unclassified information in order to prevent debate and possible criticism of administration policies, for political considerations, or from fear of embarrassment. Frequently, the information relates to the most mundane aspects of everyday life. But as the Superfund saga revealed, it may be information that the public needs.

What follows is a sampling of controversies over access to information and instances of censorship by federal agencies and departments that provide some inkling of the breadth and scope of the roadblocks that have been put in place and the kinds of information that, for one reason or another, the government deemed unfit for public consumption.

Consumer Information

March 1981

Secretary of Energy James Edwards ordered twelve thousand copies of the Department of Energy's January issue of *Energy Consumer* magazine locked up after a complaint by Idaho Senator James McClure that his constituents called it an "antinuclear handbook."

May 1981

Following the recommendation of the Office of Management and Budget, the Senate freed oil companies from the requirements of the Energy Department's Financial Reporting System (FRS), which required them to make public information about their high profits and low tax rates.

August 1981

The National Highway Traffic Safety Administration, in a reversal of policy, decided not to inform the public every time it ordered a recall of defective cars. The new NHTSA head, Ray Peck, said it may be "irresponsible" to announce some recalls, and that only those "necessary for auto safety" will be announced. Peck was suggesting that auto defects so serious that they warranted a government-ordered recall could still be so trivial that they deserved no public announcement.

July 1982

The Agriculture Department, which had planned to publish a pamphlet on nutrition, called *Food/2,* a sequel to a very popular publication about diet, excised eight pages of a section on fats and cholesterol. According to the Center for Science in the Public Interest located in Washington, D.C., meat and egg producers had been upset over mild warnings about excessive fat consumption, and lobbied the office of Agriculture Secretary John Block to stop giving that kind of dietary advice.

Health and Safety

April 1981

Thorne Auchter, assistant secretary of labor for the Occupational Safety and Health Administration, issued a memo restricting the right of OSHA employees to publicly discuss any matter the agency had not already made public. Later, he modified his order after hearing from an attorney for the American Federation of Government Employees that the memo "appears to deny employees the right to petition Congress" and "may discourage legitimate whistle blowing protected by the Civil Service Reform Act."

Under orders from Auchter, two publications and a poster listing the hazards of cotton dust were withdrawn from circulation and destroyed because they "no longer represent agency policy." The poster said, "Cotton Dust Can Destroy Your Lungs." OSHA revised the publications, cutting out photographs and quotations from workers who became seriously ill after exposure to cotton dust.

May 1982

The Veterans Administration revised a pamphlet issued under the Carter administration about the effects of a herbicide widely used in Vietnam called Agent Orange. The new edition, in contrast to the old, failed to name various diseases linked with the herbicide, and described those links as "only a theory."

July 1982

OSHA proposed that employers be allowed to withhold the identity of certain chemicals the employers consider to be trade secrets. The rule then in effect required employers to release information identifying chemicals to a worker even if they were trade secrets, since workers and their unions needed to know about any hazards in the work place.

Environment

January 1982

Allegedly in the name of economy, the Office of Management and Budget ordered the Environmental Protection Agency to ban from distribution sixty-eight publications on such topics as acid rain and carbon monoxide pollution. Thousands of copies of publications already printed were destroyed, among them, *What Everyone Should Know about the Quality of Drinking Water, The Toxic Substances Dilemma,* and *Acid Rain: A Growing Environmental Dilemma.*

July 1982

EPA reduced requirements on the asbestos industry. No longer would companies be required to keep customer lists and other data. According to Dr. Myra Karstadt of Mount Sinai School of Medicine at the City University of New York, "This change . . . will make it much more difficult for EPA and other agencies to trace asbestos to final products, and will, when taken in conjunction with reduced inspection and monitoring of work places by OSHA, make exposure data much harder to come by."

September 1982

Amid the smoke and fire of Congress's battle with the Environmental Protection Agency, Jim Sibbison, an EPA public affairs officer from 1970 to 1981, provided an inside view of the agency's information policy in an article he wrote for *The Nation*:

> From 1970, when the agency was established, until about a year after Ronald Reagan's election, I was involved in the disclosures and, yes, the deceptions of the E.P.A. press office. The latter occurred during the Nixon, Ford and Carter administrations, but their incidence increased dramatically when the Reagan team took over. The new Administration introduced heavy censorship of E.P.A. news releases, and soon the deceptions outnumbered the disclosures.
>
> My first encounter with this censorship occurred when I reported in a news release that the pesticide dibromochloropropane (DBCP) was suspected of causing cancer and that there had been cases of sterility among workers who had handled it. Someone in the administrator's office (which reviews all press releases before they are disseminated) crossed out "sterility" and substituted "adverse health effects." The reference to cancer was deleted.
>
> Soon after that, all references to cancer and hazards to pregnant women were purged from a draft of a news release about protecting workers from radiation. On another occasion, I proposed making public an E.P.A. finding that people using creosote and other cancer-causing wood preservatives should wear protective clothing. I was told not to bother. After a while, I simply stopped mentioning cancer, birth defects and damage to genes. As a colleague of mine said, "The administrator's office will take the words out anyway." But without references to those things, my news releases had little point.[74]

April 1983

The Department of Energy announced a plan to increase restrictions on nuclear information. The plan would permit the department to declare material "unclassified controlled nuclear information" and then forbid its release. Such information could describe, for example, accidents at nuclear plants, health hazards to workers and the public from radiation, or plans for protecting nuclear material in transit. The secretary of energy would be permitted to keep secret any information he chose to withhold. Penalties for violation could amount to a $100,000 fine or twenty years in prison.

Embarrassments and Obstructions

August 1982

Senator Max Baucus inserted into the *Congressional Record* an exchange of letters tracing his attempts to obtain seven censored pages of an internal audit report, which, after all the fuss, turned out to be only mildly embarrassing to the FBI. Baucus wanted to know how the FBI handled property seized from suspects; in early February he requested the results of an audit on this subject. It was sent to him in March, but seven pages were missing. A Justice Department attorney explained that the deletion was necessary to preserve privacy so that people would be "candid and forthright" with auditors. Several letters went back and forth as Baucus requested and the Justice Department refused. Weeks went by. Ultimately an anonymous person sent Baucus the "sensitive" pages. What was so sensitive? The auditors had accused the FBI of "using every opportunity to delay or hinder the auditors." Their behavior was so obstructionist, said the report, that the lack of cooperation made the audit more costly.

Baucus chastised the Justice Department. "Access to information is a right that has been used effectively in this country for centuries to improve government operations as well as society in general," he said. "Unfortunately, this view is apparently not shared by too many top officials in the Justice Department." The senator wondered whether the FBI's improper handling of seized goods had been corrected. "Certainly," he added, "if the Justice Department had had its way, we would never have known a problem existed." [75]

November 1982

The Department of Justice refused to turn over documents about a controversial presidential advisory board to a congressional committee. At issue was the President's Private Sector Survey on Cost Control, a group composed primarily of business executives assigned to evaluate some of the very government agencies that regulate their industries. In a preliminary report, the General Accounting Office suggested that the administration was going out of its way to protect task force members from federal conflict of interest laws.

Congressman William D. Ford of Michigan sought copies of legal opinions that the Justice Department's Office of Legal Counsel prepared on the advisory panel. Ford said, "Without question, there is at least the appearance of conflict of interest. . . . One would have to be blind not to be suspicious."

A Justice Department attorney maintained the documents were "sensitive," "attorney-client advice," and withheld them. Ford accused the administration of hindering his committee's investigation. "If we were seeking classified defense data or documents on foreign policy, I could understand the use of the word *sensitive*. But what can possibly be *sensitive* about legal matters pertaining to a study of management practices in the federal government? . . . Clearly there is something they don't want us to find out." [76]

The administration also turned its attention to its borders and the possibility that "bad ideas" can seep into the United States and pollute the thoughts of its citizens. The State Department, Immigration and Naturalization Service, and Treasury Department restricted travel to and from the United States. One major mechanism in this effort is the McCarran Act of 1950, also called the Immigration and Nationality Act. Passed during the flush of McCarthyism, the act provides for the exclusion of those who advocate or teach opposition to organized government or espouse the doctrines of world communism. According to legal experts, the government's erratic enforcement of the McCarran Act is in direct conflict with the 1975 Helsinki accords, which commit the United States to "facilitate freer movement and contacts, individually and collectively, [and] to administer flexibly the procedures for exit and entry." The accords explicitly provide that signatory states recognize the "close link" between "the strengthening of world peace and security and the promotion of human rights." These provisions apply with special force to those seeking to visit the United States to take part in disarmament activities. Citing the McCarran Act, the State Department denied visas to approximately three hundred Japanese citizens who planned to attend the special UN meeting on disarmament in June 1982. After threats of a lawsuit, the State Department reversed itself.

Besides the McCarran Act, the government maintains a list of organizations it has deemed antithetical to the best interests of the country. Membership in one of those can be grounds for exclusion. One of these organizations is the Socialist Workers Party, which was on the list in 1966, then removed, and in 1981 was under review for inclusion once again. In its review, the Immigration and Naturalization Service (INS) undertook "to determine whether party members or affiliates are excludable or deportable." Civil libertarians fear that if the INS does place the party on the list, the ruling could lead to deportation, denial of citizenship, and trouble for non-native-born people who work with political groups of which the government disapproves, such as Nicaraguan solidarity or antidraft organizations. The fear is based on the government's past use of such laws to deport political undesirables like social activists and prominent labor leaders, as well as socialist and communist figures.

In the sixties, shortly after the revolution there, Cuba was declared off-limits to Americans. One man who tried to visit the island legally, instead of slipping in through Mexico or Canada, was charged with violating travel restrictions. Louis Zemel took his case to the Supreme Court, arguing it was his First Amendment right "to go, to learn, and return to the United States to talk with whomever I can about what I have seen and learned." In a decision that severely limited Americans' freedom of movement, the high court ruled that the State Department's right to regulate travel for national security reasons outweighed Zemel's First Amendment rights.[77] Although the Carter administration permitted Americans to visit Cuba, the Reagan administration imposed new regulations forbidding most Americans to travel there. The Supreme Court, in a 1984 decision, upheld the president.

In 1980 Dario Fo, Italian playwright, was banned. His entry would not have been "appropriate," said an officer at the Italian desk of the State Department: "Dario Fo has never had a good word to say about the U.S." [78] The government has also refused to allow Nobel Prize–winning novelist Gabriel Garcia Marquez to enter the country except under extremely limited conditions. In May 1982, a Grenadian churchwoman and social worker connected with the Pope Paul VI Ecumenical Center in St. John's, Grenada, was expelled for "national security reasons" when she went to a theology conference in Puerto Rico. The next month, two former Salvadoran political prisoners were denied visas by the United States despite invitations to speak from members of Congress and a commission of the Roman Catholic Archdiocese of San Francisco.

As civil libertarians have warned, the government has used the deportation process to try to expel politically active noncitizens living in the United States. In December 1982, deportation proceedings were begun against a Latin American scholar at the University of Maryland who was not even told the nature of the charges against him. Angel Rama, one of the leading literary critics of Latin America, received tenure at the university in 1981, but his status was jeopardized by the government's action. Rama, who has spent years trying to obtain hearings and combat the adverse rulings, ruefully cited government regulations as he wrote of his plight:

> If someone has attacked North American policies . . . if he signs a petition proclaiming the right of the people to overthrow bloody dictatorships, even if it uses the sacred formula enshrined in the United States' Declaration of Independence . . . then he is a communist subversive. He enters that orderly system where the bad are united in one pigeonhole: 212(d)(3)(A)(28).[79]

Angel Rama was denied permanent resident status under the McCarran Act. In the fall of 1983, Rama was killed in a plane crash at the Madrid airport.

Perhaps the most devastating blow in recent years to Americans' right to travel stems from the 1981 Supreme Court decision in the case of Philip Agee, the former CIA agent living abroad. Because Agee had disclosed the names of agents and agency activities that he considered illegal or improper, Secretary of State Alexander Haig revoked his passport. Agee appealed, arguing that the revocation violated both his freedom to travel and his First Amendment right to criticize government policies. In a far-reaching decision, the Supreme Court upheld Haig's suspension of Agee's passport. It ruled that "beliefs and speech are only a part of Agee's campaign" and the Constitution has never protected speech obstructing intelligence or military operations. Citizens who "cause serious damage to the national security or foreign policy of the United States," the Court said, "are not protected by the First Amendment and may have their passports revoked."[80] The decision contained the ominous implication that First Amendment protections for American citizens may not reach beyond our national boundaries. Thus, the *Agee* decision presents the government with a powerful new tool for limiting the right of Americans to travel and speak freely abroad.

Besides the executive branch methods of withholding and censoring information described above, the Reagan administration also effectively manipulated the federal budget to reduce the amount of information available to the citizen. Given the president's commitment to reduce expenditures and to shrink the overall size of the federal government, this was a logical step, but critics speculate that the actions taken by the Office of Management and Budget were penny wise and pound foolish.

Statistics may have little attraction for most people, but the subject is essential nonetheless in this computerized age of data bases, econometrics, and high-level calculations. The Reagan administration cut heavily into government statistical programs, thus assuring that certain kinds of information would not be collected. Among the statistical programs cut back in the early years of the Reagan presidency were those dealing with the gross national product, energy, the environment, minorities, regional poverty and health, unemployment, and agriculture. Hearings held in March 1982 brought together testimony from a wide range of interest groups protesting the cuts; business executives, civil rights advocates, union leaders, academicians, and mayors, among others, took to Capitol Hill to make their objections known.[81] The federal government, they said, is the only entity that has the resources and the credibility to compile and publish national statistics on phenomena such as the census, income, health, productivity, markets, and other vital data. In addition to concerns over the effect of not compiling these figures, witnesses complained that by cutting down on sample size and instituting other economies, the government was collecting less accurate statistics as well as fewer statistics. The resulting distortions, they said, would mean that the country was operating on misinformation and therefore would make expensive errors.

Businessmen who in other circumstances deplore governmental intervention feared that the reduced statistics available to them were inadequate. "I believe that unless more attention is paid to bolstering the budgets of the federal statistical agencies we may no longer have enough quality information to know just where the economy is going, let alone funds to publish those statistics for others to interpret,"[82] warned Stephen E. Fienberg, statistics professor at Carnegie-Mellon University and chair of the Committee on National Statistics at the National Academy of Sciences. Even Treasury Secretary Donald T. Regan expressed anxiety about the cuts. "We don't know enough about our economy,"[83] he said in late 1982.

The former chairman of the U.S. Commission on Civil Rights, Arthur S. Flemming, warned the House Subcommittee on Census and Population that the cutbacks "can only weaken the civil rights movement and undermine the Nation's ability effectively to serve minorities, women, the handicapped and older Americans through the delivery of services." As columnist Ellen Goodman observed,

> You may not be able to cure unemployment, but by golly you can stop counting it. You may not be willing to help the poor, but you can stop offering up the proof of their poverty. You may not be willing to help the displaced homemaker, the abused child, the under-nourished, but you can make them invisible again.[84]

Statistics on the environment were also diminished. The pollution of rivers and the air, the effects of erosion control programs, reports on human exposures to radiation, noise, and pesticides were held back, delayed, or eliminated. From a president who once said, "If you've seen one redwood, you've seen them all," perhaps the downgrading of information about perils to the wilderness was to be expected. Certainly, if no one knows what is happening to water quality, polluters are less likely to be identified. The corporate interests that, as one EPA staffer said, make up the "primary constituents of this administration" gained a freer hand. Yet, ironically, the favored elements also suffered: Businesses were not able to conduct marketing surveys because Census Bureau figures were not available as a result of cutbacks in census funds. For the same reason, the Pentagon had to delay a study of recruitment.

As the Reagan administration went about its work, pursuing its formidable agenda for changing many of the nation's institutions, complaints were made that the effects of the changes could not be measured because of the reduction in data collection. The title of a *New York Times* article told the story: "Data on Cuts Imperiled by Cuts in Data." The staff director of the Committee on National Statistics at the National Academy of Sciences was quoted as saying, "At a time when we are seeing some very important changes in our society we . . . want to be able to monitor them—statistics are a management tool." The president of the American Agricultural Economics Association warned a congressional committee of the dangerous consequences of the weakened data base:

> This vulnerability [of agricultural policy making] goes beyond the errors in policy that will result from inadequate data and information. Democratic government itself will be at risk, because repeated errors in policy inevitably lead to a credibility problem toward government. It is not happenstance that this country, more than any other, has in the past invested heavily in data and statistics. Such investments are the basis of a free and open society in which policies are established by democratic means. We weaken that basis for public debate at our own risk.[85]

Besides eliminating free distribution of many publications, the administration also reduced public access to information by raising prices. The *Federal Register,* the basic record of federal government activity, jumped from $75 annually to $300; the U.S. Department of Agriculture's Economic Research Service, which used to give away its reports, began to charge $8 to $10 a year for its quarterly reports on particular crops. In 1983, the price of the *Congressional Record,* which once was distributed free to anyone, went from $135 to $208 per year.

Who has access to information gathered at taxpayer expense? For most of our history, the answer has been the public. But more and more, pressures from private industry are squeezing the public out. The Reagan administration even decided in March 1983 to sell government weather satellites to private industry, which could then profit from the taxpayer-funded technology estimated to have cost $1.5 billion. John Byrne, administrator of the National Oceanic and Atmospheric Administration, said that there were no reliable figures to show that such a sale would save the government money, and in fact the government would probably lose hundreds of millions of dollars annually for the next ten years. The decision to make the sale came, he said, from the White House. Ralph Nader charged that the dollar losses were "not the most important part of this. It is taking information that everyone has free access to and turning it over to a private monopoly to traffic and profit with it." Writing in *The Nation,* Anita R. and Herbert I. Schiller also drew attention to the fattening of the private sector at the expense of the public. They concluded:

> Appropriation of public resources for private enrichment, long familiar in the American experience, has now come to the newest valuable resource, information. With almost no public notice, the national stock of information, created through heavy public expenditures over the years, is steadily being removed from government custodianship and transferred to private ownership and control.[86]

The Schillers described an organization called the Information Industry Association (IIA), which numbers among its members some of the most powerful information companies in the nation. IIA was founded in 1968 "to promote the development of private enterprise in the field of information and to gain recognition for information as a commercial product." The IIA lobbies against government information services, arguing that nothing that can be done privately should be undertaken by the federal government. But information, in our technological society, is a national resource. Much of ours has been gathered at public expense: census data, congressional hearings and reports, departmental studies, federally funded research.

Historically, the Government Printing Office (GPO) has been the publisher and disseminator of government-funded and government-generated information. But the federal Paperwork Reduction Act of 1980 gave the Office of Management and Budget (OMB) discretion over what executive branch material the GPO can publish. Librarians had argued against having OMB—an entity that is typically preoccupied by matters of cost and is perceived as one of the government agencies least accessible to the public—in charge of policies "regarding citizen access to government information." Not unexpectedly, with a philosophy similar to IIA's, OMB began encouraging government agencies to have private industry disseminate their information rather than distribute it through the GPO. In the fall of 1981, David Stockman issued a memorandum requiring heads of executive departments and agencies to evaluate their major information centers to see whether the private sector could provide comparable information services. In May 1982, OMB agreed to make a list of discontinued publications available "in order to assure an orderly and equitable transfer of discontinued government publications to the private sector." One of those transferred was the *News Digest,* published by the Securities and Exchange Commision until November 1981, when a private firm was engaged to publish it at a 50 percent increase in price ($150 per year, up from $100). Bernardine Hoduski of the Joint Committee on Printing, is worried by OMB's policy of encouraging private enterprise. "If this policy were carried to the logical extreme," she warned in an interview, "you'd have very little publication by the government. Information would come out published by the private sector with no control over the price or the length of time publications would stay in print. Those who have money will be able to get information and those who don't won't." [87]

Taking its cue from the Reagan administration, the IIA has also threatened computerized government information services like the National Library of Medicine's MEDLINE and the National Technical Information Services (NTIS). MEDLINE provides access to indexes of the world's medical literature; it is an unparalleled service developed at government expense. Once MEDLINE proved successful, commercial companies developed on-line access to data bases. Now they are lobbying MEDLINE to increase the cost of its services sharply, presumably so that their own businesses will not suffer by comparison. NTIS provides access to specialized information that the executive branch has developed. It produces reports both on paper and on computer tapes. With annual sales of $25 million, NTIS is self-supporting, though some of its inventory has limited sales. The Reagan administration has proposed transferring NTIS to private enterprise. If this were to happen, and the distribution of these publications and tapes were to be governed solely by the profit motive, costs to the public would escalate and the slower-moving publications would soon be out of print. Access to information would be diminished, and some information would disappear altogether.

IIA also opposes the National Depository Library System, which for more than a hundred years has made acquisitions for the more than thirteen hundred libraries it serves. The system places government publications in libraries across the nation, providing free public access to this material. Students, teachers, researchers, writers, and any interested people can find and use information that otherwise they might not even know existed. The IIA urged replacing the depository library system with an arrangement in which libraries would pay cash for packages of information that private companies would prepare and distribute.

In bits and pieces, the right to know is slowly but surely being eroded. With far less commotion and controversy than that marking the EPA scandal or the legislative battles over the Freedom of Information Act, the Reagan administration has restricted what government reports people (and in some cases Congress) may read, where they may travel, and what they may know about hazards in their work places. "The worst sin of this administration has been cutting back on information that we all need, that we have no source for other than government," said David Vladeck, an attorney with Public Citizen Litigation Group in Washington, D.C. "If you look at the list of publications that were free to anyone who asked in the prior administration, it was twenty or forty pages. Now it's three or four. The three-page booklets on dietary guidelines, how to cook a low-cost meal, how to cut back on cholesterol, on nutrition and education—you can't get them anymore. They don't exist." He added, "It doesn't dawn on one just how basic the government information role is in our daily lives." [88] The computer-printed list of government publications terminated and consolidated by agency is half an inch thick, listing hundreds of discontinued brochures and pamphlets. As the government cuts back the flow of data, the way is opened for the private sector to assume a greater role in processing, packaging, marketing—and controlling—basic information.

With the expansion of computer technology, our society is already splitting into two groups—those with access to information and those without. If the IIA has its way, that process will be accelerated. Uncomfortably for many, the Reagan administration and private industry seem to be heading in that direction.

3

Censorship in Schools, Libraries, and Business

Many of the books and magazines now on display racks across the nation could never have been published during the more inhibited eras of the American past, when *Ulysses, Lady Chatterley's Lover,* and the works of Henry Miller were forbidden fruits to be stashed underneath mattresses and later read in secret. Contemporary sex education textbooks for children would not have passed muster in earlier days. But even though our society and our reading material have become less inhibited, influential groups today are demanding the removal of books from schools and libraries on the grounds that these books express harmful ideas. Most, but not all, of the book banners have been influenced by religious or conservative doctrines and express concern for family, morality, patriotism, and free enterprise.

Book banning, like nativism, recurs regularly in our history. The current outbreak, like its predecessors, stems from the premise that if an idea is censored, it dies out. Thus book banners have mustered vocal, angry citizen groups that try through community pressure and the courts to stamp out the words they don't like. These controversies have ruined the careers of teachers and divided communities into hostile factions. Although anticensorship groups have mobilized in opposition and book banning has been viewed with alarm in the media, the phenomenon continues unabated. In communities and courts of law throughout our nation, conflicts over school texts and library materials spring up.

A less frequently noticed kind of censorship takes place when corporations act to stifle the expression of ideas that criticize their operations or their products. This usually unnoticed obstacle in the flow of ideas only surfaces rarely because businesses rely on publishers to do their censoring for them. Because of the power of advertising, the vast majority of the media avoids antagonizing its sponsors. Sometimes the normally smooth system fails, however, and the public has the opportunity to view a company acting to censor information, or a publication censoring itself in order to not offend.

At bottom, censorship conflicts resemble those in the federal government, in that someone is telling someone else, "You can only know or say what I allow you to know or say."

MS. MAGAZINE IN CONTRA COSTA COUNTY

Censorship is more than writs and judgments; it's flesh and blood. Communities have gone berserk over schoolbooks, with irate bands of citizens pitching gasoline-filled bottles into schools and shooting people, as happened in West Virginia in 1974, or burning piles of books, as happened in Martha's Vineyard, Massachusetts, in 1983. Usually, incidents like these don't happen, although segments of communities may become inflamed with passion. Usually, the book banners are conservative family people who become outraged over words they think undermine either morality or patriotism. Sometimes a bitter controversy ensues; often the offending book or magazine is simply removed from school or library shelves with no obvious struggle. Whatever happens, though, a chilling effect remains on the teachers, librarians, and students at the school, and it becomes more difficult to examine whatever ideas caused the trouble.

One controversy over restricting a magazine typifies many of the issues and conflicts that arise when a community is polarized over printed words in schools.[1] It took place in Contra Costa County, California, beginning in 1980. About twenty miles east of San Francisco, the comfortable suburb of Contra Costa might as well be light years from fractious Berkeley intellectuals, Castro Street gays, or the celebrated hot tubs of Marin County. In fact, it's been said that the Midwest begins at Orinda, where the east end of the tunnel through the Berkeley Hills comes out into Contra Costa County.

Driving through the towns that constitute the Mt. Diablo Unified School District, you are never more than five minutes from a Long's Drugs, a fast-food restaurant, or a place to pray. At the end of the rainy season, the landscape is green; fruit trees bloom, and the well-tended lawns in developments with names like Sunset Park and Countrywood glow like emeralds. A sprinkling of professional office buildings dots the landscape, and a few townhouses have appeared not far from where horses graze in pastures. The foothills of Mt. Diablo rise up in the distance. This is an orderly place, with wide streets, neat homes, and predominantly middle-class residents. But three years ago a censorship battle began. Ygnacio Valley High School, where the controversy began, fits the scene perfectly. Single-story buildings linked by walkways fan out over the extensive school grounds. The many parking lots overflow with cars; by contrast, a small cluster of bicycles stand at the bike rack. Many of the kids drive to school.

On a spring day some students play tennis, while others chase a soccer ball around one of the playing fields, squealing with excitement. Music plays when classes break for lunch and kids stroll across the central yard. Most of the students are white; a few are Asian and Hispanic. They are well dressed in casual clothes, though a few of the girls sport more fashionable outfits and heavy makeup. In the library, some students browse through shelves of books in the spacious room; others work at desks. One is checking out the various magazines, which are arranged alphabetically in racks: *Christian Century, Ebony, Leatherneck, Life, Time, Foreign Affairs, The Rotarian.* Quite a mix. But there are signs that a label was pulled off the rack next to *McCall's,* where *Ms.* would have been. A notice advises the students that they must ask at the desk to get motorcycle, hot rod, and running magazines. Nothing is posted about *Ms.*

The banning of *Ms.* magazine was supposed to happen quietly. In January 1980, some librarians in the seven high schools of the Mt. Diablo Unified School District received phone calls asking whether they subscribed to *Ms.* magazine. The librarians, who talked among themselves from time to time, wondered what was up. Carolyne Benning felt relieved that no one had called her to ask whether her library at Ygnacio Valley High subscribed. She suspected that those calls meant trouble, and she didn't want any.

But later that month a woman whose daughter attended Ygnacio Valley, Mrs. Marlys Tash, wrote the school's principal, Dr. Ernest Wutzke, to protest against *Ms.* Tash said she was deeply offended by a story in a 1977 issue of the magazine. The frank attitude toward sex as well as the liberal use of four-letter words horrified her. (That story had not been assigned to students to read, although both the English and Social Studies Departments of the school sometimes assigned readings from the magazine.) Shortly afterward, Dr. Wutzke assured her that indeed the magazine did contain objectionable material and it would henceforth be banned. It looked as though she had won.

But that was only the beginning. Wutzke, who had been principal of Ygnacio Valley High School for almost twenty years, found himself in the midst of a controversy he never sought. Upon receipt of the letter from Mrs. Tash, he had gone to see Carolyne Benning to have the magazine removed from the premises. She objected to its removal; he ordered her to take it off the shelves and destroy all the copies the school possessed. Reluctantly, she agreed to follow his order. And there the matter might have rested, according to Benning. But, she said, unknown to Dr. Wutzke, a teacher happened to be in the stacks behind the librarian's desk and overheard the conversation between Benning and Wutzke. According to Benning's account, the teacher left the library and told students what had happened; in no time the entire school was abuzz.

The teachers held a meeting; they wrote Dr. Wutzke a letter of protest. About two weeks after he had assured Mrs. Tash that the magazine would be gone, Dr. Wutzke phoned her to say that the issue was more complicated than he had thought; pressed by his faculty, he had agreed to let students read the magazine if they had parental consent.

"He didn't have the gall to stand up for what he believed," an angry Mrs. Tash said. "He gave in to the pressure from other people." Mrs. Tash also complained bitterly about a parents' meeting Wutzke scheduled to discuss the *Ms.* issue. She had requested that the passages in the magazine to which she had taken exception—graphic, pungent language in a short story larded with four-letter words—be passed out to the assembled parents. But, she says, that did not happen; instead, teachers and librarians explained to the parents why *Ms.* had been chosen and why it was educationally useful. Tash was highly displeased.

In addition, according to one person at the meeting, Mrs. Tash was extremely distressed at being publicly identified as the complaining parent, and even entertained thoughts of suing school personnel for making her identity known. Several participants in the ensuing controversy believed that Tash had in fact been induced to complain by Mrs. Betty Arras, another resident of Contra Costa County and the publisher of an ultraconservative newsletter about California schools. Some district librarians suspect Arras of being the phone caller asking what schools subscribed to *Ms.* But both Mrs. Arras and Mrs. Tash refused to answer questions, so their sides of the story remain incomplete.[2]

Several weeks after the meeting, the pastor of a Baptist church, the Reverend Harold Carlson, took up the fight. His church placed a full-page advertisement in the March 21, 1980, *Contra Costa Times* blasting *Ms.* as pornographic and "symptomatic of a much larger problem that must be solved and that is the deterioration of morals in our society." The ad promised "to put all the pressure that we can" in order to ban the magazine because "magazines and books like *Ms.* lead to an epidemic of venereal diseases, all kinds of births before marriage, and abortion." He warned that having *Ms.* in schools was like "having poison available where people can drink it. . . . It's polluting [the students'] minds and they don't know it."

A few weeks later the church took out another ad expressing its concerns, which included the destruction of the family unit and "loss of love." The ad decried "situation ethics," "relative values," and humanism; it invited readers to attend its Easter services. Perhaps to make this invitation more attractive, the ad explained the superiority of Christianity to other religions; their leaders, like Buddha and Mohammed, were dead, while Christ was still alive.

A furious exchange of letters in the *Times* further whipped up community feelings about the issue. One man, who had written a letter in favor of keeping *Ms.* on high school shelves, reported receiving death threats from anonymous callers who promised to burn his house, kill his family, and "messily remove [his] genitals." More ministers got into the act: A Unitarian who defended *Ms.* and the advances of feminism labeled the banners a "literary lynch mob," and a second Baptist minister took out another full-page ad against *Ms.*

The Reverend Dean Grotzke, the Baptist who placed that advertisement, gave some insight into the attitudes underlying the stance of the censors. "A loving parent would not leave a toddler near a fire.... To assume that a student has the capacity to decide what is good for him is to ignore human nature. Our natural tendency is to go down, not up. ... We are more likely to choose that which is harmful." He pleaded for the removal of *Ms.* In another ad taken out some months later, Grotzke stated that "separation of church and state is a fallacy." Grotzke wrote as if the Constitution didn't exist.

In May, the month the first ad appeared, the Mt. Diablo Unified School District received a formal request from a Mormon educator named F. Bruce Packard to remove *Ms.* from all school libraries in the district, the tenth largest in California. Packard, who then had five children in elementary school, had been in contact with the Committee for Improvement of Public Schools, a group with about ten members. Along with the completed school form asking that *Ms.* be banned, Packard submitted a petition bearing seventy-seven hundred signatures. Packard contended that the magazine endorsed "a free life style which includes sexual promiscuity, abortion, homosexualism [sic] and lesbianism." These, he asserted, conflicted with the values taught in students' homes.

The filing of the request set in motion the school board's formal procedure for processing complaints about educational materials. The board appointed a committee of parents, teachers, and staff to review the magazine and make recommendations. A public meeting held in the school board offices on June 15 for the committee to hear testimony from both sides drew about fifty citizens, most of whom opposed *Ms.* Tash, Carlson, and Packard spoke against it; two lawyers for the American Civil Liberties Union and the head of Contra Costa National Organization for Women spoke in favor. When it ended, the proponents of morality lost to the advocates of free speech; the ten-member committee voted nine to zero, with the chair abstaining, to keep *Ms.* in the high school. The committee did recommend that when teachers assigned reading from the magazine, parents were to be notified and requests for alternate reading were to be honored.

Stung by their defeat, the opposing forces prepared for the next stage, a public hearing before the school board of two women and three men, at which the committee's recommendations were to be accepted or rejected. During the days before the hearing, board members found their mailboxes stuffed with fire-and-brimstone letters favoring the removal of *Ms.* At least three of the five members felt the letters were part of an organized campaign by church groups. These excerpts are typical:

> Moral impurity is one of the root causes of the problems we face in our lives as individuals and as a nation. By leaving *Ms.* Magazine in the libraries we feel the school is condoning the immorality it exemplifies.

> If we approve the ideals, life-styles and language depicted in the magazine we will be contributing to the decay which is already eating away at our families and threatening to undo all the principles upon which America was founded.

Some board members also had to purchase answering machines in order to screen out hate calls. Strangely, the callers remained anonymous, saying only, "This is a parent who cares" or "This is a person worried for your soul," before inveighing against immorality and *Ms.*

The June 26 meeting[3] drew an enormous crowd; about five hundred people jammed an elementary school auditorium. According to board member Sherry Sterrett, the churches packed the meeting by organizing groups of their parishioners. The speakers went on for almost two hours, and the minutes of the meeting indicate that it was a hostile audience for those who criticized censorship.

Mrs. Tash pleaded for "the sake of our children and for goodness sake to remove this trash from the open shelves of our libraries." Other speakers argued for the removal of the magazine because it was immoral and community sentiment was against it. They claimed that parents needed a strong voice in the education of their children, and that free speech advocates should not dictate what their children read.

Zoia Horn, the last speaker, represented the Intellectual Freedom Committee of the California Library Association. She suggested that the school board recognize the impossibility of returning to the standards of an earlier age. She summarized many of the points that had been made earlier by others opposed to censorship:

> The overall effort to portray women as human beings and the honesty with which women are portrayed override sometimes bad language in *Ms.* or points of view that some people regard as offensive. . . .
>
> A parent may have the right to determine what his or her teenager may see or read, but that same parent does not have the right to determine what other parents' teenage children may or may not read.
>
> It is what young adults do not know that gets them into trouble, not what they do know. . . . It is important for all viewpoints to be available to all young people so that they may grow maturely to make decisions for themselves.

With the impassioned voices of their constituents echoing in their ears, the board began its debate. Not one of the three male members had taken the time to read an entire single issue of *Ms.* magazine. Board member Dennis McCormac opened the discussion with a rousing speech. He said he respected community standards of decency and decried modern permissive society: *Ms.* should be banned altogether. "Goodness is the only investment that never fails!" he concluded, playing to his audience. He was roundly cheered. The next member, Harry York, agreed that community sentiment, not the magazine, was what counted, and that *Ms.* should be removed from the school district. He too was greeted with applause.

Then the women board members spoke. Both had read many issues of *Ms.*, and while obviously troubled by the excerpts that had provoked the uproar, they found the magazine to be generally suitable for high school students. Nancy Gore was booed when she claimed that if the majority of citizens in the school district had read the full magazine, they would be against banning it. Sherry Sterrett asserted, "I do believe the classroom is appropriate for this magazine. The teacher is not a dictator but a trained professional. It is with such a person that students are introduced to many ideas. To me the classroom is a healthy environment for discussion of foreign policy, auto mechanics, the energy crisis, sex education, and any topic that appears in *Ms.* magazine."

Milt Lambertson, the key vote, spoke last. This was a difficult decision, he said; what troubled him most about banning *Ms.* was his fear of what they would be asked to ban next. But he also felt that parents ought to have a say in the education of their children. He finally proposed that the magazine be placed on restricted reserve, and that students be allowed to read it only with parental permission. After a long debate, the board voted three to two to let the magazine remain in the high schools, but with the condition that only students who had permission forms signed by both a parent and a teacher could read it. McCormac and York for some time resisted allowing the magazine in the schools at all, but as the night wore on they compromised.

Just one month later, in July 1980, another vote on *Ms.* took place in the nearby Acalanes School District. Betty Arras had filed a request in April to have the magazine banned there: In a procedure like that followed in the Mt. Diablo School District, the Acalanes review committee also recommended retaining it. Unlike the Mt. Diablo school board, however, the full Acalanes board on July 30 voted to accept its committee's recommendations. In an angry confrontation with a teacher who advocated free speech at that board meeting, Mrs. Arras shouted, "What right do you have to impose your immorality on us?" [4]

The restrictions placed on *Ms.* in the Mt. Diablo high schools sharply reduced the number of students who read the magazine. About half of those who initially asked for it at school libraries never bothered to take the forms home to be signed, even though the policy was eventually softened: Students over eighteen could read it without permission from a teacher or parent; students under eighteen still needed approval from a parent. Schools were to keep a list of students who read it. Teachers were permitted to use the magazine in classrooms. Evidently, after the policy change, different schools used different standards for the circulation of *Ms.*; there was confusion within the Mt. Diablo School District over just what was required.

In September 1980, two students, two teachers, a parent, a concerned resident of the county, and *Ms.* filed a lawsuit declaring that the restrictions arbitrarily violated the First Amendment rights of students, teachers, and the magazine. The American Civil Liberties Union (ACLU) of Northern California together with an attorney from a large San Francisco firm represented the plaintiffs. The school board hired private attorneys.

During the three years the lawsuit was in the courts, the school board's restrictions on *Ms.* remained in effect. Librarians in the Mt. Diablo high schools reported that the red tape involved in checking out the magazine was just too much trouble for the students. "The policy has effectively killed the use of the magazine," said Benning. Perhaps more important, the controversy had a chilling effect on the teachers and librarians as well. "I used to recommend certain articles in *Ms.*, but I don't anymore. The concern over what happened with *Ms.* sort of permeates a lot of other stuff we would use," said Don Gallup, a teacher of social studies at Ygnacio Valley High School. Not surprisingly, the community censors who fought *Ms.* felt vindicated. "People say we didn't lick [the magazine]," said Mrs. Tash. "I say we did. It's my understanding that because of the process used in getting that material, it's not used all that much."

Many of the opponents of the magazine were hostile and suspicious when they were asked to discuss the controversy. In a phone conversation, Tash declined to be interviewed in person and refused to discuss the matter further. Mrs. Arras also refused. Reverend Grotzke made an appointment for an interview, but canceled it at the last moment and refused to make another. By contrast, Bruce Packard, the Mormon educator who formally requested the banning of *Ms.*, had no qualms about being interviewed, and took considerable pains to dispel any notion of himself or all book banners as knee-jerk puritans.

Unlike the male school board members, he had carefully read several issues of *Ms.* before involving himself in the controversy. Unlike many who wanted to ban the magazine, he understood that the offensive articles actually opposed pornography and considered it degrading. What he objected to, he explained, were the magazine's methods, not its objectives, in these two articles. "It's like teaching our youth that they can murder to stop murder, or steal to stop stealing," he explained. "Using dirty words even to show that such use is harmful was the wrong way to go about solving the problem."

Packard also felt the magazine's descriptions of sexual activity were immoral. "The scenes were so graphic that they don't leave people's minds once they are imbedded," he said. "If a high school teacher requires that for learning of today's society, I think the teacher is wrong. We can know about death without killing; we can know that there's immorality without seeing it portrayed in words or pictures. Teachers ought not to have the right to infect minds with that kind of garbage." He cheerfully admitted that he wanted to protect young people from much of modern life. "There are a lot of things in this world I never want my children or other children to see or touch or feel—because they hurt," he said. He equated those who advocate free speech and unrestricted access to *Ms.* with "humanists, who say, 'Do what feels good,' " principles that he feels lead to moral deterioration and ultimately to unhappiness.

Packard insisted he believed in freedom of choice, in exposing students to varying points of view, but only so long as the "other side" is taught as well. "I don't mind teaching both sides of the issue, teaching that, yes, sexual freedom is a choice young people have—they do—and my thirteen-year-old son will have that choice. I won't be able to force him; he'll have to make his choices. I wouldn't mind if teachers taught that kids have sexual freedom and access to drugs and so forth, but many of them teach that as if that were the kids' *only* choice, and I believe that that perverts the truth." He also seemed to believe that exposure to varying points of view was all right so long as the virtuous path was portrayed as leading to happiness, the immoral as leading to unhappiness. "I think many people teach 'whatever you want to do is fine,' not just that freedom of speech is okay. They are not teaching that there are consequences." Finally, he objected to being categorized as an ultraconservative or fundamentalist, "as if that means being so biased I couldn't think on my own." He criticized some of his allies against *Ms.* for not thinking very much, and felt they were wrong, as were those who advocate total freedom of speech.[5]

Throughout my research into the controversy over *Ms.* I was puzzled by the evident fear of Baptist and Mormon parents that if their teen-aged children read dirty words and advertisements for sexual aids like those in the back pages of *Ms.,* all the parents' years of indoctrinating strong values into the children would count for nothing. The parents behaved as if the kids risked a sort of instant corruption. Why were they so insecure?

Dr. Wutzke, the Ygnacio Valley principal, thought he knew the answer. The conservative parents, he said, are not particularly well educated. They provide solid homes, and they care about their children very much. They have had a high school education, maybe a year or two of college at the most. When their children go to high school and are a little rebellious, as kids that age are, the parents feel inadequate compared with the English or history teacher, who is more verbal and better educated than they are. The teachers in the humanities often are rather liberal; when the youngsters challenge the parents with a teacher's ideas, it can be threatening to the parents. Wutzke gave his own experience as an example. He was raised by German immigrant parents who highly valued their heritage and wanted to pass it on to their children. When the parents heard during the thirties how wonderful Hitler was and what great things he was doing for Germany, they passed that on to young Ernest, who was then in high school. Ernest came home from school with the exact opposite message about Hitler; he and his parents had knockdown, drag-out fights over the issue.

Wutzke concluded, "It's the fear of losing their children that gets the religious parents so exercised." He added, "You've got to relate this to other issues and the many changes that have taken place in the recent past—like dress and grooming, even that smoking is allowed now in high schools." The conservative parents, Wutzke said, really want the children to be like themselves and not be exposed to differing values and customs. The same seems to be true of ideas, and from this fear of new ideas grew the movement to ban *Ms.* magazine, which, with its nontraditional views about women's place in society and its advocacy of alternative life styles, contradicted parental values.

The lawsuit over *Ms.* placed before the court the difficult question of control over high school reading material. The parent's right to control what the child reads conflicted with the teacher's right to select classroom materials and the young person's right to intellectual freedom.

Opposing views of education clashed in the legal briefs: Is the main purpose of education the inculcation of community values, as the parents who wanted to ban the magazine contended, or is it the opening up of young minds to the free interchange of ideas, as those who filed the lawsuit claimed? Judge David A. Dolgin, who decided the case in August 1983, wrote a mixed opinion that recognized both the student's right to read and the parent's right to control reading material. He found, however, that one outweighed the other: "The right of a parent to bring up his child in a way the parents have experienced and found valuable exceeds the child's right to receive information or the magazine's right to disseminate information." But, he added, neither the school board nor parents could interfere with the rights of children not their own.

Thus, although upholding parental rights, he struck down the policy adopted by the Mt. Diablo school board, saying that the schools could not remove *Ms.* from library shelves, nor could the schools require parents to write letters of permission before their children could read it. The burden rests with the parents who objected; they would have to write, saying that their children could *not* read the magazine.

Although this decision directly affected only the Mt. Diablo school board, it had important implications for other schools. According to ACLU attorney Margaret Crosby, it was the only case in the country to place before a judge the issue of parental restriction of high school reading material. Other school boards considering a similar policy would probably hesitate because of the likelihood that the ACLU might file an expensive lawsuit against them. The Mt. Diablo School District spent nearly $48,000 in its unsuccessful attempt to ban *Ms.*, a large sum at a time when school budgets were particularly strained.

Certainly the conflict over the right to read and teach freely will arise again in other districts. For Mt. Diablo, the outcome was mixed, and gave encouragement to both sides.

A HISTORY OF BOOK BANNING

Attempts to remove or change textbooks have a long and rich history in the United States.[6] All sorts of groups have appeared over the years to ensure that schools were teaching what they considered to be the correct point of view. After the Civil War, groups of Southern veterans took on publishing houses, denouncing what they perceived as textbooks unfair to the Confederacy. Union soldiers similarly took on publishers who they felt placed insufficient emphasis on patriotism, the flag, and the Grand Army of the Republic. Then, as now, publishers often acceded to the demands of those who told them how to write history. One even advertised, "Books prepared for southern schools, by southern authors, and therefore free from matter offensive to southern people." Others simply published dual versions of the Civil War, one for Northern schools and the other for Southern. The interest groups succeeded in having the histories tailored to their prejudices. The language used by those who favored banning books they disliked resembled the language used by book banners today: An organization of Union soldiers labeled textbooks they considered too favorable to the Confederacy "the cup of moral poison that our school histories are holding to our youth."

Textbook critics and book banners surged again after World War I, when a series of anti-British articles in Hearst newspapers fanned ultra-patriotic flames. The American Legion took up the cause, commissioning a textbook that would "preach on every page a vivid love of America." The Legion also agitated against what it considered to be un-American texts. The mayor of Chicago, a city with large German and Irish populations, attacked school texts for being pro-British. He succeeded in having the superintendent of schools fired, and made speeches opposing texts that praised British democracy, British ideas, and British institutions. Again, publishers saw which way the wind was blowing and tacked accordingly. Sections of texts that said that the British colonies were not "desperately oppressed" and passages saying that many colonists wondered about the wisdom of a revolution against England were removed from the books.

The Ku Klux Klan, the Knights of Columbus, the antievolutionists, and others had their own axes and ground them loudly. The Klan wanted Columbus deemphasized and the Nordic Leif Ericson lauded, and the Knights wanted it clear that the Catholic Columbus in fact discovered America and was just as worthy of admiration as George Washington. Organized labor and manufacturers' groups, pacifists, and the Daughters of the American Revolution (DAR), for example, camped in publishers' offices and harassed school boards to win the changes they wanted to see in America's texts. The Oregon legislature passed a law requiring educators to select no book "which speaks slightingly of the founders of the Republic, or the men who preserved the Union."

Executives of public utilities, besides wanting to censor books that spoke favorably of municipal ownership of utilities, wished to have new books written that would improve history according to their specifications. They negotiated with publishers and seemed well on their way to achieving their goal; as an interim measure, they had 136,000 copies of a commissioned booklet entitled *Aladdins of Industry* distributed to schools in Ohio. Finally, the Federal Trade Commission investigated and publicly revealed the utilities' activities in a series of hearings beginning in 1928. The resulting public outcry discouraged most of the textbook revisers for a while.

In the late 1930s, representatives of big business took on a series of social science texts prepared by a Columbia University professor of education, Dr. Harold Rugg. Rugg's books dealt with controversial issues in an attempt to bring to life the complex problems of government and history. They won acceptance in forty-two hundred school districts throughout the nation and reached nearly half the school children in the United States. The Advertising Federation of America campaigned against Rugg's books because of a section that said that while advertising was vital to the economic life of the nation, perhaps "we must ask ourselves if all the advertising today is wise and necessary." The book criticized misleading ads and advertising's tendency to induce people to buy things they didn't need. Other probusiness forces such as the National Association of Manufacturers and *Forbes* magazine joined the fray, as did the American Legion. Newsletters of these groups urged their members to attack the Rugg books, criticizing them for promoting socialist theories and a lack of patriotism.

Rugg traveled the country, attending hearings to defend his life's work. He learned that few of those who wanted his books out of the schools had even read them. One school district after another banned his books until they disappeared almost entirely. The business interests had succeeded.

Not surprisingly, another wave of book banning swept the country in the fifties, the era of Joseph McCarthy. The Conference of American Small Business Organizations sponsored a publication called *The Educational Reviewer,* which published evaluations of textbooks. The *Reviewer* opposed favorable mention of the United Nations, unequivocally praised the free enterprise system, and blacklisted books that it felt smacked of socialism or communism. Its definition of those isms was broad indeed. Similarly, the Sons of the American Revolution saw communist influence in many school texts; they published lists of authors whom they labeled subversive and warned of "interstate traffic in propaganda textbooks and teaching materials." Other groups that appeared during this period include the Guardians of American Education, who were concerned that "our schools and colleges continue to spawn Marxists"; American Patriots, Inc., which was headed by an anti-Semite named Allen A. Zoll; and Minute Women of the U.S.A. Since then, various national and local organizations have been trying to stamp out positive references to the Supreme Court, the United Nations, Robin Hood, and others who appear to them as Godless, un-American, or communist.

Alabama passed a law in 1953 that required publishers to state in every book whether any authors cited in the book had ever advocated any left-wing ideologies. A group of publishers filed suit against the law; they calculated that twenty-eight million names and publications would have to be examined before they could sell books in that state, and succeeded in having the law declared unconstitutional. California State Senator Hugh P. Donnally in 1957 proposed a bill to outlaw schoolbooks that were contrary to "morality, truth, justice, or patriotism." It failed, but the mentality that Senator Donnally represented lives on.

The rise of the John Birch Society and other ultraconservative groups in the 1960s, as one might expect, fueled yet another round of textbook censorship and book banning. E. Merrill Root, a professor of English at a small Indiana college, became convinced that higher education was infiltrated by communists. The author of *Brainwashing in the High Schools* and *Collectivism on Campus,* Root characterized various presidents in startling ways. Eisenhower was "soft on Communism"; FDR "did not have a fundamental grasp of reality"; Thomas Jefferson "would be a member of the John Birch Society" if he were alive today. Senator Joseph McCarthy was "a great patriot and a great American" who was falsely smeared and attacked. Root evaluated books by counting the number of lines or pages devoted to particular subjects. If a book had more lines about liberal presidents than conservative ones, it was ipso facto suspect. Root was also a member of the Board of Directors of the Congress of Freedom, headquartered in Omaha, Nebraska, whose magazine in November 1957 listed the NAACP as an organization of "Jews and left-wingers" trying to drive a wedge between blacks and whites.

The *New York Daily News* took up Root's cause and, in an article entitled "Poison in Textbooks," decried New York's practice of allowing principals to choose from a list of approved texts those that would be used in their schools. Said the *News,* "Obviously, if a principal happens to be a Communist, Fascist, Socialist or America-is-no-gooder, he can force textbooks that peddle his particular ideology on his defenseless pupils, and rule out books which truly and patriotically tell the great American story. There are many of the former and few of the latter."

The DAR also adopted Root's cause and helped to stir up textbook controversies in several states in the late 1950s and early 1960s. The Daughters distributed material charging that textbooks are written by subversives; they claimed that "some central source within the educational apparatus" chose what material textbooks would include, and they cited 170 "subversive" volumes. They were concerned with Red influence on the clergy, as well as on education, mental health programs, and messages on Christmas cards, among other things. One earnest lady warned, "When you choose your Christmas cards, be alert to any outright or concealed technique indulged in to convey a clandestine Marxist message." The objects of the DAR's wrath also included many of the targets of today's book banners: insufficient patriotism, leftist ideology, calling the United States a democracy rather than a republic, "realistic literature," and weakening of the family.

Similarly, a group called America's Future, headquartered in New Rochelle, New York, launched a campaign against textbooks and subversion in schools. Operation Textbook, begun in 1958, reviews texts and attempts to influence their contents. Rudolf K. Scott, president of the organization, said in 1962 that "publishers have had a free hand too long. There were no qualified persons criticizing them. Now we are hitting the publisher where it hurts—in his pocketbook." The group commissioned and disseminated textbook reviews (written by ultraconservatives) to educators, school board members, and other organizations. Predictably, certain groups provoked their ire: labor unions, the UN, Democratic presidents, the income tax, and Social Security, as well as the minimum wage and democracy. The group's secretary, in a book about the Supreme Court called *Nine Men against America,* suggested that all the decisions since 1937 should be considered null and void. Publications by America's Future were used in textbook challenges by members of the John Birch Society, the DAR, the American Legion, and others who tried to have books banned from their local schools.

A group that shared their beliefs, called Texans for America, showed up at textbook adoption hearings in that state in 1960; their spokesman stated their criteria for evaluating books. "The stressing of both sides of a controversy," he said, "only confuses the young and encourages them to make snap decisions based on insufficient evidence. Until they are old enough to understand both sides of a question, they should be taught only the American side." He wanted more favorable treatment for "traditional" Christianity in the texts, as well as for Herbert Hoover, Chiang Kai-shek, and Joseph McCarthy. He attacked UN Secretary Ralph Bunche and black poet Langston Hughes. Another member of Texans for America objected to writings by the early muckrakers Lincoln Steffens, Ida Tarbell, and Jack London. He labeled all of them subversive.

The onslaught of criticism by this group and others resulted in publishers making many changes in their books. A dozen books were rejected because of the Texans, and twenty-seven were adopted with many modifications agreed to by the publishers. Macmillan Company, for instance, deleted a passage about the League of Nations, to which the Texans objected. The publishers of a geography book altered several passages. Laidlaw Brothers eliminated from a history bibliography three names the Texans found objectionable. The publishers seemed eager to do whatever was necessary to win approval for their books; one said he was "not only willing but anxious to delete any references" to persons whose loyalty to the United States had even been questioned.[7]

The Texans for America took on school libraries as well, and succeeded in securing the removal of ten novels (including four Pulitzer Prize winners) from four Amarillo high schools and Amarillo College. Publishers reported that their sales nose-dived after these attacks on their books; even though they made the desired changes, schools were reluctant to adopt books that had even been challenged.

The Texas House of Representatives in 1961 passed a resolution advocating that "the American history courses in the public schools emphasize in the textbooks our glowing and throbbing history of hearts and souls inspired by wonderful American principles and traditions." This resolution also set up a state committee to review schoolbooks; the hearings that took place following this mandate turned into a circus. One blushing woman, too modest to read the offending portions of a book, had her pastor read the profane lines to the committee. She felt that the eight books she challenged had been put on school reading lists as "part of the Communist conspiracy to lower the morals of youth." Those who spoke in favor of challenged books drew hisses and boos from the spectators, as did the two committee members who disagreed with the censors.

A woman legislator praised a guide to textbooks that explained how to evaluate patriotism and subversion. By counting the good words (e.g., "accomplishments," "achievement," "admiration," "bold," capitalism," "character building") and bad words (e.g., "adjustment," "aristocrats." "big business," "coexist," "community," "conform") one could tell whether the books were left wing or not. At one of its sessions, the committee viewed a film called *The Ultimate Weapon,* narrated by a movie actor named Ronald Reagan. The committee was told the film would prove that American prisoners of war in Korea succumbed to brainwashing because of a "weakness in American character" attributable to "subversive" textbooks studied in schools.

Since the early 1960s, Texas has been fertile ground for schoolbook censors. For years Mel and Norma Gabler of Longview, Texas, have held unparalleled influence over the books adopted by the state. But Texas is not the only state with a tradition of censorship. In a textbook controversy in Florida in the early 1960s, self-described patriotic groups forced publishers to make changes in textbooks. A state legislator, in the wake of censorship hearings, proposed a law that would ban from the state's texts works by communists, persons who had invoked the

Fifth Amendment when asked about subversive connections, or members of any group that presented any ideology as "superior to the American system." The bill was defeated, but another bill was passed opposing the selection of texts that presented any political ideology as preferable to the American.

Segregationists have also insisted on screening books. In the South, they succeeded in banning several texts: Three books were banned in Georgia because the Board of Education said they were not "in accord with the Southern way of life." The books paid insufficient attention to the Southern role in the Revolutionary War and implied that white Southerners had mistreated blacks. Alabamans banned a text because it included a photo of Secretary of State Christian Herter shaking hands with the black president of Nigeria. In response, publishers eliminated such photos in order not to lose sales.

Not all objections to schoolbooks originate among right-wing groups. In the 1930s and 1940s, the NAACP objected to books considered derogatory to Negroes, as they then called themselves. They particularly objected to songs like those by Stephen Foster, which referred to "darkies," and succeeded in having the word removed from school song books. *Huckleberry Finn,* now under attack by blacks in some schools, was banned from a New York City school in 1957.

In censorship activities the same books often offend particular groups. For example, *The Merchant of Venice, Oliver Twist,* and *Little Black Sambo* were accused by Jews and blacks of perpetuating racial stereotypes. At first, the Anti-Defamation League of B'nai B'rith (ADL) tried to have books it considered anti-Semitic banned from the schools. Later, it took a different approach. In 1961, the ADL published a report discussing forty-eight books. This was not done to pressure publishers, said the ADL, but to make known its ideas about the ways minorities ought to be referred to, and to suggest that the problems of American minorities have been neglected or distorted in texts.

Minorities also began to object to schoolbooks in the 1960s. Their objections were not as frequent as right-wing attacks on books, and they differed markedly. Instead of asking that certain ideas be excluded, they asked that more ideas be included. In 1961, the annual convention of the NAACP urged members to inspect texts to see that they "properly present the contribution of the Negro to American culture." And many texts in that decade and in the 1970s were revised to portray minorities more accurately.

Women also protested their absence from the history books and their stereotyped roles when they were mentioned. Texts of this era presented white males as the significant individuals, virtually ignoring the accomplishments of other human beings. Rather than censor what could be published, the women and minorities criticized books and asked for their stories to be told, too.

Interest in book banning exploded in the 1970s: By the end of the decade, Professor Edward B. Jenkinson of the University of Indiana and a scholar of censorship, estimated that about two hundred groups were dedicated to removing from schools books that they considered immoral or lacking in patriotism. One of the most celebrated incidents occurred in 1974, in Kanawha County, West Virginia. A school board member, after telephone conversations with the Gablers in Texas, challenged several books that had been selected by the school's teachers from a state-approved list. The community was polarized; some ministers supported the books, but more supported the censors. The school board, after long and tumultuous meetings, voted to use eight of the challenged books and to drop the rest. Books by black authors, "depressing" books, and even *Jack and the Beanstalk* came under attack.

During the first week of school, eight thousand students stayed home and four thousand miners stayed off the job to protest the school board's action. Pickets agitated for the removal of more books; high school students picketed to retain them. Three men were shot; school buses were shot at and vandalized; beer bottles filled with gasoline were thrown at an elementary school; one minister asked for prayers for the death of the three school board members who had advocated the adoption of some of the books that had been criticized. Court-ordered limits on the number of pickets allowed at the schools were violated and protesters were arrested. The Gablers arrived on a quick speaking tour. The Board of Education issued a rigid set of guidelines for the adoption of textbooks. Among the criteria: recognizing the sanctity of the home, encouraging loyalty to the United States, not defaming our nation's founders, respect for traditional rules of grammar, no personal inquiries to be made of students about their inner feelings or behavior.

The National Education Association, in its 1975 report, *Kanawha County, West Virginia: A Textbook Study in Cultural Conflict,* stated that if the guidelines were implemented as the protesters advocated, the public schools would indoctrinate students "to one system of cultural and religious values, inflexible and unexamined." Its report also stated that highly sophisticated, right-wing organizations inflamed the controversy, naming among others the John Birch Society, the Ku Klux Klan, and the Heritage Foundation. The battle over texts in Kanawha County became, in effect, a religious war, in which passions inflamed people to commit violent acts.

In 1977 in Warsaw, Indiana, the community was also at loggerheads over books. A group of senior citizens burned forty copies of a book called *Values Clarification,* which had been criticized by the school board.

A long and complicated struggle took place over the right of teachers to choose the books students would read. A back-to-basics movement turned into a moralistic crusade against teachers, educational philosophies, and teaching methods as well as against individual books.

In the 1980s attempts are still being made to get school materials and library books removed from circulation. Individuals and groups who are offended by words or ideas increasingly take action to see that no one else will be exposed to them; all too often, the attempt at banning or censorship succeeds.

Several organizations measure censorship. The Office for Intellectual Freedom of the American Library Association found three times as many censorship attempts between 1975 and 1979 as there had been in the previous ten years. Since the opening of 1980, the office estimates that the rate has tripled again. The office received almost one thousand reports of books being challenged, removed, destroyed, or altered in 1981. Two other organizations concerned with censorship, a writers' organization called PEN, in New York City, and People for the American Way, in Washington, D.C., a group founded to combat the agenda of the New Right, also found dramatic increases in censorship—particularly after the election of Ronald Reagan. A study by Lee Burress, an English professor at the University of Wisconsin at Stevens Point, further confirmed the reports of increased censorship. Burress, who reported his findings to a convention of English teachers on November 20, 1982, has been taking surveys since 1966; in that year, 20 percent of the high school librarians who responded to his questionnaire reported some form of censorship pressure on books. The figure in 1973 was 28 percent, in 1977, 30 percent. By 1981, 34 percent reported such attempts against books; when attempts to censor both books and other media were counted, the figure rose above 50 percent.[8]

These startling figures do not reflect the full extent of censorship attempts in the nation, only those that have been reported. Professor Edward Jenkinson estimates that for each case reported, fifty cases are not reported. Judith Krug of the American Library Association figures more conservatively; she estimates that one of every four censorship incidents is reported to her organization.[9]

Perhaps the most complete study of censorship was conducted jointly by three groups: the Association of American Publishers, the American Library Association, and the Association for Supervision and Curriculum Development. They found that efforts to censor books occurred in one fifth of the nation's schools during the school years 1978–1979 and 1979–1980—before the Reagan election gave a boost to conservatives with censorship inclinations. The study, called *Limiting What Students*

Shall Read, listed more than two hundred books that were attacked, and found that schools often capitulated quickly in the face of protests made by parents or others.[10] Judy Blume, author of novels for teenagers, led the censored author list with eight challenged books. Also under attack were several dictionaries, as well as works by Richard Brautigan, Nathaniel Hawthorne, anticensorship activist Nat Hentoff, Ernest Hemingway, Aldous Huxley (*Brave New World*), Mario Puzo, Gordon Parks, J. D. Salinger, Eric Segal (*Love Story*), Maurice Sendak, William Shakespeare (*Merchant of Venice*), Alexander Solzhenitsyn, John Steinbeck, Studs Terkel, and Kurt Vonnegut. Among the titles were *Webster's Collegiate Dictionary, A Farewell to Arms, Passages,* and *Huckleberry Finn.* Books about human reproduction and science texts cropped up quite often, as did several magazines—*Ebony, Sports Illustrated, Mad, Esquire,* and *Mademoiselle,* among others.

Dirty words and material concerned with sex provoked about half the challenges originating with local schools. (Local challenges were counted separately from challenges originating with state textbook commissions.) The study found that only about half the people bringing challenges had read the material to which they objected. Presumably the others were following the recommendations of groups that send out reviews and lists of books they think ought to be banned. Roughly three fourths of the censors were parents. About one in six referred to outside groups when objecting to books, a figure that seems to be on the rise as the groups continue to gain prominence. Most frequently mentioned were "church groups," the John Birch Society, and the famous Gablers, whose organization is called Educational Research Analysts. A few mentioned the National Association for the Advancement of Colored People and the Congress on Racial Equality as having stimulated book challenges.

According to the study, about 30 percent of the challenges to school materials originated with school personnel—teachers, librarians, and administrators. School personnel may make preemptive strikes, taking controversial material off the shelves in the hope of avoiding trouble. One superintendent reported on the survey form "No challenge. Took book out of library and destroyed it." Similarly, a principal wrote, "I have had 3–4 books and one magazine brought to me by staff members for the above reasons [obscenity, profanity, "dirty words," nudity]. We removed them from the shelves."[11] More than 50 percent of the challenges resulted in some degree of censorship or restriction of the material. Schools that did not have formal written procedures for dealing with objections were more likely to accede to the objectors' demands than schools that had such procedures. Objections made by school personnel were especially likely to succeed.

Limiting What Students Shall Read also discusses what it calls pre-censorship: That is, school personnel avoid selecting books that meet educational standards but might provoke controversy. Of this, of course, there are no studies and no statistics. But some of the comments volunteered by participants in the study give some idea of what transpires:

> Parental badgering has caused rifts between teachers and administrators. Extreme care is taken in selecting any material. Teachers are afraid of bringing in "controversial" subjects.[12]

As a result of this kind of policy, many controversial ideas simply do not enter the classroom or the library. A school administrator in Seattle, Washington, stated the problem this way: "Our society becomes alarmed when an attempt is made to remove a source of information, while we tend to ignore the fact that the greater limits to access occur at the entry point of information into the sysem." [13]

Paula Hartz of the Association of American Publishers' Social Issues in Education Committee explained that publishers cannot afford to battle the book banners. "When you fight [censorship], you're fighting the people who buy your books. School administrators don't want controversy, they just don't. If they hear about programs somewhere else, they just won't buy that book or that program," she told the *Los Angeles Times*. "So no matter how effectively you fight this battle, in one place or another, you're going to lose the war because you will make that group in the middle nervous." [14]

Beyond the question of costs to publishers and ill will in the community, there are far graver costs from censorship. Individual teachers suffer, caught between their professional judgment about classroom materials that would interest their students and their concerns to avoid conflicts or threats to their jobs. A Wisconsin teacher who found himself accused of making "anti-God" statements told the *New York Times*, "Anything I think possibly controversial I tape." Other teachers say that they no longer use books that might be considered controversial or hold classroom discussions about issues on which students might be called upon to make personal judgments. But students lose most of all. They lose important opportunities to explore new ideas and examine and test them intellectually in a safe and open environment.

RELIGIOUS AND CONSERVATIVE BOOK BANNERS

By far the largest majority of those who would restrict the ideas discussed in schools speak in the name of God and Country. While these book banners rightfully exercise their own rights of free speech, they would like to abridge the free speech of others. According to these people, the devil and communism are abroad in the land, seeking control over young, innocent minds. Rooting out the evil, the suggestive, the subversive, becomes their crusade. Those who argue for freedom of speech and for the right of students to make up their own minds, in this view, merely further a dark conspiracy to sabotage all that has made America great. Thus, while wrapping themselves in the mantle of patriotism and righteousness, fundamentalist Christians, who believe that the Bible is literally true, ally with conservatives of the New Right to stamp out ideas of which they disapprove. The religious and conservative book banners long for a mythical bygone era when things were simple—when, as one teacher said, the air was clean and sex was dirty.

The language used in their speeches and their literature reveals their positions on specific issues: the family, scientific creationism, patriotism, communism, secular humanism, vulgarity. Needless to say, they favor the first three and oppose the others. Also among their dislikes is feminism, which is perceived as an attack on traditional family values. According to Dr. Charles Stanley, a television evangelist on the board of the Moral Majority, "There is a vicious all-out Satanic attack upon the American home—the whole concept of anti-submission and independence.... When two people in the family become absolutely legally equal, there is no head; both become independent of each other and love is destroyed."[15] Howard Phillips, founder of the Conservative Caucus, echoed this view, asserting that public schools sometimes follow "a conscious policy of government to liberate the wife from the leadership of the husband. It used to be that in recognition of the family as the basic unit of society, we had one family, one vote. And we have seen the trend to have one person, one vote."[16] Clearly, the fundamentalist conservatives dislike preparation of girls for an "independent" role, and prefer books that depict women in traditional roles.

Men and women sharing Phillips's ideology hold important offices in the Reagan administration: The former executive director of the Moral Majority, Robert Billings, is director of regional liaison for the U.S. Department of Education. He said, "Censorship has become a necessity because perverted educators have felt that presenting life in the raw produced a better product than the tried and proven methods of a few generations ago . . . with their emphasis on morality, integrity and striving for perfection."[17] Tom Ascik, former policy analyst for the Heritage Foundation, was nominated to be director of planning for the National Institute of Education, and Charles Heatherley, also a former officer of Heritage, is deputy under secretary for management at the Department of Education.

Moral Majority members like Billings generally view with distaste the social upheavals of the sixties and seventies, the revelations of U.S. government misdeeds at home and abroad, new measures to achieve full equality for women and minorities, and the sexual revolution. And, in truth, there is much about life in the 1980s that is nasty, unpleasant, and confusing. Raising children at a time when dangerous drugs abound, families fall apart, sex roles have changed, unemployment rates are high, and nuclear annihilation possible is a difficult task. But even if it were possible to eliminate from schools every mention of the difficulties and uncertainties of modern life and to restrict the curriculum to Christian morality and the three Rs, social problems would still be with us.

Yet fundamentalists and conservatives still focus on eliminating books from schools and on pressuring publishers to make changes in texts. Among the most effective groups crusading against suspected textbooks is the Moral Majority, headed by television evangelist Jerry Falwell. Falwell blames books for numerous social evils:

> Our textbooks deceive our young people about premarital sex, about the role of the father and the mother in the home, and even about history. . . . We should be angry with our textbooks because they push socialism and one-world government. What makes me mad is that it is our own tax money that is underwriting the destruction of the morals of our nation, our church, and the world in which our children will live.[18]

He obviously wishes to stop some ideas from circulating:

> It's not that the schools teach the wrong answers; it is that the schools do not protect children from information that might call their beliefs into question.[19]

In one effort to protect students from information, Falwell in 1981 attacked two sex education books that questioned the rigid moral values his church espouses. He wrote in a fund-raising appeal:

> We cannot compromise our children's moral values because a small minority of people in America don't believe in the traditional moral principles this nation was founded upon! . . . The Moral Majority is already working with several organizations to remove these harmful sex education materials from classrooms. . . . Destroy this letter and the special sheet I've enclosed immediately after reading it so that it will not fall into the hands of an innocent youngster.[20]

Presumably his letter had to be destroyed because it quoted from the sex education books *Our Bodies, Ourselves* and *Life and Health.* Falwell went on to ask his readers to learn whether the books could be found in their local libraries and to send "the largest amount you can possible [sic] sacrifice" to him right away to support the effort to root out the evil books wherever they turned up. Subsequently, *Our Bodies, Ourselves* was challenged in school libraries in Texas, Illinois, California, Massachusetts, Ohio, Colorado, and several other states. In Montana, in a lawsuit argued in 1980 over the banning of *Our Bodies, Ourselves* from the Helena School District Number One, a state prosecutor had threatened to bring criminal charges against any teacher or librarian who gave the book to a minor. "Americans have genuflected too long at the altar of free speech," he said.

Despite his attacks on books, Falwell denies being a censor. In March 1983, his campaign took a different twist, playing down censorship and advocating equal time for conservative ideas. Alleging that librarians and booksellers repress the conservative point of view, he announced a large-scale effort to balance that censorship by getting more conservative books into schools, public libraries, and bookstores. "We plan to flood the nation's libraries with questioners," he said. "If they don't put our books up, then take the liberal books down, too." [21]

Other groups espousing principles similar to those of the Moral Majority have attracted large followings. Among the best known are Mel and Norma Gabler's Educational Research Analysts in Texas; Phyllis Schlafly's Eagle Forum, with its confusingly named Stop Textbook Censorship Committee; and the Pro-Family Forum, headed by Lottie Beth Hobbs. There is also Barbara Morris, who publishes an ultraconservative newsletter about education. Schlafly maintains in her Citizens' Bill of Rights About Schools and Libraries that schools "should have a decent respect for the parents' beliefs and attitudes." The school board should "reflect the values of the citizens in the area of its jurisdiction" [22] and not censor religious and conservative writings (hence the name of her group). The tirades of these and other groups against textbooks seem to be part of an overall attack on public education. Morris writes, "The best thing that could happen to education in America would be the demise of government schools." [23] In fact, religious conservatives often advocate government encouragement of private, Christian schools through tax credits and a voucher system.

Book banners have been known to go to extraordinary lengths to find the evil they expect in texts. Family IMPACT (Interested Monitoring Persons against Contemporary Textbooks), a Fresno group, used high-powered magnifying glasses to examine teaching materials. They approached C. Hugh Friedman, a member of the California State Board of Education, to show him "obscene" illustrations in eighth-grade reading texts published by Holt, Rinehart and Winston. The IMPACT members had discovered under the magnifying glass what looked like a girl wearing a "transparent skirt" and a rabbit's foot, which appeared "subliminally to represent a different part of the body." Friedman suggested to Bob Jones, West Coast representative of Holt, Rinehart and Winston, that the drawings be changed, and in fact they were. No fuss, no public meeting, no awkward due process or confrontations. Said Jones, "When you're publishing a book, if there's something controversial, it's better to take it out." [24]

Perhaps no two people are as responsible for Jones's ready surrender to the demands of IMPACT as the Gablers. The Gablers arrived at the 1982 hearings of the Texas State Textbook Committee with about six hundred pages of detailed criticism of the texts to be considered for adoption. Echoing an earlier generation of book banners, Norma Gabler objected to a Scott, Foresman civics text, because she said it presented the United States "in a bad light, criticizing the American system and slighting American achievement." The Gablers felt that the book also contained too many pictures of people protesting, which might encourage students themselves to protest. They wanted more balance in a Ginn and Company junior high health book: To offset a chapter called "When Things Go Wrong," they demanded one called "When Things Go Right."

The Gablers review about fifty textbooks a year, with the help of their small staff, and send their views to thirteen thousand individuals and groups. In a 1978 annual report they wrote, "We submitted 659 pages in our bill of particulars against 28 textbooks. God saw fit to direct the Texas State Textbook Committee to remove 18 of these objectionable texts." The Gablers feel so strongly about the evil effects of textbooks that they even warn against children studying hard. Their *Handbook Number One* advises:

> As long as the schools continue to teach ABNORMAL ATTITUDES and ALIEN THOUGHTS, we caution parents NOT to urge their children to pursue high grades and class discussion because the harder students work, the greater their chances of brainwashing.[25]

They oppose discussions of civil rights, feminism, unions, poverty, and other controversial problems of the modern world. They steadfastly reject the idea that students should think for themselves, saying that "leaving students to make up their own minds about things just isn't fair to our children." They consider texts that ask for students' opinions about issues an invasion of privacy; such questions should be forbidden in the classroom. They discourage criticism of the United States and its traditional ways. One book's discussion of the Equal Rights Amendment attracted their ire because it misled "students to believe that women are not guaranteed equal rights already. This is totally untrue." [26] They say that teaching about the Great Depression of the 1930s "will only succeed in raising doubts about our system." [27]

Among the groups that follow essentially the same principles as the Gablers is Parents of Minnesota, which states, "Classroom materials, textbooks, audio and visual aids must not portray parents as unloving, hypocritical, old-fashioned, possessive, or in any other negative way . . . [and] must not defame the nation's historical personalities." They believe, "We have been endowed by our Creator with certain unalienable rights over our children and must insist that the schools and legislators recognize and ensure those rights." [28]

These groups have also taken on some government publications: The Indiana chapter of the Moral Majority succeeded in stopping Senator Richard Lugar from sending out copies of *Your Child from One to Six* to new parents. They objected that the booklet advises against spanking, advice that the Moral Majority claims "flies in the face of Biblical doctrine on discipline." [29]

Smaller, local groups also take up the book-banning cry, sometimes following the urgent warnings spread by the larger organizations through newsletters and television. Calling themselves names like the Committee for Improvement of Public Education, Committee for Excellence in Our Schools, Guardians of Education, and so forth, they spring up in communities for the duration of a censorship controversy, then disappear again. But they are effective; mobilizing a vocal constituency, they pressure local school officials into removing books from schoolroom shelves, sometimes in violation of official school procedures.

What Do the Religious Conservatives Want?

"Until the textbooks are changed, we won't begin to solve our problems with crime, venereal disease and teen-age pregnancy," Mel Gabler said in a widely quoted interview. "The kind of textbooks we have largely determine what a nation becomes and where it goes." [30] One of the most dangerous aspects of textbooks, according to the Gablers, lies in the misbegotten concept called secular humanism. According to the fundamentalist conservatives, secular humanism is a religion recognized by the Supreme Court and taught by public schools in contravention of the First Amendment, which forbids the establishment of a state religion. This extraordinary claim stems from a footnote in a Supreme Court decision (*Torcaso v. Watkins,* 1961) written by Justice Hugo Black, listing secular humanism along with Buddhism and Taoism as religions that do not hold a conventional belief in God. A later decision (*Welsh v. United States,* 1970) also mentions it.

Starting from those footnotes, the fundamentalists jumped to the conclusions that not only is this "religion" recognized by the state, it is inculcated by the public schools into the students. Thus, they say, secular humanism is being slipped like so many Mickey Finns to unsuspecting youngsters as they learn to read and write. A pamphlet written by Lottie Beth Hobbs and published by her Pro-Family Forum, called *Is Secular Humanism Molesting Your Child?,* lists the beliefs that characterize this "religion." According to the pamphlet, humanists do not believe in God or Jesus or in the divine inspiration of the Bible; they believe in evolution and deny the existence of the soul, heaven, and hell. They fail to acknowledge moral absolutes, but rather live by self-determined, "situation" ethics that sanction lying, stealing, and killing. Also according to the pamphlet, humanists think the distinctive roles of men and women should be eliminated; they endorse sexual freedom, including homosexuality, between consenting individuals; they assert the right to abortion, euthanasia, and suicide; they feel that America's wealth should be redistributed in order to bring about equality; and they want to control the environment. The pamphlet also calls the humanists antipatriotic, opposed to the free enterprise system, and advocates of one-world socialism. Finally, according to the fundamentalist conservatives, humanists subvert the family through textbooks. Hobbs likens secular humanists to child molesters:

> [Your child's] conscience can be slowly remolded until he recognizes no need for God and parental values. Parents are portrayed as unloving and uncaring and inadequate. Slowly he is conditioned to view his parents with distrust and disrespect. Alienation often results. . . . Let's protect our families from child molesters!

Certainly many of the beliefs attributed to "secular humanism" are held by both religious and nonreligious people throughout the United States. Jews don't believe in the divinity of Christ, for instance, and many Christians believe that abortion should be permitted. Simply holding one or several of the beliefs listed in the Hobbs pamphlet hardly makes one a secular humanist. The Moral Majority and their like have simply lumped together most of the beliefs of which they disapprove, labeled them a religion, and complained that this religion is being taught in public schools. By positing this religion of secular humanism, they can condemn as illegal the teachings of which they disapprove and ask on ostensibly First Amendment grounds that secular humanist ideas be excluded from classrooms. What they want, of course, is for *their* values to be taught, and they try to have banned books that conflict with those values.

Controversial Issues

Issues of right and wrong, feminism, vulgarity, and sex education provoke a large percentage of the objections to books. But troublesome as these subjects are for schools, the most difficult issue, especially in those twenty-two states with education commissions that choose textbooks for use statewide, is evolution. This is hardly a new issue in American education: The Scopes trial of the 1920s was fought over the right to teach Darwin's scientific theory, which contradicts the Biblical account of creation. The two sides have been at it, on and off, ever since, in the courts and in the offices of textbook publishers.

In recent years, evolution has been deemphasized in textbooks, largely because the Gablers and other fundamentalists objected to texts that describe it. Evolution has been downgraded in some texts from a process about which many details are not known to a theory that is not necessarily more scientific than the Biblical book of Genesis. A 1982 survey conducted by Gerald Skoog, chair of the Secondary Education Department at Texas Tech University, showed that a "significant" decline in emphasis on evolution in high school biology textbooks that began in the 1970s continued into the 1980s. Skoog said that the deemphasis was "mostly a result of the strenuous pressures anti-evolutionists have exerted upon publishers, authors, educators and policy-makers." He added, "Statements indicating that biologists support the validity of evolution have become very modest and almost nonexistent in textbooks since 1980." [31]

Laidlaw Brothers, a publishing subsidiary of Doubleday, omitted the very word *evolution* from its new high school biology text, *Experiences in Biology*.[32] This was done, said publications director Eugene R. Frank, "to avoid the publicity that would be involved in a controversy." [33] Other publishers put the material about evolution in a special signature (group of pages), which can be omitted from a volume. Still others capitulate to the objectors. "We don't see this as a First Amendment problem," said the head of Prentice-Hall's elementary and high school division, James Peoples, in a 1982 interview with the *Los Angeles Times*. "I believe in local community control. I think the local school board ought to have the right to select whatever they want." [34]

In 1982, Holt, Rinehart and Winston inserted the phrase "according to scientific theory" at the start of a paragraph about biological adaptation of animals in *World Geography Today*.[35] Silver Burdett, publishers of *Biology,* slashed coverage of Darwin's life and his account of evolution from more than 5,000 words in 1968 to less than 200 words in 1981.[36] Follett Publishing Company changed the title of a chart from "Mountain Ranges and Ages" to "Mountain Ranges and Approximate

Ages," and added the phrase "scientists believe" to a sentence describing the formation of mountains in their text *World Geography.*[37] These changes were not made because of new information leading scientists to doubt that evolution occurred, but rather to tailor information to suit the religious beliefs of organized groups.

The fundamentalists are engaged in one of the great deceptions of modern education—presenting the Biblical account of God's creation of the world as science, and then trying to enact laws requiring it to be taught in schools. For much of this country's history, laws have forbidden the teaching of evolution. Although Darrow is erroneously remembered as winning the Scopes trial of the 1920s, the Tennessee law he challenged remained in effect, and the teaching of evolution remained forbidden in that state until 1968. For as long as possible, creationists have shut out evolution from classrooms.

In February 1981, the Alabama State Board of Education held a public hearing at which a group of parents protested against *Unfinished Journey: A World History,* a social studies text that, they claimed, inculcated the values of secular humanism. The following are examples of objectionable passages and the parents' objections:

> TEXT: During the long centuries of the Old Stone Age . . . humans developed spoken language and learned how to make and use tools.
>
> OBJECTION: How does he know that there was no language in the beginning? . . . That is a very subtle way of telling us that we evolved through evolution. . . . This cannot be proved, but it is being stated as a fact. There must have been language in the beginning . . . because . . . Adam named all the animals.
>
> TEXT: Stone Age people also developed religious beliefs. To early humans the sun, rain, wind, thunder, and lightning were alive. These forces were looked on as spirits, gods, or demons. . . . Myths evolved to explain the mysteries of nature, birth, sickness and death.
>
> OBJECTION: The development of religion indicates evolution and implies religion is man-made. We object to the fact that they are trying to say that religion is man-made.[38]

As a result of these and other objections *Unfinished Journey* along with ten other texts that had drawn criticism was removed from the Alabama school system.

Between 1964 and 1978, bills mandating that evolution be taught as unproven theory, with creationism given equal time and credibility, were introduced in twenty-two state legislatures, and since 1979 in at least another thirteen. Arkansas and Louisiana actually enacted the laws in 1981; the Arkansas law was declared unconstitutional the next year; the constitutionality of the Louisiana law is now before the courts. The Arkansas law specified that "creation science" had to be taught as if the Bible were literally true, that it required "explanation of the earth's geology by catastrophism, including the occurrence of a worldwide flood; and . . . a relatively recent inception of the earth and living kinds." That law would have meant teaching students that trilobites, dinosaurs, and human beings all lived on earth together, and just happened to settle in the flood with the trilobites at the bottom, dinosaurs in the middle, and human beings at the top, the order in which biologists think those life forms evolved on the planet.

It is perhaps most important to the creationists that students would have had to be taught that human beings and apes have completely separate ancestries—in order to preserve the cherished, if perhaps vain, idea that God created man in His own image. The judge ruling on the Arkansas law in 1982 held that "creation science" is religion, not science, and lacks educational merit.

Another significant defeat for the creationists took place in Texas, where the state Textbook Proclamation mandated the teaching of evolution as only one theory of the origin of humanity. This regulation had been adopted in 1974 after the Gablers protested the teaching of evolution as fact. In March 1984 Texas Attorney General Jim Mattox, in response to a state senator's inquiry, found the provision unconstitutional because it violated the required separation of church and state and also interfered with the free expression of ideas. Faced with the threat of a lawsuit by scientists and civil liberties groups if they failed to act, the State Board of Education voted to repeal the provision.

The battle over creationism has significant First Amendment implications: It is not only a matter of science teachers being forced by law to teach things they know are not true, but also a matter of law being used to drive out truth. Wayne Moyer, head of the National Association of Biology Teachers, worries that "educators are going to be asked to stand in front of students and say that all animals and plants and the world were created 6,000 years ago, and that a great flood covered the entire world, even the highest mountains, and hollowed out the Grand Canyon in one year." [39]

Not all school systems have gone along with the deevolutionized textbooks. New York City rejected three high school biology texts in 1982 specifically because of their inadequate treatment of evolution and their uncritical approach to creationism. In a letter to Prentice-Hall, explaining the rejection of *Life Science,* school official Charlotte Frank wrote, "This book does not state that evolution is accepted by most scientists today, and represents special creation without characterizing it as a supernatural explanation that is outside the domain of science." New York school officials took exception to passages like this one from *Natural Sciences: Bridging the Gap*: "Another hypothesis about the creation of the universe with all its life forms is special creation, which gives God the critical role in creation. In some school systems, it is mandated that the evolution and special-creation theories be taught side by side. That seems a healthy attitude in view of the tentative nature of hypothesis." [40]

The cry of equal time has a reasonable and democratic ring; it's hard to say no. But should textbooks give equal time to teaching that the earth is flat, or that the sun revolves around the earth? Biologists like Stephen Jay Gould of Harvard University do not wish to ban the Biblical account of creation from schools, but they think it belongs in the history of scientific thought. Creationism in the biology class becomes a wedge for the teaching of Christianity and a step toward state inculcation of religious belief.

The creationists' recent tactic of arguing for equal time has had some success. They continue to claim that by teaching evolution as fact, schools are infringing on the free exercise of their religion and are imposing alien beliefs. But, again, they have run into roadblocks in the courts. A California lawsuit filed against the schools by the Segraves family of San Diego, who founded the Creation Science Research Center, did not succeed in having evolution and creationism taught as theory against theory in that state. Nevertheless, with their continuing assault on textbooks, the fundamentalists and conservatives are succeeding in making some ideas so controversial that teachers and librarians avoid discussing them or buying and using books that deal with them. It is a very effective method of shrinking the free expression rights of students and teachers alike, and it seems destined to continue.

The individuals and groups seeking to eliminate texts and materials that contravene the tenets of their religion and their politics have raised serious and difficult issues. What rights do parents have in the education of their children? How much should school boards consider community standards when they are choosing books for schools? Clearly it would not be appropriate to assign *Hustler* in junior high school, or *Lady Chatterley's Lover* in ninth grade. Lines do have to be drawn, but where, and by whom? These are questions that are raised before legislatures and courts. And to date, there are no clear answers.

BOOK BANNERS FROM THE LEFT

The Moral Majority and conservatives are not the only groups critical of materials used in schools and libraries. Women challenge material they consider sexist; minorities challenge material they consider racist. But censorship attempts by these groups are not nearly as numerous, as effective, or as disruptive as the efforts of the fundamentalist conservatives. It is important to recognize that although there are certain similarities between the fundamentalist conservative censors and those who are sometimes called the censors of the left, the differences between the two groups are great.

First, let us look at the similarities. The arguments for censoring materials are the same: Certain books offend parents and damage children. Schools have an obligation to respect the wishes of parents and remove the offensive materials. To achieve this goal, individual feminist or minority parents complain to local schools, and their organized groups complain to state textbook commissions. After the Gablers, one of the most vocal objectors before the Texas State Textbook Committee over the years has been the National Organization for Women, protesting sexist stereotyping.

Perhaps the best known object of censorship from the left is the quintessential American novel *Huckleberry Finn.* Black parents in schools from Texas to Virginia have tried to remove the tale of the runaway white boy and the runaway slave from classrooms and libraries, arguing that the frequent use of the word *nigger* demeans black students and provokes white attacks on blacks. A sensitivity committee of black parents in Houston opposed to the novel stated that no book is worth the humiliation of their children, and claimed that the book was not properly taught, that teachers there made the black students "feel like dogs." Like the Moral Majority, whose members argue that controversial books ought to be eliminated because there are plenty of fine noncontroversial books available, these parents want *Huck Finn* thrown out and some nonharmful work substituted. The black parents were not convinced by a school review committee that found that "no other literary selection illustrates the mid-nineteenth century and its evils of slavery as well as this novel, Mark Twain's satirical masterpiece." [41]

Although minority and feminist book banners feel that racist and sexist books will damage their children, they do not rail against public education per se, or try to turn back the clock; quite the reverse. These groups feel that social change can improve their position in society; consequently, they generally look to the future and what they hope will be progress. In fact, most pressure on schools and publishers emanating from groups that have not been part of America's traditional power structure has been toward *adding* material about them and their contributions to society. Women, Native Americans, Asians, blacks, Jews, gays, disabled people, and Hispanics, among others, have felt that they have been unfairly portrayed in both histories and fiction taught in schools, if they were portrayed at all.

Is this pressure a form of censorship? No, say the advocates. It is not a restriction or exclusion of ideas, but rather the addition of new ones to the marketplace. It is a recognition of things that have been long overlooked, like the role of black cowboys in the settling of the West, or the dedication of the suffragettes in their struggle for the vote, or the accomplishments of women artists and engineers, or the discrimination that afflicted Asian immigrants to the West Coast. Bringing out this information is, they argue, an extension of the Fourteenth Amendment, which mandates equal protection under the law to all, including minority and female students who must be portrayed accurately along with whites and males. The censors of the left thus reject being paired with the Falwells and Schlaflys and Gablers; they are not stifling academic inquiry or the freedom to read, they say; they are instead enriching the mix of ideas and pointing out errors of the past.

One organization has monitored schools and publishers since 1965: the New York–based Council on Interracial Books for Children. Its director, Bradford Chambers, explained its objectives: "to provide librarians and other educators with the perspectives of those our society has long oppressed—minorities, feminists, older people, disabled people, etc." The council's *Bulletin* reviews books and makes recommendations; the reviewers are members of the group being portrayed because, according to Chambers, "the surest, most effective way to uncover bias and stereotyping is to ask for criticism from those who are struggling against their oppression." He seeks out reviewers who are also activists working for social justice—an approach that he called "a little eyebrow-raising" in the early years, but says is now more accepted. The book reviews appear in review annuals of children's literature as well as in the council's own publications.

Chambers condemns censorship, advocating not the banning of biased books but rather their use among other materials as a way of teaching children about prejudice. "Providing children with the skills to identify bias gives them a sort of defense, an antidote against the worst effects of bias. We are not asking that children's books remove women from the kitchen, but that they not limit women to the kitchen. We are not asking that people of color be shown as saints, but rather that they not be restricted to subservient and stereotyped roles," he said. While disagreeing with members of the religious right, Chambers supports their right to be heard. "We don't mind including the Moral Majority point of view—as long as other viewpoints are there also," he said.

But like the fundamentalist conservatives, Chambers advocates certain values. A council statement says, "Textbooks can mold human beings with counter-values that may help to restructure society." Chambers does not hesitate to say that, in his view, "political and economic power is concentrated in the hands of a relatively few well-to-do white men, and they benefit very materially from this society's value system." He criticizes the values that are "at the root of the mess" this country is in, values such as "acquisitiveness, competitiveness, aggressiveness." [42] He wants to see education used to further social justice, and to see textbooks that reflect his views made available in classrooms throughout the United States. In this, of course, he both resembles and differs from the Moral Majority, which also advocates certain values but wants to see only theirs expounded in classrooms.

An important difference between the left and the right has to do with history: The council, along with other advocates for less powerful groups, wants to see a wider variety of materials taught, with the idea that students will ferret out the truth for themselves. The Moral Majority wants a limited, super-patriotic version of history taught that will reinforce loyalty to God and Country, as well as respect for the existing law. In fact, the religious right disagrees with groups like the National Organization for Women and the Council for Interracial Books for Children, which advocate social change; the right objects to students learning about sweatshop conditions or studying the defects of the free enterprise system.

But despite the council's disavowal of censorship, their own publication included an article in praise of book banning. In "Protesting Sexist Materials: You Can Make a Difference," which appeared in the *Interracial Books for Children Bulletin* (Vol. 12, No. 3), Elaine Wagner described her successful campaign to ban a romance magazine published by the venerable Scholastic Book Services and distributed through the New York City public schools. Wagner objected when the romance magazine *Wildfire* was presented to her eleven-year-old daughter with the sanction of the school (a teacher distributed the Scholastic order form and collected the money for the publications). The *Wildfire* stories taught several lessons: Girls should learn to manipulate friends, girls need boyfriends and are incomplete without them, activities that do not involve boyfriends are worth little, and so on. For example, two girls are talking about a boy who is coming for a visit.

> "I hope your cousin likes me." . . . "He will," Sally promised. "Only don't say much. No boy wants an extra brain around. Especially when that brain belongs to a girl."

At one point in a story, one girl justifies to another her plans to snare a boy who is going with another girl: "Maybe you think I'm being selfish, deliberately planning to steal Eric away from Laurie, but Laurie doesn't really love him, not the way I do."

Elaine Wagner complained to the principal about the brainwashing of young girls implicit in the stories, encouraging them to believe that a Prince Charming would one day fulfill them. Her letter asked him to "institute policy level review standards to assure that neither my child nor anyone else's children will in the future be exposed to this kind of imprinting through the schools." Through diligent organizing, she succeeded in extirpating the offending romance series from her school district and then from the Scholastic line of books. The article in the council's *Bulletin* presenting the story of her succesful campaign sounds very much like the "success stories" of fundamentalist and conservative mothers who have had books that offended *them* eliminated from schools.

The obvious question is, which mothers have the right to eliminate what they see as trash from their children's schools? Which have the right to determine what someone else's children may read? Certainly the antiromance mother could simply have forbidden her daughter's purchase of the offending magazine, thereby removing the "imprinting" she found so wrong while leaving others free to make up their own minds about what to read. The council's rationalization for seeking to ban schoolbooks stems from the compulsory nature of education. In this context, the question is, Is racist and sexist content something that the state can sponsor by allowing it in books that are mandatory reading, paid for at public expense? The Moral Majority employs the same rationalization, substituting the words *immoral* and *subversive* for *racist* and *sexist.*

The council also suggests that forcing students to read texts that ignore or distort their heritage may violate the Fourteenth Amendment, which assures equal protection of the law to all citizens. According to the council, schools, as public institutions, *must* include every group and sex in the pages of textbooks in a way that does not insult students or their cultures. Students cannot be demeaned for their race or their sex, conditions of their being they can never change. But what about a student's moral values? Can students be forced to read books that take the name of the Lord in vain, if they consider that to be sinful? In 1982, two religious boys refused to read Studs Terkel's *Working* because of the profanity it contains. Their school refused to give them their diplomas or to assign them alternate reading—until the boys went to court. That school was trying to deprive them of their First Amendment rights just as if it had forbidden them to read that book.

Underneath this argument about which kinds of censorship are better or worse, permissible and impermissible, lies another issue rarely mentioned: the effects of corporate control of publishing and the unequal distribution of power. We act as though the marketplace of ideas were free, and as though the distribution of power were equal and fair in the democracy that is the United States. But the fact remains that because of past and present discrimination, whites hold more power than people of color; men hold more power than women. In our society, some ideas are more acceptable than others: If a book says that U.S. democracy ensures majority rule and that free enterprise is the best economic system, that book is more likely to be published and used in schools than a book that says that corporations run this country and the free enterprise system is flawed. In fact, the free market in ideas is not truly free, but subject to the demands of the profit motive; therefore, books that displease the powerful are less likely to be published, and if published, they are less likely to be distributed to major bookstores.

This fact of publishing and ideas may seem irrelevant to a discussion of censorship from the left, but it is not. For a look at the other side of the coin will show that a large proportion of the books banned from schools and libraries are by or about minorities and women. Lists of books under attack include such works as *Down These Mean Streets* by Puerto Rican Piri Thomas, *Soul on Ice* by former Black Panther Eldridge Cleaver, *The Learning Tree* by Gordon Parks, *Best Short Stories by Negro Writers* edited by black poet Langston Hughes, as well as works by Alice Childress (black and female), Richard Wright (black), and many others. The Minnesota Civil Liberties Union found in 1982 that Alex Haley's *Roots* had been banned from 88 of the state's 235 schools. In addition, it has, with rare exceptions, been far more difficult for blacks and other minority writers to find publishers for their works than it has been for whites. Even works about racism come under attack. For instance, the Gablers objected to a book about slavery that stated, "The law that allows slavery in America was wrong, so people could break the law." [43] That sentence, they argued, encouraged insubordination. They also objected to a book that suggested that students imagine themselves as sit-in protesters of the 1960s, because in their opinion that sort of activity "teaches rebellion."

Given the long history of discrimination, some blacks speak out against censorship, both because they oppose it in general and because they have suffered from it in the past and expect to again. Black psychologist Kenneth Clark said, "The last damn thing blacks should do is get into the vanguard of banning books. The next step is banning blacks." [44]

Three of the four most banned books, according to a recent study, were by or about women, or both. Like racial discrimination, discrimination against women remains an unsolved social problem that sparks strong emotion. Therefore, women should also be especially careful about banning books, because they will be among the first to suffer the consequences.

PORNOGRAPHY

Pornography in the United States is a booming business. In 1970, the U.S. Commission on Obscenity and Pornography estimated industry worth at about $573 million; Kathleen Barry in *Female Sexual Slavery* estimated its worth at $4 billion in 1979, and in 1983 Women against Violence in Pornography and Media gave an estimate of $8 billion. Pornography goes far beyond *Playboy* centerfolds, objectionable as those might be. It extends to the farther reaches of violence against women. Books, films, and photos portray torture, rape, and murder of women by men—all for huge profits. An X-rated film called *Super Vixens* exemplifies the mixture of sex and violence:

> A muscular and sadistically inclined off-duty cop, taunted by his voluptuous one-night paramour because he cannot achieve erection despite her intense stimulation, hacks apart and breaks down the door to the bathroom where, scarcely clothed, she has sought sanctuary, and in a rage beats, stomps, and hacks her into a bloody pulp; he finishes the slaughter by tossing a live electric heater into the crimson tub water, virtually electrocuting his tormented half-conscious victim. Well spiced with leers, shouts and screams, the torture and agony of a once beautiful woman takes place up close, in livid color, and precise detail. The perpetrator of this barbarity caps off his crime by burning her house down, the audience unsure whether despite her wounds she might still be alive. In this bizarre nightmare-fantasy the killer cop goes unpunished and, miraculously, shortly later the victim reappears, unscathed, in the form of another character, portrayed by the same actress and having the same oversexed qualities.[45]

Pornography has been one of the most passionately debated issues in the women's movement. Some feminists want to see it banned outright. Others fear government intervention and believe in eliminating violent pornography by means of education and consciousness-raising. Those who want to see it banned label those who don't "First Amendment fascists," or "politically self-righteous fellow-travelers of the pornographers." They deplore what they consider a misguided concern for civil liberties, as feminist novelist Valerie Miner writes:

> Liberal consumers of the media who deplore pornography would die for its right to be printed, confusing in their tender consciences Stephen Daedalus with Chester the Molester.[46]

Those who don't want to see it banned label their opponents "censors" and "antisex."

Feminists have formed organizations to combat pornography. Groups like Women Against Pornography, in New York, and Women Against Violence in Pornography and Media, in San Francisco, use various methods to promote their ideas. When these groups were formed in the 1970s, many members favored legislation outlawing depictions of degrading sexual images of women, particularly those involving violence. Such images, they held, led directly to actual violence against women, and they believed the immediate risk of harm justified elimination of the offending words and pictures. To bolster their argument, they cited studies showing dramatic rises in incidents of rape and other violence against women, along with other studies that indicated that exposure to pornography made men more likely to commit such acts. As time went on, the groups withdrew from advocating government censorship and turned instead to educational efforts aimed at raising the consciousness of society about the pernicious effects of pornography.

These groups and others with the same objectives hold slide shows illustrating the degrading ways the media and pornography depict women—as come-ons, as sexy vehicles for selling blue jeans, as objects for sexual satisfaction or displays of power including torture—in an attempt to combat prevailing media images of the weak, victimized, seductive female. They also conduct tours of sex and porn shops in areas like New York's Times Square, picket films showing violence against women, and boycott companies whose ads they consider degrading to women. Organizations against pornography exist in such towns as New Haven, Connecticut, Columbia, Missouri, and Northampton, Massachusetts, as well as in many major cities.

The antiporn groups do not always stay within the law in their attempts to draw attention to the issue. For instance, using a skunklike odor and the theme "Porn Stinks," some women in Albuquerque, New Mexico, hit several pornography shops in the early morning of July 24, 1982. They spray-painted their theme on the walls of the buildings and on the sidewalks nearby, drawing attention to the violence and hatred of women shown in the stores. A group in England, using quick-setting cement, blocked up the toilets of the studios where the X-rated film *Dressed to Kill* was made. One autumn evening in 1978, a crowd of more than three thousand women and some men marched down the garishly lighted strip-joint section of Broadway in San Francisco to "take back the night." For once, the pushy barkers who usually insult women passers-by stood quietly inside the doorways of the stripjoints as the massive throng chanted antiporn slogans and brought traffic to a halt. For many women who participated, it was an exhilarating experience and an unaccustomed display of power in a section of town in which they were used to feeling especially vulnerable.

Pornography has enemies on the other side of the political spectrum as well: conservatives and fundamentalists oppose it. Both the left and the right find pornography degrading to women and a detrimental influence on society; both groups, and probably many in the middle range, would like to see the sex shops and X-rated films shut down. But profound differences between the feminists and the fundamentalist conservatives have prevented them from forming a long-term alliance on this issue.

The feminists, who support women's rights to live as they choose, in families or out, straight or gay, mothers or not, oppose the traditional patriarchal family and restrictive sexual morality. They want available, safe, legal abortion; equality in job opportunities and pay; the enactment of the Equal Rights Amendment; education that challenges sex-role stereotyping; and recognition of women as the peers of men. To women, pornography presents a total contradiction of that image. It helps prevent the advent of the free, egalitarian society they would like to see, and thus should be eliminated. The feminist wish list could double as a hit list for the New Right, which is trying to resurrect a golden past when Dad's word was law, Mom did the cooking, Jane played with dolls, Dick threw a baseball around, and everyone went to church on Sunday.

The power relationships inherent in pornography infuriate the left; the immorality infuriates the right. Both deplore the violence. Some adherents from both sides criticize court interpretations of the First Amendment that permit pornography to exist. The feminist arguments for censorship were cogently expressed by Mills College philosophy professor Helen E. Longino in an article published in *Take Back the Night,* an anthology of antipornography writings. She defined pornography as "material which explicitly represents or describes degrading and abusive sexual behavior so as to endorse and/or recommend the behavior as described." [47] This type of material ought to be banned for three main reasons, says Longino: (1) It perpetrates emotional harm to women and leads directly to physical violence against them; (2) it misrepresents the nature of women, portraying them as passive and oversexed, and is thus defamatory; and (3) it supports male-centered attitudes that reinforce the oppression and exploitation of women.

Longino argues that the First Amendment was created to facilitate political speech, not all speech, and the Constitution was written in the interests of liberty, not license. Longino is willing to accept a circumscribed view of freedom in order to permit the censorship of pornography, and in that sense she arrives at the same position as a right-wing First Amendment scholar, law professor William A. Stanmeyer of the University of Delaware. Compare Longino's and Stanmeyer's remarks.

Longino says, "If everyone did exactly as she or he pleased at any given time, we would have chaos if not lives, as Hobbes put it, that are 'nasty, brutish and short.' We accept government to escape, not to protect, this condition." [48] Similarly, Stanmeyer says, "Pornography warps the moral sensibility. . . . To remain civilized, society must by law exclude the more blatant forms of depersonalization . . . pornography 'is inherently and purposefully subversive of civilization and its institutions.' " [49]

Stanmeyer holds that the public wants to see pornography restrained, while "intellectuals" do not. In his view, the public is right for several reasons. First, it is reasonable to assume that a depraved moral outlook can lead to depraved conduct; the harm to society outweighs the right of the publisher of porn. Second, pornography debases sex; it teaches that human beings are animals; it teaches bad values to children. Third, "uninhibited indulgence in excessive sexual pleasure, actually or vicariously," erodes human mental health. And fourth, by using the law to bring about virtue, society improves its ethical standards. Like Longino, Stanmeyer argues that the Constitution was not written to protect pornography. Stanmeyer challenges those who adhere literally to the First Amendment by saying that "while the libertarian believes the control of pornography endangers the free society, the political moralist believes that the *failure* to control pornography endangers the free society."

The conservatives have not been as visible on the antiporn front as in the schools. Many feminists, however, carry on their efforts (and exercise their First Amendment rights) in a battle to end what they view as misogynist propaganda. In a collective letter to the *Village Voice* written in August 1982, feminist leaders Susan Brownmiller, Gloria Steinem, Shere Hite, Florence Rush, and others said, "Rather than trying to shut down porn shops, we are working to effect radical changes in mass consciousness—the only way to bring about lasting and radical social change." [50]

Censorship in the interests of promoting virtue and censorship in the interests of ending oppression have a certain initial attractiveness: Both promise to shut out the bad and bring in the good. But who is to do the shutting out and the bringing in? If the colleagues of William Stanmeyer were to do the choosing, they might, as many conservatives have, wish to ban material about birth control and abortion, material whose availability Helen Longino would consider essential. If Helen Longino were to do the choosing, she might wish to ban sex-stereotyped reading texts from the 1950s, books that Stanmeyer might like to have his children read.

Any group that has been oppressed—Jews, blacks, Asians, Hispanics, as well as women—has been the object of writing and speech that incites violence. Certainly massive violence has been inflicted on those and other groups: lynchings, beatings, and rapes. But the banning of any hate-filled speech could lead to government intrusion in areas where it would be impossible for citizens to exercise control over the extent of the intrusion. Better, in the words of law professor Franklyn S. Haiman, to fight speech with more speech. Historically, the oppressed have made use of their freedom of speech to agitate for better treatment: Suffragettes, blacks, birth-control advocates, pacifists, Jehovah's Witnesses, union organizers, anti-McCarthyites, and antiwar activists have all gone to court to fight for the right to speak out. There has been another strain in history, of antidefamation movements in which oppressed groups exercised *their* First Amendment rights to point out the untruths and distortions perpetrated by such hate-driven groups as the Ku Klux Klan or the Nazis.

The current feminist movement against pornography seems to fit right in with the antidefamation tradition, so long as the movement repudiates government intervention. And as civil libertarian Aryeh Neier concluded in an article entitled "Expurgating the First Amendment," "Those who call for censorship in the name of the oppressed ought to recognize it, it is never the oppressed who determine the bounds of censorship." [51]

LAWS ON SCHOOL CENSORSHIP

The law concerning classroom and library materials is, at the very least, in a confused state. A number of important interests and rights come into conflict with one another, particularly over the issue of what students shall read. For example, what right, if any, do parents have in determining the education of their children in tax-supported schools? What are the rights and responsibilities of the school boards elected to run the schools? In choosing books, what weight should be given to community standards? There are conflicting interpretations of First Amendment rights of students to read and of teachers to teach. All these issues are not only complex but also emotionally charged.

In thinking about censorship, we need to consider two kinds of laws: those passed by state legislatures to regulate the adoption and content of schoolbooks, and U.S. constitutional law handed down by the federal courts in individual cases. Given the limits of space and time, and the wealth of publications available that examine these matters more fully, this section can only summarize some of the more important laws and recent First Amendment conflicts over schoolbooks. More new laws are proposed and new cases arise all the time, and the resulting legislative actions and court decisions continue to complicate an already confusing situation.

State Commissions

In nearly half the states, textbooks are selected from basic lists compiled by education commissions charged with considering texts to be used throughout the state. These are called adoption states. In the others, local school boards choose the books independently of state commissions. Some states from time to time make laws governing the textbook selection process.

The two adoption states that purchase the largest number of textbooks in the nation, California and Texas, lay down the most specific regulations for evaluating material their schools can purchase. California textbook standards require that textbooks treat racial minorities, women, and the handicapped equitably. The state's Standards for Evaluation of Instructional Materials with Respect to Social Context are very specific. For instance, the section on male and female roles provides:

> Descriptions, depictions, labels, or rejoinders which tend to demean, stereotype, or patronize males or females because of their sex must not appear.[52]

Such remarks as "old maid," "she's only a girl," "dumb jock," and "male chauvinist pig" may not appear in textbooks. To counteract bias, the achievements of women must be recognized fully. Both women and men are to be portrayed in traditional and nontraditional roles in approximately equal proportions. For example, women can be shown sewing and cooking so long as men are also; boys can be shown playing baseball so long as girls are shown playing soccer, for instance.

Similarly, ethnic slurs are forbidden, and minorities must be sometimes portrayed as professionals or executives in order to enable children of all races to identify with any occupational field. No culture is to be considered better than any other; the California standard requires that "diversity must be portrayed as an enriching and positive element of our society." As with women, the achievements of racial minorities must be included and discussed "when historically accurate." In addition, "minority persons should be depicted in the same range of socioeconomic settings as are persons of the majority group." [53]

By contrast, the Texas Textbook Proclamation, drawn up annually by the State Board of Education to provide standards for textbooks, has some very different guidelines. Section 1.5 of the 1982 Proclamation provides:

> Textbook content shall promote citizenship and understanding of the free enterprise system, emphasize patriotism and respect for recognized authority, and promote respect for human rights. Textbooks adopted shall . . . not include selections or works which encourage or condone civil disorder, social strife, or disregard for the law.

Thus, a favorable account of the civil disobedience that marked the antisegregation struggles of Martin Luther King could conflict with those guidelines. The Proclamation becomes even more specific: "Textbooks shall not contain material which serves to undermine authority"; "Free enterprise . . . means an economic system characterized by private or corporate ownership of capital goods, by investments that are determined by private decision rather than by state control." One catchall provision can bar almost any work with which the textbook committee disagrees: the provision forbids "material which would cause embarrassing situations . . . in the classroom."

The Texas guidelines with regard to minorities and women are not as strong as those in California. Textbooks, "whenever possible," are to treat "divergent groups fairly, without stereotyping, and shall reflect the positive contributions of all individuals and groups to the American way of life." Textbooks "shall reflect an awareness that culture and language variation does exist and can be utilized to promote successful learning." The Proclamation's attitude toward sex roles is ambivalent. It states that "traditional roles of men and women, boys and girls, shall be included, as well as those changing roles in our society," but "textbook content shall not encourage life styles deviating from generally accepted standards of society." [54]

Examining the Texas procedures for textbook adoption reveals why large publishers bend to the will of people like the Gablers. In 1983, Texas spent $66 million on textbooks for its 1,152 school districts, making it the second largest purchaser in the nation and accounting for 8 percent of the total textbook market.[55] Only five books are approved by the textbook committee for use per subject each year. Thus, the Texas procedure weighs heavily on publishers, who risk losing a lucrative market if their work is not chosen. And since it is not economically feasible to produce more than one version of a textbook these days, what Texas demands often becomes the standard for the rest of the nation.

The Texas adoption procedure allows citizens to read the proposed texts publishers submit and to file written objections to those texts, then to testify against them before the Texas State Textbook Committee. The committee, made up of fifteen teachers and school administrators, hears the complaints. It reads written rebuttals by the publishers to the objections before compiling a proposed list of books that then goes to the state commissioner of education. When he approves them, the books become part of the Texas school shopping list. The rules in effect through 1982 did not permit statements to be made in favor of texts, except for the publishers' responses. In 1983, new rules permitted other favorable comments to be submitted and expanded the membership of the committee.

The textbook committee can request that publishers make changes in their books. The changes requested in recent years have tended to reflect a conservative ideology, indicative of the Gablers' influence on the process. Among the changes requested in 1982 and 1983: the deletion of a sentence from a civics book for eighth graders published by Allyn and Bacon: "Only white, male property owners were allowed to vote by the original Constitution." [56] In a health textbook for sixth graders published by Charles E. Merrill, the original text described the development of adolescent females as follows: "A girl will grow taller. Her hips will widen. Fat will deposit in her breasts and in her buttocks." The company agreed to change the passage to: "Fat will deposit in certain areas of a girl's body." [57] In health education books for fourth and seventh graders published by Laidlaw Brothers, the committee requested that a passage be rewritten to show that families consist only of people related by birth, marriage, or adoption, and no other kind of affiliation. In another text, a sentence defining families as "couples with no children and roommates in a college dormitory or apartment" was to be changed to "a couple with no children." [58] The phrase *junk food* was to be deleted from two seventh-grade texts. The committee also requested the deletion of a sentence describing the medical use of THC, the effective ingredient of marijuana.[59]

These examples are perhaps minor, but they indicate the way certain ideas are erased from textbooks nationwide because of Texas state law and procedure. In addition, fiction is limited. Shirley Jackson's classic short story "The Lottery" was cut from national editions of four literature anthologies because in 1978 the Texas Textbook Committee refused to buy books including it.

State Laws: God and Country

Those who wish to control the content of school textbooks turn to their legislatures as well as to school boards and the courts in order to achieve the desired results. Two of the major issues that frequently arise before state legislatures in disputes over texts come under the headings of God and Country, most often in terms of creationism and patriotism. Oregon, for example, passed a law that forbade the adoption of any history text that spoke "slightingly of the founders of the republic." In early 1981, it briefly became a criminal offense in Georgia to show, lend, sell, or distribute to a minor books or magazines "likely to provoke or arouse lust or passion." The prohibition applied to librarians as well as to booksellers. This Georgia law was declared unconstitutional by the end of the year, but similar legislation is proposed time and time again in states across the nation. Also in 1981, the California Assembly passed a bill requiring the adoption of texts that stressed the importance of the family, the principles of free market enterprise, respect for the law, and the universal values of right and wrong. The Senate rejected the bill.

In an earlier section of this chapter, we saw that appeals to law have been invoked to permit or deny teachings about the origin of life. The evolution controversy continues, with both sides claiming that the U.S. Constitution supports their position.

Textbook Contents Acts

The American Legislative Exchange Council (ALEC) in Washington, D.C., drafts model laws for Congress and state legislatures. One of ALEC's goals is the restoration of "educational principles upon which this nation was founded" and "traditional moral values." The group's model Family Choice in Education Act, aimed at offering strong competition to public schools, would break the "state monopoly concerning education" and prohibit governmental regulation of private schools. Another ALEC proposal is the Textbook Standards Contents Act. The heart of this bill, section 4, opposes adoption of any text containing "partisan" or "sectarian" doctrines, and recommends texts advocating the work ethic, absolute standards of right and wrong, and respect for parents and those "duly in authority." Texts may not "degrade" the religious beliefs of students. Other proposals include the Honor America Act and the Parental Rights Act. The organization's goal is to persuade state legislatures to enact these measures, which overall would require textbooks to promote "patriotism" and "free enterprise" in public schools.

ALEC sends its recommendations to the approximately seventy-five hundred state legislators throughout the nation but does not keep track of them, according to Dan Bray of the ALEC staff, who could not say how many state legislatures were considering ALEC's model bills or how many states had adopted any of them. The organization nevertheless carries some weight, particularly since it has been endorsed by none other than Ronald Reagan.

Family Protection Act

The Family Protection Act, introduced in 1981 and again in 1983 into Congress, is another cluster of laws designed to impose ultraconservative values on the nation. Its main purpose is to strengthen the traditional family by eliminating government policies (like the banning of school prayer) that according to its supporters hurt families and by adopting government policies (giving parents more rights over the moral and religious education of their children) that would help families.

One part of the proposed law would prevent federal funding for textbooks that "do not reflect different ways in which women and men live and do not contribute to the American way of life as it has been historically understood." The law would establish income tax deductions for private school tuitions, thus encouraging parents to desert public schools. Church schools would be free of federal regulation and would be shielded against claims of racial or religious discrimination. The laws would also cut off federal funds to schools that prohibited parents or "representatives of the community" from participating in decisions relating to the study of religion; stopped parents from visiting classes; or prohibited parental review of textbooks prior to their use in the classroom. Thus, if the Family Protection Act passes, religious groups will have a much stronger hand in determining the content of books used in public schools.

The Courts

As one might expect, litigation over censorship in schools and libraries has proliferated in recent years. The results have been confusing, with decisions in one jurisdiction contradicting decisions in others. One particularly important issue—under what circumstances school boards can ban books—remains unsettled.

The starting point for an evaluation of First Amendment rights in schools is *Tinker v. Des Moines Independent Community School District,* a landmark case decided in 1969.[60] This case was triggered by high school youngsters wearing armbands to protest the Vietnam War. The school administrator ordered the students to take off the armbands and, when they refused, ordered the students to leave school. The students filed suit and, after losses at the district court and appeals levels, won in the Supreme Court. That decision established for the first time the First Amendment rights of minors—so long as the exercise of those rights does not obstruct the educational process, and so long as obscene material is not employed. The Court ruled that neither students nor teachers "shed their Constitutional right to freedom of speech or expression at the schoolhouse gate," and forbade school administrators from placing arbitrary curbs on student speech in public schools. It can be (and has been) argued from this decision that a book cannot be banned from a class or library unless it, too, disrupts the educational process or is obscene.

Sometimes this reasoning has prevailed, and at other times it has not.

This reasoning did not succeed in a 1972 case in which the authority of a school board to remove books from a school library was first tested. The board had removed *Down These Mean Streets,* the account of a Puerto Rican growing up in Spanish Harlem, from the shelves of a junior high school in New York. People offended by its sexual scenes and four-letter words asked for its removal; the board acquiesced. The appeals court that decided the case bypassed its constitutional aspects, ruling instead that:

> To suggest that the shelving or unshelving of books presents a constitutional issue, particularly when there is no showing of a curtailment of freedom of speech or thought, is a proposition we cannot accept.[61]

The court said that someone has to bear responsibility for the selection of books, and the school board has that power; therefore, its removal of the book was justified.

A somewhat similar case in 1976 in Ohio, *Minarcini v. Strongsville,* yielded different results.[62] The faculty recommended that the school board approve the purchase of *Catch-22* by Joseph Heller and *God Bless You, Mr. Rosewater* by Kurt Vonnegut for use in high school classes. The board not only refused but also removed a second Vonnegut novel from the school library. The board gave no official reasons for its actions, although in the minutes of its meeting the books were described as "completely sick" and "garbage." The U.S. Court of Appeals for the Sixth Circuit in *Minarcini* upheld the students' right to receive information and the librarians' right to disseminate it. The court rejected the absolute right of a school board to remove a book it simply disliked. The decision called the school library "a storehouse of knowledge" and said that school boards could not "winnow" the library "for books which occasioned their displeasure or disapproval." The court found that the removal of books from the school library constituted a more serious violation of a student's rights than did the ordered removal of armbands in the *Tinker* case. The court did not accept the argument of the board that the books were readily available in bookstores and in the public library, and therefore no harm would be done if they were removed from the school.

A Massachusetts case decided two years later reinforced *Minarcini.* This time a poem called "The City to a Young Girl" included in an anthology occasioned the disapproval of the school committee, which then banned the book. The poem powerfully expresses the feelings of a girl as men make suggestive remarks while she walks down a city street. The school committee argued that it had the authority to approve or disapprove material used in the schools; it also argued that since the committee had decided not to include sex education in the curriculum, the poem constituted an improper effort to introduce the subject into the classroom. The school librarian and a group formed to help her claimed that the anthology came under the protection of the First Amendment, that students had a right of access to works under such protection, and that the school committee's objection to the poem as "vulgar and offensive" was insufficient to justify the book's removal. In a ringing affirmation of First Amendment freedoms, the judge said:

> What is at stake here is the right to read and be exposed to controversial thoughts and language. . . . The most effective antidote to the poison of mindless orthodoxy is ready access to a broad sweep of ideas and philosophies. There is no danger in such exposure. The danger is in mind control.[63]

But two years after that, in 1980 in the neighboring state of Vermont, another judge dismissed a complaint by a librarian and several students protesting the school board's removal of *The Wanderers* and *Dog Day Afternoon* from the Vergennes High School, as well as the board's imposition of a freeze on buying new books and a policy of screening all major purchases. As in the New York case, the court found that although it did not entirely agree with what the school board had done, the board had every right to do it. The court also said that the books had been removed, not for political reasons, but for "vulgarity and obscenity."[64]

A very different case from Mississippi decided in the same year raised the opposite issue: not what could be eliminated, but what had to be included.[65] The Mississippi Textbook Purchasing Board declined to approve a ninth-grade history text called *Mississippi: Conflict and Change*; the five white members said the book was overly concerned with racial matters and too controversial, and outvoted the two black members, who found it suitable. Its authors, claiming that the one approved history for that grade "stigmatizes black people," went to court. The judge decided that the criteria used by the textbook committee had violated the constitutionally guaranteed rights of the authors to freedom of speech and of the press. Inclusion of controversial information about race did not constitute adequate grounds for keeping the book out of the schools, the court ruled.

But again, other recent court cases brought conflicting decisions. It is little wonder, then, given the contradictions between judicial rulings, that school boards, teachers, librarians, and civil libertarians awaited a decision from the U.S. Supreme Court that would lay to rest the conflicts and confusions. The big case was called *Pico v. Island Trees*.[66]

In 1975 three members of the school board of Island Trees Union Free School District in Long Island, New York, went to a conference sponsored by the ultraconservative Parents of New York United. There they picked up a list of books the group considered objectionable. Some time later, after a school board meeting, two of the three members persuaded the janitor to let them into the library at night, searched it for offending material, and removed nine books on the grounds that they were "vulgar," "anti-American," "anti-Christian," "anti-Semitic," and "just plain filthy."[67] The books were *The Fixer* by Bernard Malamud, winner of the Pulitzer Prize in 1967; *Soul on Ice* by Eldridge Cleaver; *Slaughterhouse Five* by Kurt Vonnegut; *Down These Mean Streets* by Piri Thomas; *The Naked Ape* by Desmond Morris; *A Hero Ain't Nothin But a Sandwich* by Alice Childress; *Best Short Stories by Negro Writers* edited by Langston Hughes; an anonymous book called *Go Ask Alice*; and *A Reader for Writers: A Critical Anthology of Prose Readings*. The last book made the "objectionable" list because it included Jonathan Swift's famous satire "A Modest Proposal," which suggests that to solve the problem of poverty, the babies of the poor be eaten.

The school board voted to remove the nine books from the shelves. "These books contain obscenities, blasphemies, brutality and perversion beyond description," the board said in a press release. They particularly disliked a reference in *Slaughterhouse Five* to Jesus Christ as "a man with no connections." The school superintendent, who disagreed with the board's decision, resigned. Several students and parents in the school district sued, claiming that the board's action violated the students' First Amendment rights.

The federal court judge before whom the case first appeared dismissed it, saying that school officials had the authority to ban the books. The appeals court, however, overturned that decision, saying that a trial should be held to decide whether the board's decision was constitutional. Lawyers for the school board appealed to the U.S. Supreme Court, arguing that their clients were trying to "cope with the moral crisis confronting our nation today." The case, they said, "raises significant and recurring problems concerning the extent of a school board's right to use its members' value systems in determining which instructional materials to utilize."

The Supreme Court heard arguments in March 1982. George Lipp, Jr., representing the school board, claimed that the transmission of moral values was one of the school board's functions. They could follow their own "social, moral, and political values," he said, and those values were not reviewable by judges. Justice Sandra Day O'Connor challenged this assertion. "If a school board removed all books referring to Republicans because it was a Democratic board should that be unreviewable?" she asked. Lipp backed up a bit. He did not mean partisan politics, but rather the study of government. O'Connor pressed further: "What is the line to be drawn where a court can review a school board's actions?" Lipp answered that review was justified only when a board had "sanitized" library shelves in an attempt to "establish a rigid and inclusive indoctrination." Lipp had to concede that the board had acted without guidelines. When Justice Thurgood Marshall asked, "How can you regulate without standards?" Lipp could not reply.

Alan Levine of the New York Civil Liberties Union, who represented the students, also ran into difficulties with the high court. Levine contended that the right to read is clearly inherent in the First Amendment. But Justice Rehnquist said he could find no restriction of the students' right to expression and added that they could buy the banned books easily in bookstores. Levine argued that there were limits to what a school board could do, though he too could not define a standard. These cases, he said, "get us into First Amendment quicksand." About as far as he could get was to argue that school boards had to respect diversity in their choices of materials.

In June, the fiercely divided justices revealed their opinions. Justices Brennan, Marshall, Blackmun, and Stevens agreed that the students were entitled to a trial on the constitutionality of the book banning. They said:

> Our Constitution does not permit the official suppression of *ideas*. . . . [Local] school boards may not remove books from the school library shelves simply because they dislike the ideas contained in those books and seek by their removal to "prescribe what shall be orthodox in politics, nationalism, religion, or other matters of opinion." Such purposes stand inescapably condemned by our precedents.[68]

The decision said that elimination of books that were obscene or educationally unsuitable was permissible. Justice White, though disagreeing with their reasoning, agreed with the decision that the case merited a trial.

Justice Lewis F. Powell, once the chairman of the Richmond, Virginia, school board, was among the dissenters. Appearing annoyed at the notion that students could challenge the authority of adults, he wrote:

> After today's decision, any junior high school student, by instituting a suit against a school board or teacher, may invite a judge to overrule an educational decision by the official body designated by the people to operate the schools. . . . I therefore view today's decision with genuine dismay.[69]

Two months after the decision, rather than go to trial, the Island Trees school board voted to return the banned books to the shelves. This case, which had been expected to produce a major decision, thus ended quietly.

Pico did not settle the conflicts over book banning in the schools because the Supreme Court was unable to muster a majority of members in support of one opinion. The plurality opinion signed by the four justices, while perhaps influential, does not set a precedent that other courts must follow. Thus, the big decisions about censorship of books in schools have yet to be made.

FIGHTING BACK

A number of organizations have mobilized to oppose censorship. They engage in a wide variety of activities designed to raise public awareness of the issue, and to provide legal assistance, advice, and comfort to those engaged in censorship battles, be they writers, readers, or besieged school and library personnel. Some of these groups are long established; some appeared in the early 1980s in response to what they saw as the rising threat to free expression.

The first group that people often turn to in censorship battles is the American Civil Liberties Union. Throughout the nation, ACLU lawyers have been in the forefront of negotiations and legal battles to prevent the removal of controversial materials from schools and libraries. They have developed legal briefs, expertise with school procedures, and, perhaps most important, a strong commitment to the full exercise of First Amendment rights for all members of our society.

The second group that people might turn to is a professional organization with a committee concerned with censorship and prepared to help members who have come under attack. Librarians have perhaps the best group, the American Library Association (ALA) based in Chicago. Its Office for Intellectual Freedom was formed in 1967 specifically to deal with attempts to curtail the professional prerogatives of librarians. The office publishes an excellent newsletter on intellectual freedom, keeping track of censorship cases both as they arise and as they work their way through school procedures and the courts. Its staff helps prepare testimony for challenges to books, and has become one of the few sources of statistics on attempts to remove, alter, or otherwise cut back on books and other library or teaching materials. Its director, Judith Krug, appears on panels and gives talks around the nation.

The ALA provides sets of ground rules for librarians, ranging from statements of principle to practical tips on how to handle problems. Its library Bill of Rights affirms the group's ideals and commitments. Among its principles are the following: Books and other sources of information should never be excluded because of the background or the views of the authors; librarians are to provide materials representing all points of view on issues; libraries should be accessible to all; libraries should challenge censorship in the fulfillment of their responsibility to provide information and enlightenment; librarians are to remain neutral in their dedication to making materials available. In elaborating on the meaning of its Bill of Rights, the ALA has developed written standards on a number of topics. Among these are the need for diversity in putting together a collection; what to do about challenged materials or the expurgation of materials; the rights of minors to library materials (librarians are not to deny minors access to any service available to adults); strong opposition to restricting access to library materials; proper evaluation of library materials; and opposition to "silent censorship"—the simple removal of controversial works.

The ALA publishes resource material such as a pamphlet on censorship called *What Is It: How Do You Cope?,* which advises librarians to develop a written policy on the selection of materials and to have it approved by their school system's governing body. Librarians are also advised to lay a groundwork of support by keeping the lines of communication open with parents and community leaders. They should explain their policies in advance of any trouble, and stay abreast of issues so that they know what is happening with books in other districts. The librarians are given common-sense advice: If a book is challenged, be courteous, insist that formal procedures be followed, and keep a written factual account of what happens.

The ALA also formed the Freedom to Read Foundation, whose purposes are to defend the First Amendment right to free expression of ideas without governmental interference, to foster libraries as institutions where every citizen's First Amendment freedoms are fulfilled, and to support the right of libraries to acquire any books they legally can. The foundation provides financial and legal assistance, and lobbies and raises funds for its activities.

Writers also have organizations to aid in book removal battles. PEN, a writers' group with about eighteen hundred members, launched a Freedom to Write campaign and a project called the American Right to Read. Writers were recruited to give speeches around the nation on the dangers of book banning, and some of the more celebrated (and banned) members such as Kurt Vonnegut, Studs Terkel, and Judy Blume were active participants.

The American Society of Journalists and Authors began the "I Read Banned Books" campaign on April Fools' Day 1981. Proclaiming April to be "I Read Banned Books" month, the society organized read-ins in public places, with authors reading from books that have at one time or another been banned. Avery Corman, standing on the steps of the venerable New York Public Library, read in 1982 from his award-winning *Kramer versus Kramer,* banned in Seattle. Other demonstrations took place across the nation: Michael Castleman, whose self-help book *Sexual Solutions* was banned in Superior, Wisconsin, took part in a reading at the San Francisco Public Library, organized by a group of West Coast writers called Media Alliance. Students from a human sexuality course at Syracuse University made posters and displays celebrating books that had been banned, such as *Alice in Wonderland, Mary Poppins,* and *In the Night Kitchen,* and books on sex education. It is not clear how effective these activities were in deterring censors, but they did attract coverage in local newspapers.

Individual writers have also taken on those who censored their work: Kurt Vonnegut wrote a furious letter to the principal of a school that removed his works from the library, and Studs Terkel staged a fiery debate with school personnel in Girard, Pennsylvania, who took exception to his book *Working* because of the four-letter words it contained.

Teachers' organizations have set up committees to defend their right to choose classroom materials and, like the librarians' group, to dispense advice and support when attempts are made to censor books. The National Council of Teachers of English (NCTE) is particularly active. Its Committee against Censorship publishes a booklet called *The Student's Right to Read,* concerning First Amendment rights for students, and another called *Dealing with Censorship.* The NCTE gives advice to teachers involved in book-banning cases, stressing the need to have in place an orderly procedure to use when trouble arises. Leona Blum, the NCTE staff liaison to its Committee against Censorship, said that in December 1981 half of the nation's school boards did not have formal procedures for the handling of complaints. These, she said, are the best and sometimes only defense against "the frequently emotional challenges of parents who want their children protected against books they consider dirty or immoral." She also warned that teachers faced two somewhat contradictory temptations: the thought that "censorship cannot happen here," with the resulting failure to implement complaint procedures, and the fear that "it might happen here," with resulting self-censorship and a chilling effect on ideas introduced into the classroom.[70]

The powerful National Education Association, with 1.6 million members, conducts workshops in communities to promote policies and procedures for the handling of challenges to books. It publishes a resource book called *Helping Teachers to Teach All the Children,* and sends staff members to help teachers in censorship cases. It advertises the availability of legal defense through the United Legal Services program.

Education Week, published in Washington, D.C., described another method of preventing challenges to books. In September 1982, it published an account of a rural Ohio teacher's successful campaign to head off book challenges in his school. Jim Creighton, head of the English Department, faced a challenge in 1977 to *A Day No Pigs Would Die,* the graphic account of a young boy's growing up on a Vermont farm. Creighton did not remove the book, but he did not claim that he had a First Amendment right to use it in class, either. Instead, he avoided a confrontation by setting up a series of evening classes for parents and community members called "Books Our Children Read." The parents read and discussed the books, and learned the teachers' reasons for including them in the curriculum. This succeeded so well that it became an annual event. As a result of his efforts, the Fort Frye High School in Beverly, Ohio, a community not far in geography or ethos from Kanawha County, West Virginia, has an English program that comfortably includes titles that have caused havoc in other communities. The Beverly community generally trusts the teachers and supports their program.

The anticensorship groups have often joined together to form larger groups: There is a ten-member coalition of teachers called the Academic Freedom Group, composed of such organizations as the American Federation of Teachers and the National Council of Social Studies. Publishers as well as school administrators also have formed organizations to combat censorship. The largest and most diverse association is the New York–based National Coalition against Censorship, which has a membership of thirty-five national organizations, and dates from 1976. Its membership includes the National Council of Churches, the ACLU, the Newspaper Guild, PEN, the Child Study Association, a number of Jewish, Methodist, and Unitarian groups, as well as groups of academics, students, and writers. The NCAC publishes *Censorship News,* a newsletter about court decisions, challenges to books, and other developments that affect the free circulation of ideas. The group also holds conferences, like the one on "the religious right and freedom of speech," which took place in April 1981. The NCAC sponsored a debate between a woman opposed to pornography and a woman opposed to banning it. The group serves as the center of a network of individuals and organizations concerned with freedom of expression.

A new group formed in quite a different way has made a significant impact on the book-banning phenomenon. Founded by television producer Norman Lear of "All in the Family" fame, People for the American Way (PFAW), in Washington, D.C., has as its purpose the defeat of the New Right's agenda for the United States. Like the other groups, the eighty-two-thousand-member organization publishes information and literature warning of the dangers the censors pose to traditional American freedoms, and like the other groups, it lobbies for and promotes its objectives through press conferences, films, and other media. Besides the usual activities, however, People for the American Way took the battle against censorship right into the territory of a major opponent. In July 1982, the organization implemented its Texas Project, to confront the Gablers before the Texas State Textbook Committee and to open up the Texas textbook adoption procedure so that the Gablers and other conservatives could no longer dominate it.

According to Barbara Parker, in charge of PFAW's Schools and Libraries Project, "Censorship activity is so well organized that the only way to combat it is through an equal amount of organization. If 93 percent of a community doesn't want *Catcher in the Rye* that's OK. That's a community decision. My disagreement is that in education today things are being run by vocal control, not local control." [71] Mike Hudson, a lawyer who directs the PFAW office in Austin, said as the Texas Project began that censors "are working to purge schools of all material that encourages thinking and discussion or is inconsistent with their narrow religious and political orthodoxy. The public schools have become the battleground for their efforts." PFAW, on the other hand, wants a "school system that teaches children how to think, not what to think." [72] The Gablers, predictably, took exception to this. "It's a double standard," said Norma Gabler. "Those liberal elements have controlled the minds of our children for years. If parents bring things up, it's censorship. If [liberals] do it, it's not." [73]

Hudson petitioned the Texas State Textbook Committee to allow him to speak before it and also to allow positive comments to be made about textbooks instead of only objections. Newspapers and magazines throughout the nation gave considerable play to the Texas showdown, thereby illustrating the disproportionate power exercised by that state and its adoption procedures on the whole textbook industry. PFAW complained that Texans who wanted to defend a book or who disagreed with protests had no forum in which to be heard. People for the American Way at first was rebuffed in its attempts to testify before the committee, but was eventually permitted to do so. After the hearings were over, Barbara Parker viewed the operation as a success. "We did open the process to positive citizen comment," she said. "In the long run, I think that's going to be positive. The publishers view this as a two-edged sword, and I hope that it doesn't get down to a shouting match and whoever makes the most noise wins." But she conceded that citizen participation would be necessary to keep the process open. "People with favorable things to say will have to show up in large numbers, as they did this year," she observed.[74]

Parker believes that much work remains to be done. Incidents of attempted censorship continue to arise, but they receive little media attention because the books under attack are more likely to be textbooks. "The media love it when Hemingway or Steinbeck are removed from libraries," she said. "It makes great copy. But now the attention is focused less on the classics. The hottest topics for the censors this year are health education and sex education."

So far as Texas is concerned, she fears that the Texas Textbook Proclamation, which has the force of law, controls the adoption process in that state. "The Gablers could disappear tomorrow, and it wouldn't make much difference," she said. "The guidelines are set in stone. They are a censorship tool which forces publishers not to include certain ideas, and that has a terrible effect because all the publishers bid in Texas. Carried to its worst extreme, the Proclamation could prevent a teacher from asking any question at all in class: It forbids materials which could cause embarrassing situations in the classroom, and any kid might not know the answer to a question and could get embarrassed." [75]

The organizations that oppose book banning have helped to slow down the censorship juggernaut. By appealing to the courts, generating publicity, and insisting that proper procedures be followed, they have succeeded in stopping some attempts to ban books. But as of 1983, incidents of censorship were considered by most observers to be on the rise, making the effect of the groups, apart from raising consciousness about the issue, difficult to estimate. Like all organizations concerned with civil liberties, the only certainty was that they would have plenty of work to do in the immediate future.

MUFFLING CORPORATE CRITICS

When angry citizens organize a book burning or the Reagan administration tries to gut the Freedom of Information Act, people notice. Whether they approve or disapprove, the issues are covered in the press, speakers pro and con appear on talk shows and in magazine articles, and the issues are investigated. But a more subtle, pervasive, and ultimately controversial kind of censorship takes place every day all around us. Because the censors are private entities, not governmental, they are not restricted by the bounds of the Constitution. Because they are so powerful, they need not even state what they want removed: Those who need their favor anticipate their wishes and carry them out without even asking.

These censors are America's corporations. They work so quietly, behind the scenes of publishing and broadcasting, that only on very rare occasions does a controversy make the news. But every now and then events occur that illustrate the use of corporate muscle to suppress information or ideas. We should pay close attention to these, for they represent the barest tip of a mighty iceberg.

One way that corporate censorship works, and perhaps the most common, is through influence over editorial content. Publishers and broadcasters know that if they antagonize advertisers, they lose money; all the rest stems from that simple principle. Of course, there are degrees of influence and control on the part of business as well as degrees of independence and resistance on the part of the media. But one rarely sees exposés of the cosmetic or tobacco industry in women's magazines, which depend on makeup and cigarette ads for much of their revenue. It is important to understand this subtle exercise of corporate censorship: Because the "bottom line" is crucial to the survival of any media operation, the advertiser doesn't even need to lift a finger; the editor or producer will do the job without being told. The problem thus becomes one of self-censorship, a difficult phenomenon to pin down and to combat.

A good example occurred in 1982 in Minneapolis–St. Paul, Minnesota. In the spring of that year, a reporter named Paul Maccabee who specialized in music wrote a colorful article in the weekly *Twin Cities Reader,* criticizing the sponsorship by Kool cigarettes of a local jazz festival. Maccabee labeled Kool officials "nicotine pushers." He quoted an American Cancer Society official calling the cigarette company's sponsorship of the festival a public relations ploy to give respectability to cigarettes. "Strange bedfellows, cigarettes and jazz," wrote Maccabee. "Duke Ellington died of lung cancer in 1974." The twenty-six-year-old reporter also connected smoking to Buerger's disease, "a degenerative nicotine-linked condition which leads doctors to amputate toes and feet one at a time, like snipping grapes off a vine. Definitely not sexy. Definitely un-Kool."

Unknown to Maccabee, his newspaper had signed a $50,000 contract with Kool that required the *Reader* to warn the company of any upcoming articles linking cigarettes and cancer. The day after the story appeared, publisher Mark Hopp fired Maccabee; the paper's editor, who like Maccabee did not know the terms of the Kool contract, resigned shortly after the firing. Hopp vigorously defended his firing of Maccabee. "The repercussion from that story could hurt our ability to cover local issues because an advertiser pulled out. What's more important, sixty local articles or one opinion piece?" Hopp fumed. According to Dr. Paul Magnus, a physician then conducting research on cigarette advertising and lung cancer at Stanford University, Hopp told him, "If I have to get on my hands and knees and go to Louisville and beg them to keep Kool ads in my paper, I'll do it."

Magnus, an expert on media coverage of smoking and health, considers cigarettes the "greatest killer and the most advertised product" in the United States. "Cigarette advertising makes up 24 percent of advertising money in *Parade* magazine and 17 percent in *Time*," he claims. "And each year 350,000 people die of cigarette smoking in the United States. Papers don't sensationalize cigarette stories. They don't call it a killer industry making a killer product," he complains. "Most articles on smoking begin 'Studies show . . .' Americans are all worried about drugs and kids' addiction, but the chance of a kid dying from drugs is 1 percent that of dying from cigarettes." [76] Magnus also noted the success of the Philip Morris Company, which for years succeeded in suppressing *Death in the West*,[77] an antismoking film that juxtaposed video ads featuring husky, handsome Marlboro men riding and roping with gaunt, hollow-eyed cowboys dying of lung cancer and interviews with Philip Morris executives. The film shows the executives pleading ignorance about the causes of cancer and denying a link between smoking and lung cancer. Made in 1976 in London, *Death in the West* was supposed to be shown on "60 Minutes." But it was not distributed in the United States because of a court order obtained in England by Philip Morris suppressing the film. A pirated print of the film was finally shown by KRON-TV in San Francisco in May 1982. Philip Morris executives were invited to appear on the program, but they refused.

The Philip Morris court order is rare, as is the dismissal of Paul Maccabee—unusual incidents in which a flex of corporate muscle, or fear of that corporate muscle, stifled free expression. The more usual situation is described in the March 1981 issue of the *Journal of Public Health Policy* in an article called "Analysis of Coverage of Tobacco Hazards in Women's Magazines." According to this study, which surveyed twelve leading women's magazines (*Good Housekeeping, Seventeen, McCall's, Vogue, Harper's Bazaar, Cosmopolitan, Mademoiselle, Redbook, Family Circle, Ms., Ladies Home Journal,* and *Women's Day*) between March 1967 and February 1979, a grand total of twelve antismoking articles appeared. Six of these ran in *Good Housekeeping,* which does not accept cigarette ads and therefore risked no economic reprisals. Eight magazines ran no articles on the hazards of smoking, and four ran no articles on smoking at all.

During the period surveyed, professional and scientific journals published studies on the dangers to women smokers who take birth control pills, the increased risks of heart disease associated with smoking, and other medical problems. The lack of coverage in the women's magazines becomes even more extraordinary when one considers that health is a major topic for these magazines and that cigarette-related diseases are major killers. Furthermore, during that period, there was a significant increase in the number of women who smoke, particularly young women, and, according to the article, statistics showed an alarming increase in smoking-related cancers. According to the article, members of the American Council on Smoking and Health who write health articles said that they have been told by editors to stay away from the subject of tobacco and its risks. One author said she submitted an article about cancer in women with a discussion of the role of cigarettes and lung cancer as the lead. As edited, the article led with breast cancer; the emphasis on smoking was weakened. Peter Georgiades of the council said, "Although it is difficult to tell how direct that relationship is [between advertising and editorial policy] it is clearly the crassest case of journalistic prostitution one will ever see. Many newsweekly magazines give only the most washed-out, bleached coverage of cigarettes' effects on human health. 'Sanitized' describes their coverage even in their health, science and medical columns." [78]

The tobacco industry buys a disproportionate amount of print advertising, and has done so ever since cigarette commercials were banned from television in 1971. It spends more than any other national industry on newspaper advertising and is the second-largest purchaser of magazine ads. The tobacco industry naturally dismisses allegations of its control over editorial policy. "Baloney," said the senior vice-president of the Tobacco Institute. "The suggestion that buying an ad buys the judgment of reportorial people is a contemptible red herring." But the *Wall Street Journal* reported that an examination of tobacco advertising and editorial policy "suggests that any big advertiser can, to a degree, blunt negative publicity about its product." [79]

The experience of *Mother Jones,* a nonprofit, muckraking magazine published in California, showed a cause-and-effect relationship between advertising revenue and cigarette exposés. After the magazine's editorial board decided, following considerable debate, to accept cigarette advertising, they published an article in 1978 called "Why Dick Can't Stop Smoking." Shortly afterward, $18,000 worth of advertising was withdrawn from the magazine by a tobacco company.[80] In January 1979, *Mother Jones* published another article on the dangers of smoking. According to Adam Hochschild, then an editor of the magazine, "Within two weeks of the article's publication, the two remaining tobacco advertisers canceled their existing contracts with us and made it clear that *Mother Jones* would never get cigarette advertising again." [81]

One author who challenged a major American corporation faced a more active form of censorship. In this story, a young lawyer from New York, Gerard C. Zilg, plays the role of David. One of the oldest corporations in the United States, run by one of the most prominent American families, plays Goliath.

Zilg, after years of dogged investigation and research, wrote a book called *Du Pont: Behind the Nylon Curtain,* published by Prentice-Hall in 1974. Du Pont had refused to cooperate with Zilg as he did his research: In fact Irénée du Pont, a senior vice-president, instructed his subordinates to investigate Zilg. One internal Du Pont company memo labeled Zilg a "professional radical." [82]

Zilg relates the story of America's oldest and most successful maker of munitions, not always in a flattering light. Said one writer," The stench of war profiteering hangs very heavy over the pages of Zilg's book." [83] The book also portrays eccentric, rapacious, and spoiled members of the family and it describes ventures associated with scandals and fraud. One family member performed stupidly before a Senate committee in the 1930s; subsequently, he had "to content himself with playing baritone horn for the Wilmington police band." [84] The book received some excellent reviews and was chosen for distribution through the Fortune Book Club, a subsidiary of the Book of the Month Club (BOMC). It was scheduled to be sent to members on November 14, 1974, the date of publication.

But then it was Goliath's turn. The Du Pont Company managed to obtain an unauthorized copy of the manuscript.[85] The legal office of the company pored over it and, in a June 17 memo, gave a rather unfavorable evaluation. Zilg, it said, wrote "as if he wants to plant the idea that there is an identifiable group in the U.S. who should be 'overthrown' because of vast greed and social injustice perpetrated over the past two centuries. The book is aimed more at the family than at the Du Pont company, probably because social injustice is more appealing when personalized." Charts in the book detailing Du Pont control over or interests in other corporations, said the memo, "could prove annoying." [86]

A month later, a Du Pont executive named Harold G. Brown, Jr., phoned an editor at the Book of the Month Club and told her that several people at the company had read the book and found it to be "scurrilous" and "actionable." [87] In a display of virtually instant spinelessness, BOMC first told Prentice-Hall that it had decided to defer distribution of the book, then canceled it entirely. No one informed Zilg of these developments until October. Far from issuing press releases trumpeting the corporate pressure from Du Pont and the BOMC compliance, Prentice-Hall quietly reduced the size of the first press run from fifteen thousand copies to ten thousand, again without telling Zilg.

Zilg's editor at Prentice-Hall, who wanted to capitalize on the attempt at suppression, was told to keep quiet. Zilg tried to generate some publicity on his own. He persuaded the *Delaware State News,* one of the few papers in the state not owned by a Du Pont, to publish portions of the book. As a result, Zilg made the best seller list in that state for a short time. But Prentice-Hall, far from following up on his success, did nothing. Finally, Zilg's editor at Prentice-Hall got the story of Du Pont's opposition and the BOMC retreat to the *New York Times,* which published it on January 21, 1975. A BOMC spokesperson denied to the *Times* reporter that the Du Pont call had influenced the decision not to issue the book; the Du Pont executive said his call had not constituted any threat. Although sales rose with the publication of the article, again Prentice-Hall did nothing in response, and the book was allowed to go out of print as demand was peaking. By that time, the book was finished.[88] Goliath had won. The corporation, merely by complaining that the book was "actionable," had quashed it.

But David, though grievously set back, did not concede defeat. Zilg filed a lawsuit, accusing Prentice-Hall of breaching its contractual agreement to publish and promote his book and Du Pont of improperly pressuring the publisher.[89] Although Du Pont lawyers argued that the company was merely exercising its First Amendment rights to speak out against a book of which it disapproved, Zilg's lawyer claimed that Du Pont avoided speaking out in the public arena but rather spoke privately to the book club in order to prevent Zilg's views from being heard. This was not a proper exercise of constitutional rights, the lawyer argued, but rather a perversion of the First Amendment.

In April 1982, federal court judge Charles L. Brieant, who heard the case, ruled that the Du Pont company had every right to express vigorously its opinion of Zilg's book and had committed no wrong in so doing. But he also ruled that Prentice-Hall had failed to use its "best efforts" to promote the book "fully and fairly." Had Prentice-Hall lived up to its contract, the judge estimated, Zilg's book would have sold 25,000 copies, instead of the 12,500 actually sold. He held the publisher liable for $24,250 to compensate for the loss.

Both sides appealed their losses—Prentice-Hall saying they were not liable for any damages, Zilg saying that Du Pont had violated his rights. In September 1983, the appeals court ruled against Zilg on both issues.[90]

He appealed to the U.S. Supreme Court, which in 1984 decided not to hear his case. But Zilg, who now uses his mother's maiden name, Colby, may yet have the last word despite his defeat in the courts. Another publisher, Lyle Stuart, planned to put out an expanded edition of the book, to be titled *Du Pont Dynasty: Behind the Nylon Curtain,* in the fall of 1984.

4

Libel

Centuries ago, libel law marked a small advance in civilization. In 1605 England's Star Chamber said, "If [the libel] be against a private man, it deserves a severe punishment, for although the libel be made against one, yet it incites all those of the same family, kindred or society to revenge, and so tends *per consequens* to quarrels and breaches of the peace." In those days the rule was simple: The truer the accusation, the guiltier the libeler. Spreading accurate bad reports about someone was more punishable than spreading inaccurate bad reports.

Times have changed. If you say something bad about me and injure my reputation, I no longer rally my relatives and friends to chase after you with broadswords. I go to court to prove that you injured me by demonstrating the falsity of your words and the extent of my injury. A judge or jury will decide whether you did wrong and how much, if anything, you must pay to compensate me. Truth, rather than being an aggravation to the charge, has become a defense against the charge.

A complex and changing body of law governs defamation, the term that includes both libel (written words) and slander (spoken words). In the last few years, the number and variety of defamation suits have increased markedly. In addition, a wider variety of people and groups are suing and being sued for ever higher amounts of damages. Practices that once were considered safe have now become risky because they might trigger a defamation suit. Political activists as well as journalists find themselves in court, charged with defamation. Besides print and broadcast media, novels and stories have become the targets of lawsuits. Fiction is no longer exempt. Because of the large amounts of money involved, lawyers and insurance companies determine what can and cannot be published or broadcast.

Lawsuits have become the weapon of the citizen, the group, the corporation, and the public official who feels wronged by the written or spoken word. And the weapon is being used in ways that constrict First Amendment guarantees of free speech and free press.

FACTS AND FIGURES ABOUT LIBEL

Libel law has gone through many changes over the years and continues to evolve, sometimes seeming to favor the plaintiff, sometimes seeming to favor the media. Unfortunately, nothing about libel in the modern United States is simple. In order to preserve robust and uninhibited debate, the First Amendment mandates free speech. But libel is by definition punishable speech, and therefore not free. The relationship between libel law and the First Amendment has always been uneasy, as different concepts and values clash with one another.

Perhaps even more basic in this country than the notion of free speech is the idea that if someone makes a mistake and injures you, that person should pay. If the *National Enquirer* reported that Carol Burnett was drunk, and in fact she was sober, the paper should compensate her. But what's fair and what's permissible under the First Amendment are not necessarily the same things. From time to time, criticism of our political leaders is not fair; sometimes it's not even accurate. Should presidents and other officials collect money from every newspaper or television station that disseminated inaccurate information or unfair criticism? Even if that were desirable, our system of law could not handle such an arrangement, and we would have no free press left, either. Where, then, are the lines drawn between what can be said without fear or retribution and what cannot?

Current libel law recognizes two categories of people: public figures, including public officials, and private persons. To libel a public figure, the media must act with what courts call "actual malice," which is far more than a hostile state of mind. Publishing with actual malice means publishing with knowledge that the material is false or else with "reckless disregard" for the truth of the material. This has come to mean that in order to be held liable, a publisher must have entertained serious doubts about the truth of the material and published it anyway. To libel a private person, a publisher must be shown only to have been negligent in some way.

This distinction between public and private figures provides one standard for the person who has placed himself or herself in the public eye, and another for the more ordinary or less visible citizen. A private person needs more protection because he or she is presumed to be less able to command media attention for any rebuttal to the allegedly libelous statement, and because a private person has not sought out the glare of public attention with its attendant risks. A public official or public figure is presumed to be fair game for comment, in part to encourage vigorous debate over political policies and hence to promote an informed electorate.

Because it is difficult to prove that a statement was made with the knowledge that it was false or with reckless disregard for the truth, most libel cases brought by public figures do not go to trial. The judge hearing the case usually dismisses the suit in what is called a summary judgment, because even if everything the plaintiff says is true, and the material published is inaccurate, the plaintiff cannot show actual malice by the defendant, and therefore the case cannot be prosecuted. The U.S. Supreme Court decision establishing these standards was handed down in 1964 in the landmark case *New York Times v. Sullivan.* The *Times* had published an advertisement on behalf of Southern civil rights activists, and in particular Dr. Martin Luther King, Jr., who were then demonstrating against segregation and being thrown in jail. Citing factual errors in the ad's descriptions of arrests and harassment of black students and Dr. King, a city official of Montgomery, Alabama, sued the *Times* for libel even though the official's name was not mentioned. He won at trial and on appeal to the Alabama Supreme Court.

The U.S. Supreme Court overturned the verdict, saying:

> Erroneous statements are inevitable in free debate and must be protected if we are to maintain free discussion. Unless a privilege to err absent malice is recognized, grave danger exists that requiring publishers to guarantee accuracy will result in unreasonable self-censorship.[1]

The rule boiled down to this: The press could be outrageous, false, and wrong about a public figure, but as long as it was not reckless or knowingly inaccurate, it would win. The two Warren court members best known for their commitment to First Amendment freedoms, Justices Douglas and Black, dissented from this decision because they feared it gave insufficient protection to the press. Black worried that if libel cases were tried before juries, the jurors would find recklessness even where it did not exist and would award damages to plaintiffs.

For the ten years following *Sullivan,* the press rarely lost a libel case in the Supreme Court. In fact, a federal judge in 1977 felt that courts had so limited the rights of libel plaintiffs that public figures could no longer obtain satisfaction by law. Judge Charles L. Brieant asked rhetorically as he dismissed a libel case against *Barron's,* a financial weekly, "Are men and women of honor who happen to be public figures to right vicious slanders hereafter by resort to fisticuffs or duelling?"[2]

But there was no return to the violent customs of the past; instead, the tide turned in such a way that many experts now believe, as Black and Douglas feared, that *Times v. Sullivan* no longer provides adequate protection for the media. A number of developments, some actual and some merely ominous, have made the media more vulnerable to libel suits than before and have made the libel suits themselves more damaging. Among these developments are increases in the number of libel suits filed, sky-high legal expenses, the risk of losing hundreds of thousands or millions of dollars in damage verdicts, a more hostile attitude toward the press in the courts, particularly on the part of juries, and a strong public perception that the press is not fair and ought to be made so.

The press feels beleaguered and anxious in this climate. The risks of publishing or broadcasting hard-hitting investigative stories have escalated. Court protections have been cut back. The complications and expense of defending against a lawsuit are considerable. Lawyers have become as essential to the news as reporters. Let us consider, for example, the recent phenomenon labeled the megaverdict—awards in the millions of dollars to libel plaintiffs, like the $26.5 million a Wyoming jury directed *Penthouse* to pay a former beauty contest winner. Such huge monetary awards dwarf those of previous years and bear no relationship to injuries actually suffered by the plaintiff. Of the $26.5 million, $25 million was awarded to punish the magazine. Even though this jury award was first cut in half and then, nearly two years later, disallowed altogether, it nonetheless caused great anxiety at the magazine and in the media at large. Combined with the soaring costs of presenting a legal defense—ABC reportedly spent about $7 million to defend against one suit, and CBS spent at least $3 million in the pretrial phase of another—libel costs and the possibility of a megaverdict that is not overturned could bankrupt small publishers and broadcasters and cause serious damage to others.

The megaverdicts, however, are more a nightmare than a reality because they usually do not hold up through the appeals process; an award of $2.05 million from the *Washington Post* to a shipping magnate was overturned; an award of $9 million from the Alton, Illinois, *Telegraph* to a building contractor was settled for slightly more than $1 million after the paper declared bankruptcy; $1.6 million awarded to Carol Burnett from the *National Enquirer* was reduced on appeal to $800,000 and then to $200,000. Nevertheless, the possibility of a megaverdict that does hold up through the appeals process remains real, and strikes terror into editorial hearts.

According to libel law specialists like Floyd Abrams, judges are allowing juries more latitude in libel cases; this spells trouble for the media, because juries decide for the plaintiffs more often than judges do, and grant higher damage awards as well. This trend on the part of the judges, encouraged by Chief Justice Warren Burger, means that judges are less likely to decide for the media on summary judgment, and therefore will permit more cases to go to trial. And the difference between summary judgment and going to trial is considerable. For example, as reporter Anthony Lewis noted, the *Washington Post* printed an article in 1979, saying that Philadelphia policemen had beaten a black man. Three police officers, not named in the story, sued for libel. The trial judge, though acknowledging that the reporter had been very careful, refused to grant a summary judgment, and permitted the case to go to trial. Several months later, the trial began; after one day of hearing evidence, he dismissed the case against the *Post,* which he could have done earlier. The delay cost the paper $170,000—the annual salary of five or six reporters.[3]

The Supreme Court in recent years has been particularly hard on the press. The Burger court has declined to review most cases that have resulted in libel verdicts against the press.[4] Some legal decisions handed down by the Burger court and others have diminished press protections. The definition of a public figure was cut back: A scientist who was roundly criticized by Senator William Proxmire for allegedly wasting federal funds was found to be a private person and therefore able to pursue a libel suit against the senator.[5] The wife of a Palm Beach socialite, Mary Alice Firestone, despite her practice of holding press conferences to attract attention, was held to be a private person and thus could sue *Time* magazine.[6]

Perhaps more damaging to the media was the Supreme Court's ruling in 1979 in *Herbert v. Lando*[7] that a public figure who filed suit could inquire into the state of mind of reporters and editors who wrote the offending story. A former U.S. army colonel portrayed unfavorably on the CBS program "60 Minutes" won the right to ask why certain material had been included in the show and other material left out—in other words, to examine the reporters and editors for possible prejudice and to force them to explain how the story was pieced together.

In recent years in some courts, judges have been permitting juries to decide what constitutes "actual malice" and who qualifies as a "public figure." Lawyers for the media decry this practice, because they say that juries do not adequately understand the law or the First Amendment. In addition, jurors are considered to be more likely to respond to changes in public opinion, including changes in attitudes toward the press, a phenomenon that cannot be precisely measured, but seems to reflect both increasing skepticism about journalism and a sense that the press has gone too far. In a 1980 survey of one thousand people, the Public Agenda Foundation reported that the press was perceived as unfair. The public felt that there ought to be some mechanism for making the press be fair. Sentiments like these, among other factors, are held responsible for high damage awards and punitive fines levied on the media. One longtime observer of press law and cases said in 1982 that "juries had grown downright reckless with the treasuries of news organizations," especially in libel cases.[8]

According to media attorney Bruce Sanford, author of a book on libel, the courts also "tend to react to what's going on in the industry and mirror public opinion." Some observers feel that judges have been equating "recklessness" with "negligence," which is supposed to be a lesser fault. Attorney Floyd Abrams of New York, one of the leading First Amendment lawyers in the United States, cites public anger at newspapers—both for bearing bad tidings and for irresponsible behavior—to explain the hostility of juries and judges toward the press.

The fears and impressions of those involved in the area of libel, however, are not always supported by the evidence. In 1980 and 1981, Professor Marc A. Franklin of the Stanford University Law School began keeping records on libel suits to see who was winning and what they were winning. His work was continued in 1982 and 1983 by the Libel Defense Resource Center (LDRC) in New York, an organization formed by publishers, broadcasters, insurance companies, and societies of journalists to aid in the defense of media organizations and journalists who are sued for libel.

Professor Franklin predicted in 1981 that "dollars may soon be flying in defamation cases," citing several multimillion-dollar verdicts returned around that time against the media. These awards were far greater than anything previously reported, he noted. But Franklin found that of three hundred media libel cases in the courts between 1977 and 1980, only ten damage awards were finally sustained. He also learned that the media appeared more likely to settle cases out of court than proceed to trial, in order to avoid the possibility of very high damage awards.

The amounts of damages awarded rose sharply during the years covered by the LDRC study. Franklin recorded only four out of twenty-three awards (17 percent) above $250,000. The LDRC found that twenty-one out of forty-seven damage awards (45 percent) reached $250,000 or more for the plaintiffs. The LDRC study concluded that "the mega-judgment trend continues unabated, with a total of 9 of the LDRC awards in the million-dollar category and only one of the Franklin cases at that level." To make a bad situation worse, noted LDRC, the awards also included "massive doses of *punitive* damages—17 punitive awards of a quarter million or more are included in the LDRC data; 7 of a million or more."[9]

The major problem for the news media defendants was the punitive damages. No insurance can be purchased that is guaranteed to cover these damages; several states have laws stating that punitive damages cannot be paid by insurance, and in those states insurance companies have refused to pay punitive awards. The *Enquirer* sued its insurance company to force it to pay the punitive damages awarded Burnett, but the newspaper lost, since the court ruled that the very purpose of punishment would be defeated if the insurer covered the loss.

Even as media defendants in lower courts lost cases and were ordered to pay damage awards at high rates, the appeals courts continued to throw out or cut down the damage verdicts. Of forty-seven damage awards entered in the LDRC study, only seven were affirmed on appeal, all in cases involving small damage awards. In sum, about three out of four verdicts against the press were overturned by appeals courts. The standards used by most juries in the efforts to reach a decision seemed to differ widely from the constitutional standards ultimately applied by the courts. Nevertheless, the LDRC survey concluded that "more and larger damage awards are still being made."

The survey also found that the press almost always lost a libel suit that went to trial. The LDRC data showed that if libel cases were decided by a jury, the plaintiff won 89 percent of the verdicts; if trials were decided by judges, plaintiffs won 83 percent. The survey noted that since most libel cases are won by the media in summary judgments, the cases that reach the trial stage are those in which the media have weaker defenses. Nevertheless, the percentage of losses boded ill for any newspaper or writer or broadcaster whose work led to a trial.

A second study published by the LDRC in October 1982 examined the frequency of summary judgments, particularly with respect to the effect of a Burger footnote in *Hutchinson v. Proxmire,*[10] cautioning against dismissals in libel cases where malice was alleged. This study concluded that summary judgment continued to be the rule rather than the exception in libel cases; 75 percent of the cases were dismissed before trial. Before the Burger footnote in *Hutchinson,* according to the LDRC, summary judgment had been the "preferred remedy, at least in constitutional libel cases, because the very pendency of defamation litigation can have a chilling effect on free expression."[11] (The Chief Justice had suggested that the question of actual malice ought to be decided by a jury and not by a judge during preliminary proceedings.) The *Hutchinson* footnote apparently did not alter the trend as much as the media had feared. Some courts, LDRC found, chose to adopt a neutral attitude toward summary judgment rather than one favoring it.

Despite studies showing that the media usually win, the number of lawsuits filed against the media has grown. Alice Neff Lucan, attorney for the Gannett newspaper chain, estimated in 1981 that a new suit or threat to sue appeared about every ten days against one of Gannett's eighty-three papers. Time, Inc., said at any one time it had about ten libel suits pending. In 1980, Roger Rudnick, head of the libel department for Employers Reinsurance, Inc., told the *National Law Journal* that libel claims handled by his company had tripled in frequency in two years. He attributed the increase to two factors: more lawsuits filed and more media clients insured by his company. He reported 692 claims (including lawsuits and notices from attorneys of intent to sue) in 1979, an increase from an average of about 200 annually in previous years.[12]

Even more suits may be filed if a recent court decision allowing the family of a libel plaintiff to sue after the plaintiff's death is upheld. Judge H. Lee Sarokin of Newark, New Jersey, decided in January 1983 that the family of Kenneth MacDonald, who had been indicted in the federal Abscam investigation, had the right to continue his suit against Time, Inc., after he died. MacDonald and his family, said the judge, "suffered untold humiliation, anguish, mental suffering and possible financial loss." Noting the "awesome power" of the press, the judge said that a lawsuit for defamation ought not to be cut short by death.[13] This unusual decision may well make things difficult for historians as well as more contemporary reporters. It will certainly add to the difficulties of media defendants, who would not be able to question a deceased plaintiff about the truth or falsity of what was published, or about the damages suffered. It could well add to the burgeoning number of complaints.

Organizations have also turned to libel suits more often and some have adopted formal policies of suing media that report on them. Perhaps the most well known of these is Synanon, a California-based foundation established to help drug addicts, alcoholics, and those with "character disorders." The National News Council of New York City, a group set up to adjudicate disputes involving media, wrote a report on Synanon in 1979 detailing the organization's assault on the media. This report was written in response to a request from United Press International (UPI), which alleged that Synanon lawyers had been "flooding the nation's news media with letters threatening libel suits as a part of the systematic pattern of intimidation designed to suppress all stories they considered unfavorable." [14] In fact, Synanon, which has always been a controversial operation, set up what it called a Retraction Project. In 1978 and 1979, Synanon sent 960 letters demanding retractions to newspapers and broadcasters. These letters, said Synanon attorney Dan Garrett, were sent pursuant to California law, which requires libel or slander plaintiffs to demand retraction of material within twenty days after learning of the publication or broadcast alleged to be libelous if they are to retain their rights to proceed with a subsequent libel suit.

In the 1970s, Synanon filed fifty-five libel suits. Among the targets were large and small media companies: Time, Inc., the *San Francisco Examiner* (twice), American Broadcasting Company and its San Francisco affiliate KGO, and the tiny weekly *Point Reyes Light,* located north of San Francisco (the paper won a Pulitzer Prize for its reporting on Synanon). Synanon also declared a "holy war" against Time, Inc., to be waged by a separate Synanon organization called SCRAM (Synanon Committee for a Responsible American Media). This group, according to lawyers for Time, Inc., threatened those responsible for an article about Synanon in *Time* magazine with bombs and "grave danger," and threatened specific acts of intimidation against Hedley Donovan, then *Time* editor in chief. After the magazine came close to obtaining material that could have been damaging to Synanon members then accused (they subsequently pleaded no contest to the charge of a rattlesnake attack on a Los Angeles attorney), Synanon dropped its lawsuit.[15]

Although Synanon did not profit from its suit against Time, Inc., which fought back, it profited greatly from other suits. It won a $2 million settlement from the *San Francisco Examiner,* and $1.25 million in a settlement with ABC. According to the National News Council Report, Synanon also succeeded in getting retractions from some papers that feared further trouble. Capitol News Service (CNS) of Sacramento, which services small weeklies in California, made reference to a UPI story about a child custody hearing involving Synanon members in San Rafael, California. After receiving demands from Synanon, two CNS subscribers insisted that the news service run a retraction because they could not afford a lawsuit. Fred Kline, editor and owner of CNS, said he estimated that "about 25 percent of my clients simply won't publish any stories about Synanon now.... Their liability insurance for the most part calls for them to pay the first $7,500, and that's a lot of money for a small paper." [16] UPI's lawyers had gone over the child custody story and found it unobjectionable.

The editor of the *San Mateo Times and News Leader,* also in California, published a retraction of the same story as well as a retraction of another story. "I don't want to be harassed," he explained. "Running a retraction hasn't hurt our credibility." [17] The editor, J. Hart Clinton, told the National News Council he believed that Synanon had been encouraged by its large settlements with the *San Francisco Examiner,* and sought retractions "when the story is the slightest bit defamatory, whether it's true or false. That's harassment." [18] His reporters have been instructed to publish material about Synanon only when it is extremely important. The *San Francisco Chronicle* reporter who covered Synanon agreed. "Once the *Examiner* folded in response to this litigation, most of the press folded. If there had been a little courage displayed these people would never have gotten their start,"[19] he told the National News Council.

The report of the News Council concluded that "many editors and news directors, especially those associated with small news organizations of limited resources, are refraining from publishing or broadcasting news they deem legitimate regarding Synanon."[20] The News Council also concluded that Synanon had a First Amendment right to carry out its policy and recommended only that the media fight back. For an organization concerned with ethics in reporting, the group took rather a weak stand: "The history of press freedom makes it plain that there is no substitute for courage in such cases," it said, adding that perhaps the California law should be reconsidered. In contrast, Henry Kaufman, general counsel for the LDRC, feels the National News Council's conclusions did not go far enough. "My conclusion would be that what Synanon does is an abuse of libel law and [shows] how a powerful organization can chill the news,"[21] he said.

Certainly Synanon has followed an extreme policy against the press, but it is not the only group that has succeeded in chilling reporting. The Scientologists and the Unification Church have also managed to frighten the press by threats of legal action. L. Ron Hubbard of the Church of Scientology told his members, "We should be very alert to sue for slander at the slightest chance so as to discourage the public presses from mentioning Scientology."[22] According to the *National Law Journal,* between 1970 and 1979 the Church filed more than 100 lawsuits against reporters, individual critics of the church, and print and broadcast media.

One result of these and similar lawsuits is that the media are now more likely to settle out of court in order to avoid a trial with its attendant risks of high damages and an expensive, time-consuming defense. Given the temper of the current Supreme Court, as well, some papers decide to compromise rather than fight. The National Broadcasting Company and E. W. Scripps Company, both defendants in libel cases scheduled to be heard by the high court in 1982, settled out of court rather than proceed. Says libel defense lawyer James Goodale, "No press lawyer looks forward to taking a libel case to the present Supreme Court."[23] Attorney Bruce Sanford, who worked on the Scripps case, said his client was not so much afraid of losing as of generating an opinion that might further add to the media's uncertainty about libel law. Sanford said that "a great deal of confusion has been added to the law" by recent decisions.[24]

Legal writer Lyle Denniston labeled this current policy "simply to surrender when sued," and worried that if enough media defendants give in, the "word might get around that it pays to sue a newspaper, a station, or a network. The price of settling doubtless would go up, in dollars and in constitutional terms, too," he wrote. Denniston also recognized that a plaintiff against the media who takes an appeal to the Supreme Court these days has "promising prospects." [25]

What is to be done to alleviate the chilling effects of libel on the media? Among the more modest proposals is one advocated by attorney James Goodale, former vice-chairman of the *New York Times* and now a leading libel defense lawyer. Goodale believes that when the media injure a person because of recklessness, that person should have redress for the injury suffered. But he also believes that insurers ought to be able to write policies that cover punitive damages so that media defendants do not run such terrible financial risks.[26]

Judge Irving Kaufman of the U.S. Court of Appeals for the Second Circuit, who is known for his strong support of the First Amendment, wrote an op-ed piece for the *New York Times,* stating his concern about the effect on journalism of "virtually unlimited damage awards" in libel suits. He concluded that the *Sullivan* decision no longer gives sufficient protection to the media in libel and slander cases. He also believes that juries cannot give sufficient protection to the media:

> At best, a juror can be expected to rely on common-sense notions of fairness. In the usual case, the award represents a rough monetary accommodation of the claim for compensation weighed against the media's culpability. At worst, a jury will permit its verdict to reflect its disapproval of the views espoused by the defendant or its frustration with the state of world or national affairs reported by the media generally. In any event, the verdict is largely uninfluenced by the constitutional imperative of an unrestrained press that undergirds the Sullivan case. The First Amendment protections emanating from that case now play little or no role when and if a defamation action is submitted to a jury.[27]

Like Goodale, Judge Kaufman believes that libel law should exist in order to provide a remedy for those "who have suffered real injury" from a press "which does not always exercise its responsibilities wisely." But he balances this with the observation that "it is unfortunate that the exercise of liberties so precious as freedom of speech and of the press may sometimes do harm that the state is powerless to recompense: but this is the price that must be paid for the blessing of a democratic way of life." [28]

Anthony Lewis, a columnist for the *New York Times,* is also troubled by recent trends in libel cases. In a lecture at Columbia Law School he expressed doubt about the efficacy of the *Sullivan* decision to give the press adequate protection in libel suits.[29] Lewis's grounds for criticism differ somewhat from Judge Kaufman's because Lewis knows what the procedures are both in court and in the news room. Since the *Sullivan* decision (and the *Herbert* decision) permit extensive investigation into the way the questioned article was put together, and allow testimony about editorial decisions to be probed, any sensible publisher fears that his news operation will be severely damaged by the months or years the suit drags on. And any evidence that internal criticism of an article took place before publication can be used by the plaintiff to impugn its veracity; in a sense a good system of prepublication criticism only stands to harm the media defendant.

Lewis made several proposals to improve the situation: (1) Limit damages to sums that compensate for actual financial loss; (2) eliminate punitive damages; (3) have judges "play their full part" in libel cases, since the *Sullivan* protections "are largely mythical unless the constitutional issue of knowing or reckless disregard is decided by a court on summary judgment"; and (4) institute an "absolute" privilege against libel action in the limited area of "criticism of the way public officials do their public duty. . . . The First Amendment permits no libel actions against critics of official conduct." This protection would be limited to comment about officials, and not extended to commentary on public figures unless the commentary related to "public issues."

The most far-reaching proposal for change has come from the National Board of Directors of the American Civil Liberties Union, which adopted a new position on libel in October 1982. Rather than focus on the person discussed and the distinction between public and private figures, the ACLU placed the emphasis on the issue that provoked the discussion. Ira Glasser, the ACLU's executive director, believes such a solution would permit the exercise of free speech both by the media and by political groups without the chilling effect of sky-high damage suits. Glasser argued that "libel actions place a price on free speech, a price that the speaker or writer frequently cannot pay. Libel actions are increasingly being used, almost always by the powerful—government officials, union officials, corporate officials, landlords—to stifle criticism, suppress speech and chill organized resistance. The number of these suits is growing rapidly, and placing a kind of 'poll tax' on vigorous criticism."[30]

In the past, ACLU policy specifically decried defamatory attacks on individuals, saying that "false statements involving character assassination do not forward the process of a marketplace of ideas." This seemingly inoffensive and just statement had and still has critics, and these critics ultimately prevailed with the ACLU board. Why would anyone defend false statements? Thomas I. Emerson, professor emeritus of law at Yale, believes, "False statements, whether intentional or not, perform a function in a system of freedom of expression by forcing individuals to justify and rethink their positions." [31] He argued that even a false statement may make a valuable contribution to public debate by bringing about a clearer perception of truth through its collision with error.

The premise behind Emerson's position is that our Constitution is designed to encourage free speech, not fair speech. What is fair and what is constitutional are not identical. While fairness is and ought to be a goal in reporting, there are strong reasons why it ought not to be the test of what is libelous. A reporter cannot always, in the heat of a breaking news story or when working with limited sources, get the full story. The best possible coverage under the circumstances may not look good to a jury equipped with hindsight. If the media must offer a 100 percent guarantee of accuracy for everything printed or broadcast, our news would be vastly impoverished.

Given the conflict between the First Amendment rights of free speech and the property right of a reputation, the ACLU chose the First Amendment. The directors concluded, after vigorous debate, that there should be no right to sue for libel in any case involving an issue of "public concern." The new policy states:

> A free society is one in which there is freedom of speech and of press—where a marketplace of ideas exists in which all points of view compete for recognition. Whether viewpoints or ideas are wrong or right, obnoxious or acceptable, should not be the criterion. Speech cannot be restricted without the danger of making the government the arbiter of truth. Therefore, the ACLU regards the existence of the right of action for defamation to be violative of the First Amendment, in the course of public debate which is defined to occur when the speech relates to:
>
> 1) a public official on a subject matter related to his/her public position;
> 2) a public figure on a subject matter related to his/her public status;
> 3) anyone (public or private) on a subject of public concern. For this purpose public concern can be deemed to relate to anything having an impact on the social or political system or climate.[32]

Glasser does not expect any state to adopt the ACLU policy in the near future, "much less the Supreme Court." But he still holds that "the law is going to evolve in the direction of our policy."

If laws were changed to reflect the ACLU recommendations, Glasser would not expect to see much change from large newspapers or broadcasters. Rather, he thinks that smaller groups and publications that are now more vulnerable would publish more vigorous criticism. In addition, he thinks that if libel laws were eliminated, a demand would grow for a "right to reply." For example, if a newspaper criticized a corporation, someone from that corporation would have the opportunity to respond to the charges in that newspaper rather than head for the courts.

No one expects the law of libel to change overnight in response to the ACLU policy or other criticisms and warnings. But the idea that libel requires further scrutiny is gaining attention among the media, civil libertarians, political activists, and some legal scholars. According to Goodale, "Ultimately the essential rationale for giving the press the power it has is to create a countervailing force to the use of political power as well as to the other pockets of power that exist in our society—economic and social. . . . Unless the press is able to speak freely about the country's enormous power centers, [they] will develop an arrogance of their own that would be intolerable." [33]

LIBEL SUITS AGAINST BOOKS

The growth in libel suits has not failed to touch book publishing; as in journalism, the number of lawsuits has risen, and the amounts sought can be staggering. Moreover, publishing has changed from a rather genteel business conducted by small, privately owned firms to a mass market industry with millions of dollars riding on a single title. New York literary agent Arthur Klebanoff said, "The book industry is experiencing what everyone else is experiencing—a tremendous explosion of litigation. It isn't going to go away, and the fact that it happens doesn't mean that anybody necessarily did anything wrong—just that people do a lot of suing." [34] He believes that commercially successful writers attract most of the legal action: Best-selling writers Alex Haley (*Roots*), Linda Goodman (*Sun Signs*), Gay Talese (*Thy Neighbor's Wife*), and Barbara Gordon (*I'm Dancing as Fast as I Can*) were among those hit with lawsuits.

As in journalism, only a small percentage of libel suits against books acutally go to trial; only some of those that go to trial are won by plaintiffs; and only some of those verdicts are sustained by higher courts. The authors and publishers usually prevail. Henry Kaufman of the Libel Defense Resource Center believes it may not be possible to show empirically that the number of suits that go to trial has risen dramatically, but he says that publishers' perceptions are probably influenced as much by the suits that are filed and not pursued, or filed and dismissed, as by the suits that proceed.

In recent years, the fear of libel suits among writers and publishers has grown so strong that it now acts as a prior restraint. Caution is a watchword in the book industry, and lawyers, as in journalism and broadcasting, play an important role in determining which books will be published and which will not. Frequently lawyers insist that strongly worded passages be removed from manuscripts; editors tone down other passages, and authors censor themselves. As a result, some writers avoid controversial projects and some publishers stop promoting books that draw criticism from powerful people. Experienced writers and publishers do not pull back from projects because they think they might lose a libel suit but rather because of the tremendous financial and personal costs of defending against one.

Unlike journalism, the book-publishing industry is set up in such a way that authors usually bear the legal responsibility for libel suits. The indemnity clause, part of the standard agreement between publisher and author, requires the author to reimburse the publisher for expenses incurred in a defense against libel or in the settlement of a libel suit. The publisher has the power to decide whether or not to settle and to negotiate the terms of the settlement. As a practical matter, however, publishers do no always stick to the letter of the agreement and sometimes pick up the tab. Insurance companies have taken a careful look at the problem of libel suits and suggested innovations: Since a recent Authors' Guild Foundation study showed that authors make an average of $4,775 for a year's work, some insurance companies realized that most authors were too poor to hold up their end of the agreement and, in the early 1980s, arranged for insurance policies to cover both author and publisher. Unfortunately, only a few publishers purchased these policies; most held to the view that authors will become careless with facts unless their bankbooks are on the line. (Publishers have always carried insurance for themselves, but no one has argued that having insurance makes *them* careless.)

A look at three cases will illustrate the twists that have characterized some recent lawsuits against books and made libel more fearsome than it had been considered before. In the least known of these cases, libel law intersects with claims of national security to complicate a defamation suit filed by a former CIA agent. Donald Freed, the author of *Death in Washington,* is a conspiracy buff and political activist who lives in Los Angeles. He has written controversial books about many subjects, including police informants, civil rights, nuclear war, Watergate, and CIA plots. His case illustrates some of the penalties inflicted merely by having to defend against a libel suit and, in addition, the extra difficulties imposed when the federal government intervenes for the other side. This is an unusual case in that Freed is facing twin threats to his First Amendment right to free speech: libel law and the CIA. His case may set a dangerous precedent for the media.

Stung by critical portrayals of the Central Intelligence Agency in books and the press, several retired officers resolved to fight back in the courts. In 1980, members of the Association of Former Intelligence Officers received a fund-raising appeal from one of the organization's directors, David Atlee Phillips. The letter asked the members, estimated to number about thirty-five hundred, to contribute to Challenge, a legal action fund that would sponsor lawsuits against the authors of books and articles that allege misdeeds by intelligence operatives.

Phillips started to work for the CIA in the fifties and rose through the ranks to become chief of its Western Hemisphere Division before retiring in 1975. In 1981, he filed a $90 million libel and slander suit against Donald Freed and several researchers who worked on his book; he also sued its publisher, Lawrence Hill and Company.[35] The book accused the CIA and Phillips of complicity in the 1976 assassination of Orlando Letelier in Washington, D.C. Letelier, a minister in the government of assassinated Chilean President Salvador Allende and an opponent of that country's subsequent ruler, Augusto Pinochet, was killed in the explosion of a bomb attached to his car. Ronni Moffitt, a passenger in the car and an associate of Letelier's, also died in the blast. Freed's book stated that Phillips disseminated to the press forged documents supposedly found in Letelier's briefcase when he was killed. The book charges that the fake documents were designed to make the murder look like the work of Cuban agents, diverting authorities from the CIA-connected killers. In response, Phillips alleges in a lawsuit that the book has "greatly injured and damaged . . . his distinguished name and reputation" as a CIA covert operative, and that he has been and is held "in contempt, calumny, distrust and ridicule among the public" and his associates.

Phillips also filed a $70 million action for libel and invasion of privacy against writer Gaeton Fonzi and *The Washingtonian* for an article discussing possible links between Phillips and the assassination of John F. Kennedy as well as CIA plots on Fidel Castro's life.[36] By the spring of 1983, that lawsuit had been dismissed from court no less than three times, but after each dismissal Phillips and his lawyers tried again. John Sansing, the weary lawyer for *The Washingtonian* said, "I expect them to go to the court of appeals. It's been two and a half years, and [it's] not over yet." [37]

Phillips and his legal action fund, Challenge, are not the only ones filing libel suits having to do with intelligence operations. Other officials taking to the courts to defend their actions are Nathaniel Davis, former U.S. ambassador to Chile, and two other former American officials stationed there. Davis and the other two filed a $60 million lawsuit against Costa-Gavras and the film *Missing*; the film implied that U.S. naval intelligence authorities permitted the murder of an American reporter in Chile during the Pinochet coup against socialist premier

Allende. In addition, General William C. Westmoreland filed a $120 million libel suit against CBS for a documentary alleging that he knew about intelligence reports that deliberately underestimated the strength of North Vietnamese troops.

In his fund-raising letter, Phillips said that both nonfiction and fiction would be fair game for Challenge:

> Ex-intelligence officers have been battered around in recent years, and we've taken the beating. . . . I believe a test case should be mounted against writers who defame ex-intelligence officers, dead and alive, by using their names in egregious novels.

Phillips had a particular novel in mind—*Spymaster,* also by Freed, a tale about a lusty operative who becomes director of Central Intelligence, in which real and fictional characters are intermingled.

The position taken by Phillips is that CIA agents are just ordinary citizens defending their rights. Yet they are far from ordinary, since the actions of CIA agents have had important repercussions in national and international affairs. Their "ordinary citizen" claims ring hollow. More importantly, the court and the federal government are not treating Phillips as though he were an ordinary citizen. The rules of court procedure provide that after a suit for damages is filed, each side may first put questions called interrogatories to the other in order to establish the facts of the matter. Since Phillips was accusing Freed of writing falsely about his CIA activities, Phillips would have to prove the falsity of the Freed account, and in the process tell the truth about those activities. If Phillips refused to answer the questions, Freed reasoned, Phillips would have to drop the case because he could not comply with the court's rules. Freed's attorneys thus began the questioning. Phillips answered the questions about his personal life, but citing the *Snepp* case, claimed a Fifth Amendment privilege against answering many questions about his work in the CIA. Phillips argued that he would open himself to prosecution for breaking his employment agreement with the agency if he revealed classified information and for violating the Intelligence Identities Protection Act if he identified other agents. Freed's attorney, Melvin Wulf, then filed a motion to dismiss the case, arguing that Phillips cannot pursue a lawsuit if he refuses to comply with court procedure.

U.S. District Judge Thomas Jackson ruled that Phillips could refuse to answer the questions and still pursue his suit. He also permitted lawyers for the CIA and the U.S. Department of Justice to become parties to the action, a highly unusual move. Asked why he did not object to having the government's lawyers join the case, Wulf responded, "I wanted them out in the open. If I had refused, they would have been lurking around anyway. I wanted people to see that not only is Phillips refusing to answer questions, but the U.S. government is telling him not to answer questions. I want people to see how interested the U.S. is in this case, and the role it is playing." [38] Freed has appealed Judge Jackson's ruling. He is also spending much time and energy raising money to pay for his defense.

Another libel suit employing a different legal tactic was filed in May 1983 by South Dakota Governor William A. Janklow. Janklow claimed that *In the Spirit of Crazy Horse,* a book about the American Indian Movement by Peter Matthiessen, defames him with accusations of shooting dogs, rape, drunk driving, and public nudity. He asked $4 million in actual damages and $20 million in punitive damages. The twist is that he is suing not only the book's author and Viking, its publisher, but also three bookstores in South Dakota that sold the book. He claims that continuing to display and sell the book constitutes a "republication" of the alleged libel and is part of "a single libelous wrong" done to him. Janklow personally phoned Donna Dyer, proprietor of tiny Golden Mountain Books, a store occupying about eleven hundred square feet in Hot Springs, South Dakota, to tell her the book was libelous and to ask her to remove it from her shelves. According to Dyer, she refused and Janklow became angry and hung up on her.[39]

If Dyer must go through the legal process, the cost of depositions alone would range between $15,000 and $25,000. She is unlikely to have to pay those costs, though, because a printer has begun organizing a defense fund on her behalf, and Viking has stated its commitment to protecting the booksellers. Nonetheless, if Janklow is permitted to sue the sellers, bookstores may become reluctant to stock controversial works.

It is not only nonfiction that attracts libel suits but fiction as well. Perhaps the most important lawsuit involved Paul Bindrim, a southern California psychologist who conducted nude group therapy sessions in a swimming pool. During her research for a novel about California life styles, entitled *Touching* and published by Doubleday, writer Gwen Davis observed Bindrim leading a nude marathon group encounter. Bindrim read the novel and sued, claiming that she had invaded his privacy by basing one of the characters on him and that she had violated a signed agreement not to write about his therapy.[40] Bindrim, who had been cleanshaven and short haired when Davis observed him, appeared at the trial with long hair and a full beard, like the therapist character in Davis's book. A jury awarded Bindrim $75,000 in damages in a verdict that rocked the publishing industry. Hitherto, fiction had been considered virtually immune from libel suits, since it is a work of imagination rather than reporting. Anthony M. Schulte, an executive vice-president of Random House, told the *New York Times,* "The question is, will [this decision] temper the publisher's willingness to take risks in certain kinds of fiction and will it reduce the quality of writing? And how about writers who are writing frankly realistically based fiction?"

Davis described the effect of the lawsuit on her writing to the *Los Angeles Times*: "A censor is suddenly imposed on all my thinking." She began work on a book about museums and found, "I have to watch what I say because there are all those museum ladies who might get terribly offended if I use any adjectives they do not find flattering." [41]

Bindrim's award was upheld by higher courts; in 1979, the U.S. Supreme Court refused to hear an appeal. Doubleday then filed suit against Davis, who, said the publisher, was responsible under the indemnity clause of the contract she had signed. Doubleday's suit, which created consternation among writers, was settled out of court for an undisclosed sum.

The *Bindrim* case opened two Pandora's boxes for future litigants: lawsuits against works of fiction and lawsuits by publishers against authors. Neither of these boded well for the future of free expression in fiction. In fact, in October 1983 author Kitty Kelley, who wrote best-selling biographies of Jacqueline Kennedy and Elizabeth Taylor, was sued for $2 million by Frank Sinatra—before she had published a word. 'Ol' Blue Eyes' learned that she was researching a book about him, and went to court to stop her. When it was "appropriate," he said, he would tell his own story.[42]

Robert Fremlin, an attorney with the California firm Lillick McHose and Charles, which has as clients publishers, magazines, and broadcasters, finds the increase in and variety of libel suits against books to be indeed threatening. "There's a big change in how you advise clients now," he observed. "In the last five to ten years more cases have been going to trial. Clients don't publish some things—it's just not worth the candle." [43]

A POLITICAL WEAPON AGAINST ACTIVISTS

If you mentioned libel in 1981, the odds were that a person would remember that a jury had just awarded spunky Carol Burnett $1.6 million from the *National Enquirer,* which had published a rather seamy article portraying her as drunk. In the same year a civil libertarian named Elmer Gertz was awarded $400,000 in damages for a 1969 redbaiting article in the John Birch Society journal *American Opinion* that called him, among other things "Communist-fronter Gertz." The good guys, it seemed, were getting back at the bad guys.

But a very different, generally less publicized sort of libel suit was also proliferating throughout the courts. In those cases, people using the political process to redress grievances or to bring about change were being challenged by huge damage suits brought by the interests they offended. A housewife named Pat Haworth of San Lorenzo Valley, California, protested a land development in a letter to a newspaper and was sued for $3 million.[44] The NAACP and Bayview of San Francisco protested alleged police brutality and cover-ups; the Police Officers Association sued for $50 million.[45]

Although most of these suits were either settled out of court or dropped and the huge sums not paid, they scared the individuals who were sued, disrupted the organizations, and damaged efforts to recruit new members for the causes. The lesson seemed to be that political activity was becoming dangerous to one's pocketbook. This upsurge of lawsuits filed by individuals and corporations because of alleged damage from the expression of political opinions began to have a chilling effect, according to observers in communities where the legal actions took place. The suits appeared to provide a way for the rich and powerful (or the well-organized) to retaliate against those who challenged their interests. The anxiety, expense, and nuisance of defending against such suits, whether or not the suit ultimately succeeds, become a form of punishment. Furthermore, the simplest procedures for depositions, rulings, motions, appeals, and so forth take so long that even to have a case dismissed is an ordeal.

The national hot spot for political lawsuits in 1981 was Santa Cruz, California, better known for its beautiful beaches and fine university. A few years earlier, a coalition of senior citizens, environmentalists, students, and other progressives had become active in local politics. They successfully worked for the election of officials who favored restrictions on housing and land development. In 1978, a wealthy conservative landowner named Telford Smith took out a series of advertisements lambasting these new forces. Smith poured money into a campaign for a recall vote on the county's two environmental supervisors. An antirecall group formed, and responded with an ad asking, "Who is Telford Smith?" The ad claimed that Smith was pushing the recall campaign in order to advance his economic and political interests.

Smith eventually won the recall, but he was not satisfied. He sued the antirecall campaign coordinator, Tim Jenkins, who was then a stock clerk, along with one hundred John Does.[46] Smith sought $500,000 in damages for defamation. Eventually, Jenkins named forty-five others who had participated in the antirecall campaign, and Smith subpoenaed the most politically prominent of these for depositions. They were asked for the names of those involved with the ad and were confronted with questions calculated to frighten them, such as, "What is your net worth?" Smith proceeded very slowly with the suit and, according to Hugh De Lacy, a former congressman who was subpoenaed, the developer "just kick[ed] things up around election time," as if to remind the forty-five of the risks of political activity.[47]

Tim Jenkins explained Smith's suit this way in 1981, "This is one community in the nation where left and progressive politics have been successful. I think the local development interests, the conservatives and business interests realize they can't beat us at the polls—they're losing their pants in the electoral process. These suits are a way of intimidation to target the most effective people and scare us into silence." [48] Jenkins's lawyer asserted that an injustice would be done if the case ever went to trial; he said that the advertisement was the exercise of free speeech during an election, and thus totally protected under the First Amendment. After a few years, Smith stopped prosecution of the suit, which as of early 1983 lay domant in the courts. According to Jenkins's lawyer, once Smith learned that he would not be able to harass the opposition into silence, he lost interest.[49]

The key issue—what constitutes free speech during an election—in the Santa Cruz suits and several others as well was argued in April 1981 before the California Supreme Court.[50] That case arose when a development company planning to build a condominium in Beverly Hills filed a libel suit against the president of the League of Women Voters, as well as the leader of a successful antidevelopment initiative, a local citizen, and no fewer than one thousand John Does. The offending acts: a ballot initiative and two letters to editors of local papers. The damages sought: $63 million. The company claimed that libelous and slanderous statements caused it to lose the condominium project and its reputation.

Stephen Bomse, a volunteer lawyer for the American Civil Liberties Union, argued an amicus curiae brief for the defendants. He said then that "if the court allows this case to proceed with discovery, motions and a trial and appeal, that will have a tremendous economic impact on these people. This kind of lawsuit is a major, major weapon. I can assure you that all of the very nice people of Beverly Hills would have thought long and hard before getting involved if they thought they might end up with a huge legal bill." According to Bomse, the suit was really "an effort to use the legal system for what I would consider inappropriate ends." [51] In other words, the company sued because it lost the Beverly Hills election and could not build its condominiums.

During the argument before the California Supreme Court on April 6, 1981, over whether the suit could proceed or not, Chief Justice Rose Bird wondered aloud whether people would have to consult a lawyer before writing a letter to a newspaper. Justice Stanley Mosk asked whether a suit against one thousand voters in a community estimated by the developer's lawyers to have between two thousand and three thousand voters altogether would not chill political activity there. The court decided that the activities of the League of Women Voters and the letters to the editors were in fact expressions of opinion and thus fully protected under the First Amendment. The court found that the facts had not been knowingly misrepresented in the ballot argument or the letters, and therefore no libel had been committed.

Despite the ruling in the Beverly Hills case, attorney Bomse felt that similar uses of litigation were still on the rise. "We're seeing this all the time now; the Sierra Club brings an environmental lawsuit and gets sued. At one time it was not considered part of the rules of the game," he said. "If a public interest group sued you, you defended and you spent lots of money, but it wasn't considered cricket to sue them back. But all that has changed, and now you're telling this bunch of do-good folks 'the price of poker has gone up. You sue us and we're going to sue you back.' Think what that means to someone earning $10,000 a year." [52]

A West Virginia man who faced such a lawsuit earned less than $10,000 a year. A vegetarian who raised blueberries and honeybees on a West Virginia farm, Rick Webb complained to the Environmental Protection Agency that a coal company had polluted the Buckhannon River, causing the trout to die. He also aired those charges in a newsletter he wrote and published, describing the effluents he had found in the river and the death of the fish. In July 1980 the DLM Coal Company hired one of the most influential law firms in West Virginia to press a libel suit against Webb for $200,000.[53] A young lawyer with the West Virginia Citizens Action Group, David Grubb, took on Webb's defense. Realizing he did not have sufficient experience to handle the case, Grubb sought assistance from a top-ranking law firm in Washington, D.C., law professors from the state university, and supporting arguments from environmental groups. The state circuit court rejected their motion to dismiss the suit, and it looked as if they would have to spend thousands of dollars and countless hours preparing for a trial.

In an unusual legal move, Webb's lawyers asked the West Virginia Supreme Court for a writ of prohibition—a request saying that the lower court's decision was such an egregious violation of Webb's rights that it had to be overturned. In the summer of 1981, the long-haired environmentalist won. The state supreme court ruled that the coal company's suit should be dismissed. According to law professor Robert Bastress of the West Virginia University, one of those who helped with the defense, that ruling was very important: "The factual issue before us was very complex. We would have had to bring in a lot of expert witnesses and do massive research to prove that Rick's charges were accurate, and we would have had to do this in a county that relies on coal mining as its major industry."[54]

The West Virginia high court expressed its opinion in strong language:

> The people's right to petition the government for a redress of grievances is a clear constitutional right and the exercise of that right does not give rise to a cause of action for damages. . . . We shudder to think of the chill our ruling would have on the exercise of freedom of speech and the right to petition were we to allow this lawsuit to continue. The cost to society in terms of the threat to our liberty and freedom is beyond calculation.

Justice Darrell McGraw, who wrote the opinion, continued, "[the right to petition] includes, among other things, activity designed to influence public sentiment concerning the passage and enforcement of laws as well as appeals for redress made directly to the government."[55]

Although that court's decision set an important precedent for West Virginia, it does not hold for other states and jurisdictions. Furthermore, the legal tactic used by Webb's attorneys, the writ of prohibition, does not exist in all states. As a result, the victory for free speech, while important, is limited.

Although the coal company lost its attempt to collect damages from Webb, it did succeed in making his life miserable for a year. He spent most of his time during that period worrying, planning his defense, and researching his case. His wife objected to the media coverage, which invaded their privacy. Their neighbors were upset by the furor, and Webb was made to feel like a troublemaking outsider in the small town of Sutton, where he lived. He eventually left his farm for another West Virginia community. Yet despite the disruption of his life, Webb was lucky. He and the women in Beverly Hills, like most defendants in the suits described in this chapter, were able to find volunteer lawyers to defend them, and thus were not financially ruined. But if these suits proliferate, not everyone will be able to find lawyers to work for nothing.

Perhaps the most egregious instance of abuse of the libel laws is the suit filed in November 1980 by a former city councilman of Seaside, California, after he was recalled in an election.[56] Among those sued were two women whose only action was to sign a petition to recall the councilman. The issues in the case were complicated by the fact that the ousted councilman, Louis Haddad, claimed that there were violations of election rules, in addition to the libel. Haddad, a white, sued nearly one hundred defendants, among them black churches and their ministers, as well as almost every politically active black person in Seaside. He included one hundred John Does in his suit besides those named; this device enabled him to threaten those who crossed his path. In a January 22, 1981, letter to the local *Monterey Herald* after his suit had been filed, Haddad warned, "I'm not going to take your bullshit any more. My lawsuit included 100 John Does. . . . Be careful, John Doe." The defendants remained anxious for a long time, worrying whether they would be served with legal papers. They asked their lawyer, "What happens in the next election? What if we start going to City Council meetings? Are we going to get served?" The suit has dragged on for years in the courts, casting a shadow over city politics.

Richard Criley, then executive director of the local ACLU, said that Haddad was regarded by the black community as a racist who created all kinds of problems for them as they struggled to gain a voice in local government. Criley was troubled by this suit and others like it. "The First Amendment is being threatened and the threats have a certain class basis," he said. "It's only those who have enough money to play around with litigation who can afford to do this." He thought these suits cropped up at that particular time in reaction to gains that had been made in the courts in the exercise of First Amendment rights. "I think some people who are not that keen on popular democracy see this as a means of gaining ends that couldn't be gained by other forms of litigation," he added.[57]

Three antinuclear groups have also been the subjects of lawsuits that also illustrate the use of litigation to halt political expression. Libel is only one element in one of the suits. In 1980, an action was filed against the Seacoast Clamshell Alliance by the governor of New Hampshire, John Sununu. He asked that a group that had staged a demonstration and the Clamshell Alliance pay for police expenses incurred during the demonstration even though no illegal actions were alleged to have occurred. That lawsuit bounced from one court to another on various technicalities; in 1982 it was remanded from the New Hampshire Supreme Court back for trial.[58] Thus the Seacoast Clamshell Alliance had a lawsuit hanging over its head for two years and every so often had to go through court procedures that reminded the members that trouble sat on their doorstep. Eventually Sununu dropped his claim.

In 1980, the Long Island Lighting Company (LILCO) sued the antinuclear SHAD Alliance for $2 million.[59] LILCO served legal summonses on people and groups whose names appeared in SHAD literature, as well as on some people who had only attended a single SHAD meeting, and had not taken part in any demonstrations. LILCO also sought the names of contributors to SHAD, as well as petition signers. LILCO argued that antinuclear demonstrations interfere with the company's private property rights. The utility cited higher fuel costs, delays in construction, and property damages in its complaint. Eight unions joined the utility in its suit.

SHAD, claiming that LILCO had engaged in improper surveillance, countersued, demanding that LILCO executives testify about surveillance of the alliance's members. Ultimately a settlement was arranged in which both sides dropped their claims. LILCO dropped its demand for $2 million. SHAD agreed to a court order forbidding trespassing and blockading the power plant. SHAD's lawyer, Gordon Johnson, said this was hardly a major concession, since those activities are illegal anyway.

A lawyer defending a West Coast antinuclear group from similar charges disagreed with Johnson's evaluation. "It's a moral loss if you settle," said Leonard Post of Oakland, California. "It's saying that although the utility is threatening the people that live near the plant by operating a nuclear reactor, you give in because of the threat of civil damages." [60]

According to Johnson, the settlement was worthwhile because it removed the possibility that SHAD members might have to stand trial or risk being assessed huge monetary damages. In addition, the suit had damaged SHAD's ability to organize and to raise funds. Even worse for the group, the suit had diverted time, energy, and resources from SHAD's purposes, which were to halt the development of nuclear power in the vicinity of New York City. Johnson acknowledged the effectiveness of the utility's tactic: "A signal was sent by a large corporation: run afoul of our interests, and we will attack you. . . . People are less likely to speak out on issues if their target, a corporation, indicate[s] it might sue them for millions of dollars." Equally dangerous, Johnson believed, was the way utilities and other corporations can act against protesters. Since LILCO claimed it was a private party, the restraints of the First Amendment did not apply to it, and the demonstrators' assertion of First Amendment rights to speak out and assemble had no merit. Johnson concluded, "Surveillance of so-called dissidents, a major province of the FBI at one time (and even now), is likely to be conducted by the economically powerful private sector in the future. Those corporations very likely will share their intelligence with the government in an informal manner, thereby permitting the government to evade restrictions on spying that may be imposed upon it." [61]

Finally, several right-wing organizations in California filed a $3 million damage suit in November 1981 against the Abalone Alliance after it conducted massive demonstrations at the Pacific Gas and Electric

Company's Diablo Canyon nuclear power plant.[62] Taxpayers and rate-payers argued that the demonstrations raised the costs they had to pay for energy and demanded money damages from the group. The Abalone Alliance contended that it could not be penalized for exercising First Amendment rights. Later, San Luis Obispo County joined the plaintiffs. That case had yet to come to trial by January 1984.

Eva Paterson, an attorney at the San Francisco Lawyers Committee for Urban Affairs, which has played a role in the defense of the NAACP, pointed out that with these lawsuits, "the right [wing] has learned the tactics we used in the 1960s." She considered this unfortunate because, in her view, "the government and the system work in their interests anyway, so these suits are icing on their cake." She sees no way to stop the filing of libel suits against political protesters: "The other side does have free speech, and you can't cut off access to the courts to people you don't like. This is one of the unpleasant side effects of democracy." [63]

POLICE LIBEL SUITS

Ana Serrano did not intend to bump into the burgeoning "blue lib" movement. All she had in mind was to stop policemen from banging a woman's head into the pavement near Twentieh and Mission Streets in San Francisco on February 12, 1981. But for intervening in the arrest, she wound up with an arm broken in two places. For talking about the incident to the *San Francisco Chronicle,* she wound up with a $2 million libel suit against her, filed by the officers whom she accused of breaking her arm.[64]

All across the nation, police have been filing suits against those who criticize them, both those who do so publicly and those who merely report to official police investigation boards. Police unions steer a member to a lawyer who takes the libel case at no cost to the officer who is suing, and they help with publicity and moral support. In fact, so many of these blue lib suits have been filed that a publication entitled *Police Plaintiff* keeps track of the litigation. "We've been encouraging our members to sue," said Billy Norton, editor of *Police Chronicle* magazine of the Boston-based International Brotherhood of Police Officers. "Where we have struck back, the number of police brutality complaints has dropped sharply." [65] This is a perfect example of the chilling effect in operation.

At issue in these cases is nothing less than free speech, including the right to criticize public officials, which historically has been the bedrock of American democracy. Let us consider, for example, the Serranos' account of what happened to them. Ana Serrano and her husband Ramon were walking along Mission Street, the main concourse of the Hispanic community in San Francisco, when they saw two policemen push a woman down on the sidewalk, then kick and beat her. Ana ran over and told the police to stop the beating. An officer shoved her hard from behind; she got so upset that she picked up a thin tabloid newspaper and threw it at him. The paper separated into pages and fluttered to the ground without hitting anyone. Then two policemen grabbed her, threw her against a parked car, and, while twisting her left arm behind her back to get handcuffs on, broke the arm in two places. Upon seeing this, Ramon ran to help her. He was grabbed by police before he could reach her, thrown into the back of a patrol car with Ana, and taken to Mission Station. Ana repeatedly told the officers to take her to the hospital because her arm was broken, but they made her wait, crying in pain, until a paramedic arrived an hour later. Half an hour after that, she was taken to the hospital, where she had to remain for four days because of her injuries. Her arm was in a cast for six months; a year later, she still could not straighten it.[66]

Now consider the police account of what happened. The officers committed no brutality. The woman they were arresting had fired a gun in a restaurant; a hostile crowd had gathered. Ana Serrano yelled obscenities and threw a book, which hit an officer in the head; while they were handcuffing her, her husband threw himself on the arresting officers, forcing them all to fall forward and thus causing the broken arm. The Serranos are not sincere in their complaint and never even filed a charge with Internal Affairs (the police investigating bureau). She received prompt medical attention. She did not stay in the hospital for days, but was seeing a lawyer the next day and was in a bank that afternoon.

After the incident, legal papers began to fly. Charges of resisting arrest and assaulting officers were filed against the Serranos. They filed an administrative claim against the city on May 19 for $88,500 for the injuries she suffered, and a complaint of excessive force against the officers with the Internal Affairs Bureau. (This was on record, despite the police denial.) The criminal charges against the Serranos were dropped after they agreed to perform twenty-five hours of community service. Then on June 30, 1981, the *San Francisco Chronicle* ran an interview with the Serranos with the headline "Woman Says Cops Broke Her Arm." A month later, the city denied the damage claim and the Serranos filed a lawsuit. A month after that, officers Kenneth Mathis and Jeffrey Levin filed a $2 million libel suit.

Ana Serrano is a small, thin, soft-spoken woman who wears large spectacles. Neither she nor her husband had a prior criminal record. She was studying to be a dental assistant when she was injured; her husband was a busboy for a Hyatt Hotel. They saw the police as aggressors. "Here in the Mission there is a lot of discrimination," explained Ramon, who like his wife is of slim build and small stature. "The police beat people up very often; they bang you around, especially near the doughnut shop at Twentieth and Mission." Ramon was disappointed at the way he and his wife were treated. "I never thought the police would be that brutal; they were not professional, but more like the police in a fascist country like Chile or El Salvador."

The police hold a similarly hostile impression of Hispanics. "These people in the Mission like to fight," said Officer Levin. "Serrano wasn't coming to help his wife. A lot of these people just like to fight. They don't control their emotions like ordinary people."

Neither officer held out hope of collecting damages from the Serranos. "I'm not going to get any money out of them," conceded Levin. "But she accused me in the newspaper of crimes. Police are not punching bags in blue. I can refute everything she said point by point." Mathis felt that the principle was what mattered. "We want our names cleared," he said. "The policeman is not looked upon too favorably by the public anyway. People have looked funny at me since that article was printed; they don't know what to believe." He also lamented the difficulties of his job. "We're expected to be model citizens. I think we get kind of screwed in a way. Just because I have this position doesn't mean I don't have a life outside. If we get found guilty of something for punitive damages, we have to pay out of our own pocket. That's what we're facing. We want our names cleared." [67]

John Prentice represents the policemen. He works for a firm called Bley and Bley, which specializes in police clients. In Prentice's view, "Policemen have historically sat on their hands, and when people have done things to them, they have been reluctant to fight back. I think that's changing now. It's a matter of maintaining the personal integrity of the police officers." [68] By contrast, the Serranos believe the libel suit was filed to silence them and other critics, and to frighten them into dropping their damage suit for Ana's injuries. Their lawyer, Dennis Riordan, pointed out that the police failed to sue the *Chronicle,* a powerful institution in San Francisco, and one that could be expected to mount a vigorous and thorough legal defense. The police might very well have been wary of antagonizing the city's largest newspaper. Riordan agreed with the Serranos that the lawsuit was filed, in part, to stop criticism of the police, particularly when citizen review of complaints against police was a major issue in city politics.[69]

Four libel cases filed by police were in San Francisco Bay Area Courts in 1981.[70] In each one, the defense lawyers claimed that even if every word spoken by the officers were true, the lawsuits still ought to be thrown out of court because a citizen's evaluation of a public official is a right protected by the First Amendment. One lawyer explained, "A police officer is not a private citizen; he or she is the cutting edge of government to most people. And in this country we have an important right of criticizing the government. The police may not like that, and I'm sure they don't, but that's the way it is." Indeed, the police and their lawyers do not like that; they disagree completely. "The First Amendment right to freedom of speech is one of our most important rights," concedes Prentice. "But it should be balanced on a scale of what inaccurate information does to people."

Amitai Schwartz, an attorney with the Northern California ACLU, elaborated on the position of the police held by the defense lawyers. "Police are not ordinary citizens. They can take away people's liberty, they can carry weapons, and in certain circumstances they can kill people. Certainly they can stand a little embarrassment. Otherwise they're in the wrong line of work." Thomas Jefferson would have liked that view. "When a man assumes a public trust, he should regard himself as public property," he wrote to a German baron in 1807.

The ACLU's Schwartz, an expert on police, either worked on or followed closely six California cases of officers charging their critics with libel. He felt that the swift entry of the ACLU into some of the cases was important because "that really raises the stakes considerably. The police know that we will fight them at every legal turn." Otherwise, he felt, the police might have been more able to intimidate the defendants.

Schwartz worried that police were (and are) trying to reduce First Amendment rights, both by filing libel suits and by changing existing law. For example, until 1982 anyone in California could file a complaint against police officers with the Internal Affairs Bureau and not be sued for what was said. But a new law allows police to sue for defamation anyone who knowingly or with ill will files a false complaint. The police officers' association, which sponsored the bill, denied it was intended to chill free expression, but rather to protect officers. Schwartz, however, contends that the new law is dangerous. "First, it creates a special category of public employee, which is strange. This only applies to peace officers. Second, if you remove the absolute privilege protecting complaint, the police will threaten to and absolutely will sue people who complain, merely by claiming the complaint was filed maliciously. To say the bill wouldn't have a chilling effect—that's absurd. A person without money would think twice before filing; he'd have to mortgage his house even to put up a defense."[71]

Their success with this bill did not appease California police; on the contrary, in 1983 a new bill was introduced that would make it a criminal offense to file a false complaint in an internal police hearing. If that bill should pass, a person complaining to the police about police misconduct would face not only the threat of a civil suit but also the possibility of criminal charges.

The first lawsuit filed by the officers against the Serranos on February 17, 1982, failed to survive an objection raised by their defense; a second complaint, on June 2, met the same fate. Finally, more than two years after the incident, the police dropped the lawsuit. But it had done its work.

Sitting in the sparsely furnished living room of their Mission District home, Ana and Ramon Serrano were asked whether they would speak up again if they saw what looked like police violence on the street. Ana looked down at the rug and answered, "I would have the feeling to interfere, but I have learned now not to. I wouldn't dare go and talk to them anymore." Ramon felt the same way. "I learned how powerless you are," he said sadly. "I don't even dare to look police in the eye anymore. I just want to be away from them."

5

Suppression of Dissent

On the surface, dissent seems to be alive and well in the United States. Large demonstrations against nuclear power or government cutbacks are so commonplace that they hardly rate more than a mention on the evening news. Books, magazines, films, and television programs openly attack government policies. Yet, a number of civil libertarians have publicly worried that the Reagan era may usher in a 1980s variant of McCarthyism. This fear is based on the recent spate of presidential statements as well as laws, executive orders, and court decisions that, if fully implemented, could combine the intimidation and blacklisting of the McCarthy era with the brutality and disruption of dissent that characterized COINTELPRO, which was an FBI operation that used infiltration, false rumors, and other dirty tricks to cause trouble in political groups from 1956 to 1971.

A number of Reagan administration actions have made opposition to its policies more difficult by using the McCarthy tactic of equating dissent with disloyalty. If you differ with us, according to this argument, you are giving aid and comfort to the enemy. Simultaneously, the censorship advocated by the religious right and the New Right gave expression to the fear that too much openness was bad for society and only made trouble. The belief grew that there ought to be some wise head with the authority to say what people could and could not know or do: the church, the father of the family, the president. Tonda Rush, an attorney at the American Newspaper Publishers Association, in Washington, D.C., noted how intolerant these attitudes were of differing points of view: "The thought processes of the right wing lead directly to dictatorship," she said. "They can take your destiny out of your hands for your own good while saying, 'You shouldn't know this; it's not good for you.' "[1]

Inhibiting dissent agrees with the agenda of the Reagan administration, since the president's policies call for increased spending on the military and on nuclear energy as well as on increased covert operations abroad. These highly controversial objectives lend themselves to the claim that they are vital to national security, and anyone who disagrees with what the president is doing is helping enemies of the United States as well as flouting duly constituted authority. Thus there has been a confluence of administrtaion and right-wing aims, a shared objective of limiting dissent and free speech in the interests of order, security, and stability.

An example of this meshing of attitudes is the nuclear freeze: The president and his administration assailed it as subversive, and so did Jerry Falwell, who planned to mobilize the Moral Majority against the movement. In such an atmosphere, an assault on the post-Watergate regulations enacted to protect dissenters and critics of government policy from retaliation and surveillance by the FBI and CIA was bound to succeed. At the same time, as we have seen, the Reagan administration has tightened government secrecy to an unprecedented degree, thus making it more difficult for the public to be informed about what is going on and therefore correspondingly less able to comment or protest.

The Reagan administration tries to suppress dissent from the public and also from critics within the government. By attempting to manipulate federal funds, it tries to silence groups that disagree with its policies. Whether or not in concert with these actions, the Internal Revenue Service conducts audits of nonprofit groups known to oppose the president's policies, spreading the fear that the IRS will harass those who try to speak out freely.

THE SENATE SUBCOMMITTEE ON SECURITY AND TERRORISM

The phenomenon of the early 1980s that has most revived fears of McCarthyism is the Senate Subcommittee on Security and Terrorism (SST) established under the chairmanship of Jeremiah Denton, a Republican from Alabama. A prisoner of war for seven and one-half years in North Vietnam, the ultrapatriotic Denton staunchly believes that the Soviet KGB backs domestic political opponents of the Reagan administration and that terrorism is one of the most important problems facing the United States today. Politically active people fear a witch hunt in which dissenters would be branded not only as pro-Soviet but also as proterrorist. If the subcommittee can forge links between terrorism and dissent, or between foreign influences and dissent, it might try to lay the groundwork for discrediting domestic opposition to administration policies. In a talk before the National Network of Grantmakers on September 23, 1981, Kathy Engel, then director of the Fund for Open Information and Accountability, Inc., in New York spoke of this danger:

> Terrorism becomes an excuse, then, for developing a repressive mechanism to be used against those who oppose administration policies. It becomes an excuse for breaking into houses, tapping telephones, infiltrating meetings, investigating progressive organizations, telling lies, withholding passports, withholding government documents and, in essence, taking away civil liberties, civil rights and keeping government activities secret. Terrorism is the new bugaboo.[2]

Senator Denton is viewed as both ridiculous and frightening. "He's a far-right crazed guy who's trying to make America like a POW camp, that's his ideal. He is viewed as a nut," said a congressional committee staff counsel. The born-again Denton advocated the death penalty for adulterers and proposed legislation requiring citizens of communist nations to obtain written permission before attending sessions of Congress. But the very existence of his subcommittee, which numbers among its members Senators John East of North Carolina, also considered a member of the far right, and Orrin Hatch of Utah, chief antagonist of the Freedom of Information Act, and as initial staff counsel Dr. Samuel Francis, a policy analyst with the Heritage Foundation, is disturbing. The alarm heightened after a Hatch aide predicted before the Reagan election that the subcommittee would investigate the North American Congress on Latin America, known for its criticism of U.S. policies, *Mother Jones,* the muckraking California magazine, and the Institute for Policy Studies, a left-liberal think tank in Washington, D.C.

Dr. Francis presented in *Human Events,* a major right-wing tabloid, a main concern of the subcommittee:

> One goal of the new Subcommittee should be to show that modern terrorism is not simply limited to violence, atrocity, and fear that gain headlines. Terrorism as a weapon of political warfare, also has an important nonviolent dimension that consists of propaganda, the garnering of support for the terrorists and their causes, legal and financial support and operational assistance.[3]

Francis wrote the intelligence section of the Heritage Foundation's recommendations to the Reagan administration, advocating increased monitoring of dissent and giving national security priority over civil liberties.

Victor Navasky, editor of *The Nation* and author of a book on the

McCarthy era, speculated that the subcommittee would not, like the old House Committee on Un-American Activities, smear dissent by association with former communists, but would instead encourage state and local Red squads and vigilante groups seeking to repress dissent. Further, Navasky speculated, the subcommittee, by associating dissent with terrorism, would give legitimacy to a new series of operations like COINTELPRO, whose purpose was to break up groups that advocated social change and whose methods violated both the letter and the spirit of U.S. law.[4] The subcommittee's most vocal members, Denton and East, have not hesitated to label groups procommunist or to associate them with the KGB. In fact, the first group to be castigated, the antinuclear Mobilization for Survival, was labeled an affiliate of a "Soviet-front" group.

Despite a statement by FBI Director William Webster that "there is no real evidence of Soviet sponsored terrorism within the United States," the subcommittee held its second hearing on that topic, in April 1981.[5] Apparently to strengthen the subcommittee's thesis, FBI statistics that showed that terrorist acts had actually declined from 111 in 1977 to 29 in 1980 were revised upward, by the addition of "threats" of terrorism, thus increasing the numbers to a level more satisfactory to Denton. Denton reported a 20 percent increase in incidents of domestic terrorism from 1981 to 1982.

The subcommittee's activities during 1981 and 1982—a total of twenty-seven hearings in the 97th Congress—concerned the FBI, Cuban involvement in the international drug traffic, Soviet influence over the antiapartheid African National Congress, and relationships between terrorist groups. These activities garnered considerable news coverage and contributed to concerns that domestic political groups would be subjected to hostile, redbaiting hearings. But those did not take place. The subcommittee contented itself with advocating increased powers for law enforcement, most often with mutually congratulatory exchanges between Senators East and Denton and whatever law enforcement officials they had called as witnesses.

In the summer of 1982, for example, the subcommittee held hearings on the Levi guidelines for the FBI, instituted in 1976 after the Watergate revelations of FBI and other agency misdeeds. FBI Director William Webster focused on problems posed by free speech in his opening statement:

> One of the more troublesome issues in domestic security matters is how to respond to persons or groups who advocate illegal conduct. The question is whether words, unaccompanied by conduct, can be the subject of an investigation. We must be careful, of course, to preserve the right of free speech and to insure that investigations are not used in a way that

would inhibit statements that present no serious threat to society. That is not to say that statements alone, particularly statements that advocate criminal violence, or indicate an apparent intent or ability to engage in violence, are protected against investigation.[6]

Denton made his views even clearer: "I have serious reservations and concerns that the present view of an unfettered, unrestricted first amendment may not be promoting the general welfare." Denton also warned that "propaganda, disinformation and 'legal assistance' groups" may be "even more dangerous than those who throw the bombs." He singled out the National Lawyers Guild for opprobrium. An association of liberal and left-wing lawyers, the guild has been active for more than forty years in promoting such causes as civil rights, union organizing, and peace. In Denton's view, the guild "seeks to exploit the law in order to bring about revolutionary change." He accused the Guild of providing logistical support to Soviet- and Cuban-backed terrorist groups.[7]

East explained why legitimate political activity should be subject to investigation by the FBI:

The conduct of subversion itself consists in large measure in the utilization of legal activities to undermine, or to make illicit use of legally permissible activities and legally established institutions. . . . Hence front groups (widely used by both Nazi and Communist groups), terrorist support apparatuses, and propaganda apparatuses seek to make use of legal channels and activities and of unwitting individuals exercising legal rights to achieve goals that are ultimately destructive of legality.[8]

He advocated giving the FBI the right to maintain limitless investigations of political activities. He maintained that since such investigations would not be conducted for prosecution, but merely for intelligence, no guilt would be implied, and no harm, presumably, done to anyone's liberties.

Two witnesses who received accolades from Denton and East were W. Mark Felt and Edward S. Miller, the FBI agents convicted of conducting an illegal burglary in the course of an investigation of the Weather Underground and then pardoned by the president. Miller expressed his fear of dissent in the conclusion of his statement to the subcommittee:

How much dissent and revolutionary talk can we really stand in a healthy country? Revolutions always start in a small way. Economic conditions are bad, the credibility of government is low. These are the things that the homegrown revolutionary is monitoring very closely. The FBI's atten-

> tion must be focused on these various situations. If it were not, the Bureau would not be doing its job for the American people. The American people do not want to have to worry about the security of their country. We must be able to find out what stage the revolution is in.[9]

Denton shared Miller's view that domestic intelligence collection ought not to be governed by the same restrictions as criminal investigations—they ought to be broader. And if such monitoring failed to result in prosecutions, no matter—the bureau would know what was going on. A year later, Denton urged the FBI to focus on "organizations and individuals that cannot be shown to be controlled by a foreign power, and have not yet committed a terrorist act but which nonetheless may present a substantial threat to the safety of Americans and, ultimately, to the security of our country. These subversive groups seem to have 'slipped through the cracks.' " The senator seemed ready to label as "subversive" groups and individuals who have given no indication of wrongdoing whatsoever. He pointed out potential sources of such "subversion," saying, "In the future, the enemies of society" may be found among groups opposing nuclear power and racism, and among groups favoring prison reform, civil rights, and a nuclear weapons freeze.[10] The Big Brother aspect of these thoughts seems never to have crossed the senator's mind.

One other disturbing aspect of the Denton-East distrust of political activity was exemplified in the testimony given by a police detective from Los Angeles, the head of its bomb squad, Arleigh McCree. Denton mentioned during the hearing that Tom Hayden was considering running for the U.S. Senate. McCree characterized Hayden as "one of the founders of the SDS which, of course, evolved into the Weather Underground Organization. So I think that puts him in his proper perspective." [11] If McCree had been speaking ten years earlier, his words might not have been so misleading. But for many years, Hayden had been an impeccable member of the Democratic party's liberal wing and a familiar figure in California politics. The imputation of violence was completely unwarranted, and gave a chilling view of Denton's willingness to accept inaccurate appraisals of those who hold different political views.

After the hearings, the Reagan administration promulgated new FBI guidelines in agreement with the subcommittee's concerns. But thus far, the subcommittee has not subpoenaed politically active people and subjected them to cross-examination about their activities, with attendant implications of disloyalty. Some political observers believe that Denton and East are so politically isolated that they have little credibility. Nonetheless, politically active groups, especially those that have been singled out for opprobrium by the subcommittee, are concerned about the possibility that such hearings may yet take place.

THE NUCLEAR FREEZE MOVEMENT

Perhaps the major political movement of the early 1980s in the United States and Western Europe is the nuclear freeze. Millions of men, women, and children have demonstrated in many nations to halt the spread of nuclear weapons and reverse the arms race. An extraordinary coalition of groups and individuals took up this cause in the United States. By late 1982, 11 state legislatures, 56 county councils, and 446 New England town meetings had voted to endorse the freeze; more than 2.3 million people signed petitions in its favor.[12]

Religious bodies, representing Protestants, Jews, Catholics, Unitarians, and others favored the freeze, as did groups of scientists, teachers, doctors, lawyers, and women. Labor unions and some former military officers supported it, as did former CIA Director William Colby and many members of Congress. The largest demonstration in the history of New York City took place on June 12, 1982, when nearly a million rallied as the United Nations special session on disarmament began. The arms race troubled many, many people, who lobbied, sang, signed petitions, and wrote endlessly to their representatives in favor of a mutually verifiable halt to the manufacture and development of nuclear weapons.

This unprecedented popular protest drew common responses from the Reagan administration and the right wing, which unleashed a series of statements portraying the freeze movement as KGB inspired and, perhaps unwittingly, unpatriotic. In doing this the administration repeated history, for during World War I, President Woodrow Wilson authorized the dissemination of allegations that German spies were everywhere, and the State Department used selective information to "prove" that Germany, the enemy, was funding American pacifist organizations.[13]

The antifreeze rhetoric reached a climax in the fall of 1982, just before the November elections. On September 29, Jeremiah Denton took the floor of the Senate to oppose a resolution for a "national peace day" on October 10. He said this measure was "set up by those who are foreign to our interests," alleging that the advisory council of a group called Peace Links included members of two organizations "which have been publicly identified as, or linked by the Department of State with, Soviet controlled front organizations." He referred to Women Strike for Peace and Women's International League for Peace and Freedom, and labeled groups to which other members of the council belonged "radical left-oriented." Having a peace day, he said, "undermines our position in the disarmament negotiations." Groups like Peace Links, founded by Betty Bumpers, wife of Arkansas Senator Dale Bumpers, he said, "lend themselves to exploitation by the Soviet Union." [14]

Denton repeated the charges two days later, inserting into the *Congressional Record* no less than forty-five pages of reports, articles, and other material denigrating the freeze movement, its members, and activist groups. Among these articles was one by *Reader's Digest* Senior Editor John Barron, linking the KGB with peace groups. (One liberal organization, the Campaign for Political Rights, promptly capitalized on what had become known as the Denton Enemies List, so named for its predecessor in the Nixon White House, by inviting them all to a big fund-raising party to honor Peace Links and other activists for disarmament.) A few days later, President Reagan got into the act by telling the Ohio Veterans Organization that the nuclear freeze movement "is inspired by, not the sincere and honest people who want peace, but by some who want the weakening of America and so are manipulating many honest and sincere people." Later on, after receiving considerable criticism for these remarks, the president explained that he was not referring to *Americans* who wanted the weakening of America. Presumably, he was referring to the Soviets.

The October 6 *Washington Post* editorialized against the Reagan and Denton attacks on the freeze movement, but only halfheartedly. While conceding that Peace Links had the right to include whomever it wanted, the *Post* wondered, "Why does Peace Links abide the taint that even the slightest connection to a Soviet stooge group imparts?" After swift and vigorous responses from the woman's peace groups and the ACLU, the *Post* dropped its reference to "Soviet stooge groups," but again, less than wholeheartedly. In an editorial on October 9, the paper admitted that "the available public record" did not support its charge of being a "Soviet front." But, the editorial continued, members of Women's International League and Women Strike for Peace had participated in activities with international groups dominated by the Soviet Union. Further, it warned, "Moscow often seeks to exploit Western citizens who, as private individuals, enter issue-oriented forums in which the Soviet bloc participants, while claiming to be otherwise, are creatures of the KGB." With this phrase, the *Post* echoed Senators Denton and East.

The two women's peace groups attacked the *Post*'s charges of Soviet domination and spoke up for their freedom to work with all people for disarmament without attracting McCarthy-like smears. The ACLU responded with an ironic letter to the editor of the *Washington Post* wondering whether peace groups should impose loyalty tests on those with whom they worked, or should consult with Senator Denton before working with a particular group. "Will the *Post* publish its own list [of suspect groups]?" the letter asked, and continued, "Joseph McCarthy used innuendo and guilt by association. Let us not have that again."[15]

But the innuendoes continued. At a press conference on November 11, Reagan was asked if he had evidence of foreign involvement in the U.S. peace movement. He answered, "Plenty." The next day, Deputy White House Press Secretary Larry Speakes mentioned two State Department reports on Soviet infiltration of the peace movement and noted three magazine articles on the subject, including the October *Reader's Digest.* The FBI confirmed the accuracy of the president's remarks about "Soviet attempts to influence the peace movement." But New York Senator Daniel Moynihan of the Senate Select Intelligence Committee asserted that "there has never been from any of the intelligence agencies—any part of that community—the least suggestion . . . that Soviet influences were behind the nuclear freeze movement."[16] Congressman Don Edwards, Democrat of California and a former FBI agent, took the FBI to task for supporting the president without presenting evidence. "Ambiguous half-truths and innuendo must not be left to poison public debate on this important national issue," he wrote FBI Director William Webster.[17]

In December 1982, Reagan continued his theme. "All I'm saying is that one must look to see whether, well-intentioned though it may be, this [freeze] movement might be carrying water that they're not aware of, for another purpose. Incidentally, the first man who proposed the nuclear freeze was . . . Leonid Brezhnev."[18] Yet a few days later, the chair of the House Permanent Select Intelligence Committee, which had investigated Soviet influence on the freeze, announced that it was not to be found. "Soviet agents," said Congressman Edward Boland, "have had no significant influence on the nuclear freeze movement. The bottom line is that the hearings provide no evidence that the Soviets direct, manage, or manipulate the nuclear freeze movement."[19]

What was the evidence on which the president, Denton, and the other accusers relied? It began with John Rees, who has made a career out of challenging movements for social change. According to Rees, a person whom he could not identify said that the Women's International League for Peace and Freedom was a Soviet-affiliated group. He had no other proof. "Let's have WILPF show they're not [a front]" was his answer. He also noted that WILPF cooperated with a Soviet front group, the World Peace Council.[20] WILPF acknowledged that both groups sometimes attend the same meetings. But attending the same meetings falls far short of domination of one group by the other.

Despite the lack of proof, the allegations had considerable impact. They were first published in the conservative press, John Birch Society handouts, and *Congressional Record* inserts placed there by the late Congressman Larry McDonald of Georgia, known for his right-wing diatribes against political activists. The allegations spread to articles in the *Wall Street Journal, Barron's,* and the *Reader's Digest.* Then Denton took them to the Senate floor with his charges that "the KGB's involvement in the so-called peace movement is well documented." [21]

Even though the *Washington Post* concluded that the State Department reports on which it had based its editorial did not constitute documentation for its charges about "Soviet stooges," the White House cited those reports to back up the president's accusations. But nothing in the reports showed Soviet domination of the U.S. freeze movement. In April 1983, FBI Director Webster exonerated the freeze movement, saying he found no evidence of "active measures" by the Soviets that influenced its course.

Despite these findings, Reagan continued his redbaiting unabashed. In a speech to Christian fundamentalists in March, he exhorted the audience to take part in the battle of good against the communist evil, turning up the fire and brimstone rhetoric as the band played "Onward Christian Soldiers" and the flags waved. After that, he made headlines as the debate over funding the MX missile peaked in Congress. "Reagan Sees Crude Red Hand on MX Voting," blared the headlines of a *San Francisco Examiner* article about the sinister Soviet influence on those who opposed this hugely expensive addition to our stock of armaments.

Even though the allegations and smears have not stood up to examination, they have been widely circulated. There is no way of knowing how many people did not join the freeze because of the *Washington Post* editorial, which was reprinted in other publications, or the president's comments. The smears provided a divisive element that slowed the momentum of the freeze movement and hampered the formation of a broad coalition. More seriously, the smears opened an avenue to the repression of the movement. They provided an apparent justification, even though a spurious one, for FBI or CIA infiltration and surveillance of peace groups. If the government can show that it has reason to believe that an organization or individual is an "agent of a foreign power," it can use break-ins, wiretaps, and other intrusive techniques against the group. As the history of such surveillance shows all too well, agents supposedly monitoring the group turn readily to infiltration and disruptive measures designed to diminish its effectiveness.

The smears also poisoned the debate about disarmament, which is widely considered to be the most important issue of our age and deserves to be considered on its own merits, not as a test of patriotism. If the two major powers on the earth are to reach agreement to disarm, the negotiations must proceed on the basis of facts. While attention should be paid to Soviet efforts to snare technological information and to clear attempts at espionage, mindless opposition to all things espoused by the Soviet Union does not aid the cause of peace.

Edward J. O'Malley, FBI assistant director for intelligence, testified before the House Permanent Select Committee on Intelligence on July 14, 1982; his words had ominous implications for dissent:

> Soviet political influence operations are designed to cultivate contacts with political, business, academic, and journalistic leaders, and secure their collaboration. This does not necessarily require the actual recruitment of the individual; only his cooperation. Typically, the Soviets will play upon such themes as peace, disarmament, detente, and peaceful coexistence to secure this cooperation. . . . The major objective of these exercises is to inject the Soviet force into foreign government, political, business, labor and academic dialogue in a non-attributable or at least non-official manner.[22]

O'Malley said that the Soviets were aware that the U.S. Communist party (CPUSA) was vulnerable to FBI infiltration, and therefore they were instead going after "collaborators," who might well be ordinary citizen peace activists. Thus, the FBI would have to spread a far bigger net to catch subversives than mere investigation of communist and leftist organizations. Ordinary people speaking out in favor of disarmament, according to O'Malley's logic, might be advocating Soviet policy rather than American. As Alexander Cockburn and James Ridgeway noted, "The logic shown by O'Malley clearly tilts toward involving [citizen activists] in criminality. . . . In the O'Malley scheme of things, speech is propaganda, and propaganda can be a crime." [23]

UNLEASHING THE AGENCIES

The fear of political activity that marked both the activities of the Senate Subcommittee on Security and Terrorism and the smearing of the nuclear freeze movement found legal expression in edicts issued by the Reagan administration. The administration altered the rules governing the FBI and the CIA in a way that made government repression of dissent not only possible but easy. The theory underlying this "unleashing" of the FBI and the CIA, as critics called the new rules, holds that a sort of continuum exists from peaceful political activity on one end to terrorism on the other—from the League of Women Voters, for example, to the Weather Underground. At any moment, according to the theory, a legitimate political group might move into violence, and extraordinary measures must therefore be enacted to prevent such violence from occurring.

President Reagan's Executive Order 12333, on intelligence, signed on December 4, 1981, gave the CIA a number of powers that could be utilized to monitor and disrupt domestic political activity. The order permitted the agency to conduct counterintelligence or counterterrorist investigations within the United Sates, and, if approved by the attorney general, to use any intelligence technique against a foreign power or an agent of a foreign power (which might be a group acting in solidarity with a Central American nation, for example). In a provision eroding the historic prohibition against the agency's assuming an internal security function, the CIA was permitted in some circumstances to assist local law enforcement agencies.

The presidential order created an expansive catchall; agents may "conduct special activities approved by the president." "Special activities" means covert actions. While such actions are not supposed to be undertaken with the intent to influence U.S. political processes, public opinion, policies, or the media, there is no protection in the order against the possibility that they might. Furthermore, in accordance with certain procedures, undercover CIA agents are now permitted to participate in domestic political organizations; with some exceptions, such agents are not to participate for the purpose of influencing the activity of the group but, again, should that happen, there are no protections.

What these provisions mean is that the CIA can use intrusive surveillance of Americans at home and abroad, even though they are not suspected of breaking the law. The agency can use "pretext interviews" to gain "significant" foreign intelligence from Americans. "Foreign intelligence," by the CIA's definition, could concern private organizations, companies, and persons, as well as foreign governments. As explained by ACLU attorneys, this means that if an American had traveled to Nicaragua and, on his or her return, declined to speak with the CIA about what he or she had learned, an agent could pose as a reporter or professor, attend a private meeting, and get the information surreptitiously. Since much domestic political opposition in the 1980s is related to U.S. foreign policy—in Central America, in Europe, in Asia—it is easy for the CIA to claim that participants in such opposition are agents of a foreign power. That unlocks the door to agency surveillance and the possibility of disruptive actions.

Michael Ratner, an attorney with the Center for Constitutional Rights in New York City, assisted with the preparation of an unsuccessful lawsuit to have the executive order declared unconstitutional. He said, "The [order] gives the agencies permission to investigate and disrupt merely on a hunch, or on the basis of unreliable information. No criminal conduct or even the possibility of a violation of the law is required. There is clear intent to make groups engaging in lawful solidarity work around El Salvador, Namibia, Palestine and Cuba subject to investigation. Even a visit to the U.N. could trigger surveillance." [24] In the *New York Times* ACLU legislative counsel Jerry Berman also expressed concern about the combination of censorship with expanded CIA power:

> First, the Administration wants to expand on the CIA's authority to spy on Americans and violate their rights, then it wants to make it more difficult to find out about what it is doing. . . . All together, the proposals raise troubling questions about what the Administration is up to.

There is a historical basis for these apprehensions: The government justified its interference in civil rights and antiwar organizing in the sixties and seventies on the basis of illusory foreign influence; the FBI even wiretapped Dr. Martin Luther King, Jr., alleging a communist connection.

The changes in the FBI guidelines were announced on May 7, 1983, by Attorney General William French Smith. The new rules permitted the FBI to launch a full-scale investigation of a group whose statements "advocate criminal activity or indicate an apparent intent to engage in crime." This constitutes a rather broad license, since it can apply to groups advocating draft resistance, civil disobedience in antinuclear or civil rights demonstrations, and other peaceful means of protest. Congressman Don Edwards, a former FBI agent and now chair of the House Subcommittee on Civil and Constitutional Rights, criticized the new guidelines. "The Supreme Court has made it clear that mere advocacy is not enough to warrant prosecution, yet the FBI wants to investigate speeches," he said, complaining that such investigations "chill legitimate First Amendment activity." [25] Excerpts from a newsletter, phrases from a speech, plans discussed at a meeting, and comments made by group members may be examined wholly out of the context in which they were made and combined in such a way as to supply a basis for investigation.

After lobbying from civil liberties groups, the Department of Justice issued clarifications of the guidelines, saying that advocacy would be investigated only in the event of a "credible threat" of harm or an apparent intent to commit a crime. The clarification also stated that infiltration of groups would be conducted only in "compelling circumstances" and only with high-level approval.

Throughout the new guidelines runs a thread of concern that violence, "serious disruption of society," or damage to "substantial property interests" must not occur. Those seem like unimpeachable goals, and under a different administration or different circumstances might well be. But even as civil rights activists under the Hoover FBI were labeled subversive and peace activists now are labeled dupes of the KGB, there is the possibility that groups organized to oppose the use of nuclear power, for instance, or to oppose the draft will be similarly labeled and considered to be serious disrupters of society.

Curiously, the new FBI guidelines do not apply to the entire United States. A month after they were announced, a federal judge deciding a lawsuit over political spying in Chicago overturned the provision permitting the FBI to investigate a group because it advocated illegal activity. Judge Susan Getzendanner issued a permanent injunction barring investigations based on a group's exercise of free speech or assembly unless there was evidence that actual lawbreaking was likely or intended. A columnist for the *Chicago Tribune,* Stephen Chapman, analyzing the judge's action, concluded:

> There is reason to suspect that the administration may be more interested in discouraging radical dissent than in attacking terrorism. The old guidelines have worked well to protect the constitutional rights of Americans, and no one has offered credible evidence that they impair legitimate FBI work. The new ones are liable to sacrifice those rights while doing little for law enforcement. If President Reagan values individual freedom as highly as he claims, he should take the judge's cue to scrap the guidelines.

The Reagan administration and the right wing confuse free speech and dissent with propaganda and disloyalty. Now, the FBI and CIA guidelines open the door to monitoring and disruption of those who exercise their rights to dissent. As this book goes to press, activists wonder whether or not agents are infiltrating their organizations.

The decision by Judge Getzendanner may appeal to the minds of activists and other citizens concerned with preserving their rights of speech and assembly, but other courts have been moving in the opposite direction, more in accord with the goals of the Reagan administration. On September 21, 1982, the U.S. Court of Appeals for the District of Columbia decided that victims of the CIA's disruptive Operation CHAOS were not entitled to the information needed to pursue damage suits against the agency for violating their civil rights.[26] Upholding the government's "state secret" privilege, the court said the antiwar activists were not entitled to learn details of the operation. A week after that decision, a federal appeals court ruled on September 28 that the CIA can refuse to confirm or deny the presence of CIA informants at particular universities. Nathan Gardels, in 1976 a student at the University of California at Los Angeles, filed a Freedom of Information Act request to learn whether CIA informants were present on campus. In deciding the case, the court said, "To admit that the CIA had such contacts at this university would allow foreign intelligence agencies to zero in and identify . . . the nature of those relationships or with whom." [27]

On October 21, 1982, the U.S. Court of Appeals for the Sixth Circuit ruled that the National Security Agency can provide information about U.S. citizens to law enforcement agencies, even if the information was obtained without a warrant.[28] The NSA, a vast, secret intelligence apparatus, monitors communications with highly sophisticated computers. Messages are intercepted in apparent contravention of the Fourth Amendment prohibitions against unreasonable search and seizure even when no criminal activity is alleged against the sender or recipient. An Arab-American activist named Abdeen Jabara filed suit against this policy, claiming the government violated his constitutional rights by intercepting his communications and giving them to the FBI. John Shattuck, the ACLU lawyer who represented Jabara, said that it was "difficult to imagine a more sweeping judicial approval of a governmental action in violation of constitutional rights than the decision of the panel in this case." [29]

In contrast to these decisions was a federal district court ruling forbidding government restrictions on those who hold dissident opinions. The case involved Dorothy Blitz, a member of the Communist Workers party, who in 1982 was denied permission to complete a bricklaying course in the federally funded CETA work-training program because she refused to sign a loyalty oath. The oath, mandated by an amendment tacked on to a congressional appropriation bill in reaction to Blitz's initial participation in the program, asked applicants to swear they did not advocate, or had not advocated within the past five years, the violent overthrow of the government. Blitz, who had begun the program before the passage of this restriction, left to have a baby and was subsequently denied permission to reenroll. She sued.

The federal court ruled that she could not be barred from the program because of her political beliefs.[30] The Justice Department appealed. In January 1983 the U.S. Supreme Court declined to hear the case but vacated the judgment of the lower court over the protests of the ACLU attorneys representing Blitz. This meant that the lower court decision stood but did not set a binding precedent. Despite the high court's action, advocates of free speech were relieved that the only court to judge the merits of the *Blitz* decision had found it unconstitutional.

Each legal decision discussed above except *Blitz* has reinforced the principles embodied in President Reagan's executive orders on intelligence and national security. Orders and court decisions have been used to build a wall around ideas and information and then extended to subtle but steady attacks against people who challenge those walls. Each brick of security tapped into place blocks out another citizen and chills another voice.

DR. PETER INFANTE: A SCIENTIST UNDER SIEGE

When the letter arrived, it was already after five on a Thursday afternoon in June 1981. Dr. Peter Infante, the forty-year-old director of the Office of Carcinogen Identification and Classification in the Occupational Safety and Health Administration (OSHA) was, as usual, still at his desk. As a government scientist, Infante evaluated the dangers that chemicals pose to the health of American workers. Every year, according to congressional estimates, twenty to sixty thousand workers die as a result of work place carcinogens.

Infante had attained a remarkable record of public service: He had been a consultant with the World Health Organization and an epidemiologist in the Ohio Department of Health, and, for the past six years, had played key roles in OSHA's decisions to regulate fourteen chemicals as work place carcinogens. In each case, extensive tests had been done on rats and mice, then checked against other tests. After this process, a regulation was issued barring or limiting the use of the unsafe substance in the work place. Infante was known as an outspoken advocate of regulating carcinogens and a friend of the worker.

Industry, however, did not consider him a friend. Every time a chemical was regulated as a carcinogen, it cost the companies time and money to replace it or take adequate precautions in using it. In fact, protests from the formaldehyde industry had lately become increasingly shrill as OSHA moved toward regulating that dangerous substance. Formaldehyde had been shown to be carcinogenic in mice, and thus was labeled a "potential carcinogen" in humans. Industry's protests to this had found a sympathetic ear in the Reagan administration. Since the advent of the supply-siders to Washington, OSHA's regulatory efforts, begun under the previous administration, had slowed to a snail's pace. Even so, as Infante opened and read the letter, his bushy eyebrows rose above his wire-rim frames: He was being accused of "insubordination" and "misrepresenting the position of OSHA." [31]

Several months earlier, Infante had written a letter. Upon reviewing a report of the International Agency for Research on Cancer (IARC), a multinational agency that researches the causes of cancer and is partly funded by the U.S. government, he was surprised to see that IARC had failed to consider key data on the carcinogenicity of formaldehyde, an apparent violation of its own procedures. He wondered whether the IARC working group on formaldehyde had considered these data; had it done so, he believed, it would have concluded that formaldehyde was considerably more of a threat to the human beings who had to handle it. With this concern in mind, he wrote IARC Director Dr. John Higginson that "according to IARC criteria, there appears to have been sufficient experimental evidence at the time of the working group meeting to regard formaldehyde as carcinogenic in animals. . . . I feel it is in the best interests of the scientific, public health, and industrial community that IARC reconsider its evaluation to be consistent with the IARC criteria." Infante concluded, "I would hope that you give full consideration to this request in light of the magnitude of occupational and environmental exposure to this substance."

As government scientists frequently do, Infante expressed his views on official OSHA letterhead. He attached a copy of a *Current Information Bulletin* (*CIB*) on formaldehyde, which he described as a "U.S. Department of Health and Human Services publication" containing studies on the carcinogenicity of formaldehyde. The *CIB* had been approved by OSHA under the Carter administration.

Perhaps Higginson felt upstaged, or simply insulted. In any event, he quickly fired off a biting response to Infante, rebuffing the suggestions that IARC had failed to follow its own criteria and that it should have considered the *CIB*. "I would add that your letter, its content and style, also its wide dissemination, could be interpreted as an attempt by OSHA to influence a working party of the Agency, and to cast aspersions on the scientific integrity and objectivity of its members whose reputations are internationally recognized," Higginson replied. Higginson also complained to Infante's boss, Thorne G. Auchter, who had been appointed by President Reagan as assistant secretary of labor for OSHA.

Things might have ended there. But the Formaldehyde Institute, the lobbying arm of the massive formaldehyde industry, had also obtained a copy of Infante's message to Higginson. The IARC study carried important implications for the Institute. If the working group concluded that there was only minimal evidence that formaldehyde causes cancer in human beings, then the institute would have a powerful weapon to wield against any OSHA attempts to regulate it in the United States. But if IARC agreed with the vast bulk of scientific opinion that formaldehyde was quite likely a dangerous human carcinogen, the threat of regulation would be that much greater. The institute's concern over this, and over possible interference by an outside scientist like Infante, was spelled out in an internal institute memo written only weeks before the controversy began. The memo decried Infante's past testimony on the ill effects of formaldehyde and concluded, "It is imperative that IARC remain unencumbered and independent of the activities of regulatory agencies. . . . Preliminary drafts from IARC have actually concluded that there is limited evidence for the carcinogenicity of formaldehyde in experimental animals." [32]

Infante had realized some of the institute's worst fears by voicing a scientific criticism of the IARC assessment. The institute's chief lobbyist, S. John Byington, a former member of the Consumer Product Safety Commission, took the offensive with a hand-delivered, acerbic missive to Auchter's special assistant, Mark Cowan. "How do you control members of the bureaucracy who seem to be operating freely within and without government and who seem to have made a decision and are now advocating a position rather than processing information for the appropriate policy decision makers?" Byington demanded in the first paragraph.[33] He cited Infante's letter to the IARC and another scientist's efforts to participate in the IARC review. "The Formaldehyde Institute questions whether it is appropriate for these government officials with an active predisposition towards government regulation of formaldehyde to insist on participation in an independent international scientific organization of the stature of IARC," Byington concluded. "Would you be so kind as to provide guidance as to OSHA's policies on these matters so that we might properly respond to our client?"

Less than a month later, OSHA's answer to the Formaldehyde Institute's question came in the form of the late afternoon letter to Infante from his boss, OSHA Director of Health Standards Bailus Walker. Walker charged that Infante's comments to the IARC "constitute an act of insubordination which cannot be tolerated." Walker specifically accused Infante of misrepresenting the position of OSHA by endorsing the *CIB* on formaldehyde and the tests on which the information in the *CIB* was based.

Infante hired an attorney, David Vladeck, counsel with the Public Citizen Litigation Group in Washington, D.C. Vladeck was familiar with both the scientific issues and personnel matters entangled in this case. His analysis pointed to only one conclusion: At the behest of the Formaldehyde Institute, the Reagan administration's political appointees at OSHA were attempting not only to stifle Infante's First Amendment right to discuss public issues but also to intimidate other scientists and regulators. Here was a clear conflict between political policy and unfettered scientific debate.

In a brief for Infante's defense, Vladeck countered the charges. The doctor was not guilty of "insubordination" at all by writing to the IARC but was merely doing his job. Infante's job description specifically stated that he is to maintain "technical liaison with national and international agencies . . . and research organizations on matters relating to health standards development." Moreover, IARC's charter invites participation by scientists such as Infante. "Anyone who is aware of published data that may alter the evaluation of the carcinogen risk of a chemical for humans is encouraged to make this information available to the Division of Chemical and Biologic Carcinogens, IARC . . . in order that the chemicals may be considered for reevaluation by a future working group." The charge that Infante had endorsed a *CIB* that he knew OSHA had repudiated seemed bogus, because just three months earlier Dr. Walker himself had recommended to Auchter that ten thousand copies of that *CIB* be distributed as part of an effort to reduce worker exposure to formaldehyde.

Congressman Albert Gore (D-Tenn.), chairman of the Subcommittee on Investigation and Oversight of the House Committee on Science and Technology, heard of the controversy over Infante. Coincidentally, his subcommittee had scheduled two days of hearings on the national toxicology program,[34] to begin on July 16, 1981—just weeks after the Infante incident was reported by the press. On the first day, five top government scientists confirmed the data in the controversial *CIB,* testifying that formaldehyde poses a cancer risk to humans. The second day focused on the proposed firing of Infante, and was marked by several heated exchanges between Gore and OSHA officials. Some subcommittee members actually threatened to remove Auchter physically from the witness table, where he had stationed himself. One congressman called Auchter's behavior "an attempt to boldly intimidate this committee and the witnesses."

Dr. Bailus Walker was the first to testify; he had already made plans to leave OSHA to become director of public health in Michigan. Under questioning from subcommittee members, Walker became a strong witness for Infante, even though he had signed the proposal for his dismissal. Walker revealed that he actually agreed with the data in the *CIB* on formaldehyde that Infante had sent to IARC. He could think of no scientist in OSHA who disagreed with the *CIB.* When he was asked who had decided that the *CIB* data were not valid, he replied, "I don't recall specifically whether it was Mr. Cowan or Mr. Auchter. But the decision above my level was made." Walker also said he had never instructed Infante not to refer to the *CIB.* And as for the fact that Infante had written the IARC on OSHA stationery, Walker explained that he, too, under previous administrations had expressed his personal views on agency letterhead to scientific organizations.

During Walker's testimony, Gore produced a confidential memo that subcommittee staff had unearthed in OSHA files. Entitled"Memorandum for Thorne Auchter from Mark Cowan, Subject: Formaldehyde," it said:

> I met this morning with individuals representing the Formaldehyde Institute, who presented me with what I consider to be significant evidence leading to the conclusion that the Current Intelligence Bulletin ought not at present be released.

Cowan and Auchter were not scientists; nor were they institute lobbyists. Although Walker had told Cowan that he believed formaldehyde should be treated as carcinogenic, Cowan had insisted that there were questions about the quality of the data in the *CIB*. Cowan did not tell Walker where his questions came from, Walker testified. "Well, it appears that the Formaldehyde Institute engineered a decision in the agency by people who are not scientists to change the agency's view of the scientific data on formaldehyde," Gore concluded. "And then when a scientist had the temerity to express that same scientific data, the Formaldehyde Institute complained."

OSHA Chief Auchter and his special assistant Mark Cowan next took the stand together. Auchter claimed that he was not familiar with Infante's dismissal notice, and stated—in direct contradiction of Walker's testimony—that he did not order Walker to send the dismissal. Gore asked Cowan whether he personally doubted the *CIB*'s scientific conclusion that formaldehyde was a potential cancer-causing agent in humans. "I personally am not able to judge that information," Cowan answered, "as you know that I am not a scientist."

Gore turned to Auchter. Since he, too, was not a scientist, on whom had he relied for his decision that the *CIB* data were not invalid? Had he discussed the data with OSHA's own scientists? "I have discussed opinions of scientific data, not the data itself," the OSHA head explained. "I wouldn't understand it. It would be a waste of everybody's time." Gore pressed further:

> MR. GORE: Well, when the CIB was issued [under Carter] the agency had confidence in the data on which it was issued. Now, something has changed. The Formaldehyde Institute contacted your deputy and said We don't like this whole business of saying that formaldehyde causes cancer. And Mr. Cowan wrote up the conversation and handed it to you. Now, there was a change. Now, was that change because of you?
>
> MR. AUCHTER: The change was because of a change in the executive branch of government. When I came in—
>
> MR. GORE: Did that change the scientific facts?

MR. AUCHTER: No, it changed apparently the interpretation of our responsibilities under the law. Now, the first thing I did when I got to Washington—

MR. GORE: The law hasn't changed.

MR. AUCHTER: That's right, but the interpretation has, apparently.

MR. GORE: . . . You do believe that scientists should be free to express their scientific opinions, even if they work for OSHA?

MR. AUCHTER: Provided they are not in conflict with the agency policies. . . .

MR. GORE: Now, do you understand my concern that if a scientist who expresses a scientific opinion different from the one that you have is proposed to be fired for essentially that, that that has a chilling effect on other scientists in your agency and elsewhere in government?

MR. AUCHTER: I understand the concern that you have, Mr. Chairman. . . . I repeat, I am not into the facts in detail. But from a policy standpoint, once the policy decision is made, the personnel of the agency are expected to follow that policy, period. . . .

MR. GORE: The question is the distinction between policy and scientific data. I mean, the Soviet Union used to do that with Mr. Lysenko. A particular scientific theory was upgraded to the status of government policy and any scientist with the temerity to express a different scientific theory . . . was judged to have violated the Soviet Union's governmental policy.[35]

Three weeks later, in August 1981, Infante received notice from Auchter that he would not be fired. On the surface, it appeared that the OSHA head had undergone a change of heart. "I want to make it clear that it is my policy not only to permit but to encourage full and free debate on occupational health and safety issues amongst all personnel employed by this agency," wrote Auchter. "Such debate facilitates the consideration of all available evidence pertinent to a matter in question and assists me in arriving at reasoned and fully informed decisions."

Infante still had his job, but the whole incident did not bode well for him or for other government scientists. His battle consumed more than two months. In the wake of his victory, OSHA reduced his authority within the agency. Moreover, his case seemed to have a chilling effect on others. The widely publicized Infante case sent two distinct messages, according to his lawyer: To industry, "Relax; regulation is out of favor right now." To federal scientists: "Watch out! Speak out against official policy, as Infante did, and you, too, may be threatened with your walking papers." Indeed, Vladeck was surprised at the reactions to the case.

"One of the things I found surprising when I first got involved in representing Dr. Infante was the number of calls I got from his colleagues, who were both concerned about his welfare and wanted to express, 'My God—if they can do this to Infante, think what they can do to me!' "

Worst of all, the Infante episode has become only one in an unprecedented series of such incidents. "There has been a consistent attack on government scientists within this administration," reported Vladeck, who has represented more than a half-dozen federal scientists who have been threatened with loss of their positions or otherwise harassed after speaking too freely on scientific issues. Vladeck continued, "Tony Robbins was fired at NIOSH (National Institute for Safety and Health). Mel Ruber was dismissed at EPA, and Hugh Kaufman nearly lost his job there. Other cases have not come to light, as scientists under siege often seek to resolve them quietly."

These cases have common elements. Each scientist under siege had attained some level of expertise, was in a fairly visible position, and was a conscientious regulator frowned upon by industry. "In each incident, if someone had sat down and thought, 'Who can I get that will have the most pervasive impact on other scientists,' the correct decision was made," observes Vladeck. "I don't mean conspiracy. But it certainly is not serendipity, it is not haphazard."

Vladeck does not view this trend as a result of traditional party politics. He is quick to point out that the Occupational Safety and Health Act was signed into law by Nixon, and that OSHA was as vigorous a regulator under Ford as under Carter. The difference: "There certainly is a disincentive to engage in scientific debate in this administration. The important thing about science is the freedom to debate, the freedom to take different positions, the freedom to speak out. That freedom has been eroded. I would hate to spend a lot of time in a work place under this administration." [36]

MANIPULATING FEDERAL FUNDS

Passing laws to restrict the flow of information and threatening outspoken federal employees with the loss of their jobs are direct ways to inhibit informed dissent. But the government has far more subtle methods at its disposal, and gives every appearance of employing these as well. One of these methods is the manipulation of federal funds. Government regulations determine the way most businesses, nonprofit groups, and foundations are structured. A change in regulations could put some organizations out of business, or at least require radical changes in their operations.

Thousands of organizations at present receive some government funding for their programs through federal grants or contracts for specific projects. Alcoholism programs, help for the elderly and disabled, counseling services, arts and theater groups, vocational training, and a vast variety of others depend at least in part on financial support from the government. A large proportion of these groups serve constituencies like minorities, women, and the disabled—those who are particularly critical of Reagan administration policies.

In January 1983, the Office of Management and Budget tried to change the rules governing these organizations so that groups receiving federal funds would face severe financial penalties if they engaged in any political advocacy. Circular A-122, entitled "Cost Principles for Non Profit Organizations," was supposedly issued to ensure that organizations that have a grant or a contract with the government did not "create political armies that are paid for with federal money." Existing law already forbids the expenditure of federal money on lobbying, and groups with some federal funding must keep records in order to show that any lobbying they did was supported by private funds. The proposed regulations, however, vastly expanded the meaning of *lobbying* and tightened the restrictions on the groups.

Under the proposed rules, a theater troupe that received a grant from the government could be considered to be engaging in "political activity" if it staged an antinuclear play. An executive of Planned Parenthood, which has federal contracts from the Department of Health and Human Services to provide counseling, could not comment to a government official about the controversial "squeal rule" requiring the notification of parents when prescription contraceptives are issued to a minor. An association of rural cooperatives that had a contract to distribute surplus food could not publish a newletter that wrote about "political" topics. (*Political* is not defined.) If a day-care-center worker, paid in part by federal funds, photocopied her letter criticizing President Reagan's budget on her office machine, the center might have to repay the entire cost of the copy machine, even if she could prove she put her own dime in the jar.

In addition, the proposed rules mandated separate staff and facilities for lobbying activities. Thus, the director of an agency like Planned Parenthood could not run a public information program advocating certain policies; the agency would have to hire a separate person and put that person in a separate office with separate phone and copy machine, entirely paid for by private funds. Under present rules, the portion of that person's time spent on public education is paid for by private funds; the time spent on federally funded activities is paid for with government funds. The same principle applies to payment for rent, equipment, and other expenses. Defense contractors, another group that receives federal contracts and is subject to government regulation, would have to buy separate company planes for transporting congressmen on lobbying trips, in addition to the planes they use for transporting their executives.

The proposed rules did permit groups to speak at public hearings if they received written invitations from governmental agencies. But this provision gave rise to more suspicions: The Environmental Protection Agency, for example, could hold hearings and invite only representatives of industry associations to comment on pending legislation. An opposition group that was not invited could speak only at the risk of losing any federal moneys it might have.

Liberal groups, distressed over the implications of the proposed rules, complained that the government was trying to silence them and make it more difficult for them to obtain government funds—an objective of the New Right. Budget officials denied any political intent, and said their objectives were merely to remove any appearance of federal support for lobbying by private groups and to keep taxpayers' money from influencing political causes.

But the suspicions remained, for a year earlier in April 1982, New Right strategist Richard Viguerie, writing in *Conservative Digest,* had advocated what he called "de-funding the left." According to Viguerie, "billions of taxpayer dollars . . . have been going for the last dozen or more years to help advance the liberal's domestic and foreign political agenda." He depicted a network of left-wing activists who kept in touch with one another and paid their rent thanks to taxpayer dollars, and urged the president to stop this flow of funds immediately.[37] The *Wall Street Journal* took up Viguerie's cry, criticizing organizations that receive a government contract and "use it to run that Xerox machine, man that phone bank, get out the troops for that political rally." The paper urged that such funding be cut off, along with funding for shady defense contractors who use government money to lobby for more business.[38]

Out of the controversy over Circular A-122 was born an unlikely alliance, called the Catch 122 Coalition, to oppose the new rules: The U.S. Chamber of Commerce, the ACLU, the Urban League, and the American Lung Association, together with the Computer and Communications Industry Association and the Appalachian Mountain Club, all went on record, along with hundreds of others, as opposed to the proposal.

"The worst thing about this is the psychological impact," said Jack Duncan, a lawyer who had as clients such affected organizations as the American Association of Museums and the American Council for the

Arts. "A lot of people are already nervous about advocacy. They're afraid the federal government will get them one way or the other. This regulation would add to that paranoia about how to deal with the government."[39] The *San Francisco Chronicle* editorialized that OMB Director David Stockman and the Reagan administration "disapprove of activist lobbyists and the things they advocate." The editorial noted that according to Stanford president Donald Kennedy, "anything from a university with a federal grant trying to influence anything—a Paul Ehrlich testifying on the need to protect endangered species, for example," could be silenced, or risk losing federal funding.[40] Another goal of the administration was not lost on congressmen either. "What we see here is an effort by the administration to appease some right-wing constituents by de-funding the left," said Congressman Barney Frank (D-Mass.) at a hearing on Circular A-122.[41]

Ultimately, after receiving six thousand communications opposing the proposal (communications that would not have been permissible if the regulation had gone into effect), Stockman rescinded it, saying that he would issue a revised proposal in a few months. Thus, one attempt to stop groups from speaking out by threatening to remove federal grants and contracts was temporarily beaten back. Some observers thought the administration feared antagonizing the big business interests, and wondered whether an attempt that covered only the nonprofits might not be more successful.

THE IRS AND DISSIDENTS

The government giveth and the government taketh away—or at least claims the right to take away. A number of nonprofit groups dependent for their very existence on their tax-exempt status who oppose government policy fear that their exemptions may be challenged by the Internal Revenue Service. In particular, those whose major activity is publishing information critical of government actions or funding social change have found IRS auditors on their doorsteps. Does this mean that we are returning to the days when the IRS sought out and harassed individuals and organizations President Nixon considered enemies?

That question cannot readily be answered today. The tax laws are both complex and vague enough to lend themselves to subjective interpretation. Section 501 of the Internal Revenue Code contains one volume of more than six thousand pages on tax exemption, plus an additional three volumes of explanation. One rule that lends itself most easily to arbitrary interpretation specifies that the material published by an educational group must be a "full and fair" exposition of the issue discussed. Who is to say what that phrase means? The IRS.

This means that everything a group composes in words or on film is subject to the scrutiny of the IRS staff. In an article called "When Auditors Turn Editors," Angus Mackenzie emphasized the freedom given to individual IRS agents in determining the application of such terms as *full and fair, educational,* and *propaganda.*[42] As Mackenzie reported, the publishers of a small Colorado feminist paper called *Big Mama Rag* had their tax exemption denied because an IRS official disliked the paper's approval of lesbianism. The paper refused to accede to the agent's stipulation that it "abstain from advocating that homosexuality is a mere preference, orientation, or propensity on par with heterosexuality," and fought its case in the courts. In a landmark decision in 1980, the first handed down against the IRS on such grounds, Judge Abner Mikva of the Federal Circuit Court of Appeals in Washington, D.C., ruled that the IRS definition of *educational* was unconstitutionally vague, and thus open to discriminatory enforcement. *Big Mama Rag* could not lose its status because it approved of lesbianism.[43] A decision in a later case involving a racist newsletter called *Attack!* held that the IRS requirement of "full and fair exposition" was similarly vague and therefore unconstitutional.[44]

Concern over the freedom given IRS agents is not new. It worried Supreme Court Justice Harry Blackmun, who wrote in a 1973 opinion that the lack of "clear statutory definition" in tax law had given the IRS commissioner "almost unfettered power. . . . This may be very well so long as one subscribes to the particular brand of social policy the Commissioner happens to be advocating at the time . . . but application of our tax laws should not operate in so fickle a fashion," he concluded.

Why do groups seek a tax status that puts them under the thumb of the government? The advantages are manifold: no tax on incomes from their exempt activity; donations to their operation are tax deductible; and special low postal rates. Without such benefits, a number of organizations simply could not remain economically viable. Those that criticize corporations, in particular, have little profit-making capability but can survive as nonprofits if they have tax-exempt status. Thus, the benefits of this status outweigh the disadvantages of undergoing bureaucratic scrutiny. (Congress in 1982 diminished the benefits somewhat by raising sharply the postal rates for nonprofit organizations. Religious, education, labor, and other groups had to pay from 20 percent to 30 percent more to circulate their ideas. Third-class nonprofit rates also rose, making direct-mail fund-raising, on which many of these organizations depend, much more expensive.)

As long as the laws and regulations are administered evenhandedly, people may grumble about the inconvenience of tax audits but they have no real grounds for complaint. Certainly, in granting special status, the government has the right to declare certain conditions and rules. But if maintaining the tax exemption depends on not criticizing the current administration, the right of free speech is abridged. Further, if political harassment is suspected, paranoia takes hold, and every move an organization makes becomes a subject for internal debate and worry. The chilling effect takes over.

According to New York lawyer Richard Wagner, a few years ago the IRS asked only objective questions about an organization in processing its tax-exempt status. "But gradually, there's been this shift to substantive, political questions," he said. An IRS agent recently asked a left-wing publication, "What is the position of the organization in regard to the following? A. The Masses? B. The Bosses?" [45] Such questions, and the knowledge that they might be asked, cannot fail to trigger memories of the Nixon days, when a special IRS task force called the Special Service Staff (SSS) responded to White House pressure to harass "ideological organizations." During its four years of operation, the SSS opened files on 11,458 individuals and groups and assessed hundreds of thousands of dollars against them. John Dean, dissatisfied with that effort, wrote a memo to H. R. Haldeman, complaining, "We have been unable to crack down on the multitude of tax-exempt foundations that feed left-wing political causes. We have been unable to obtain information in possession of IRS regarding our political enemies." [46] Another memo, this one to Dean from investigator and security expert Jack Caulfield, asked that "discreet IRS audits" be performed on Emile de Antonio, New Yorker Films, Inc., and Daniel Talbot, responsible for the movie *Millhouse,* a distinctly unflattering portrait of the president.

Political use of the IRS is hardly a Republican prerogative. In 1961, after President John Kennedy made an oblique hint in a press conference, the IRS began going after groups he considered unfriendly. San Francisco attorney Thomas Silk, who now advises exempt groups on tax law, recalls that in his days in the Justice Department under Robert Kennedy, "the right-wingers were being hit, the Christian Anti-Communist Crusade, and so forth." Silk observed that it is the noncentrist view that is challenged by the IRS. "The little guy, the unpopular guy, out of the mainstream," is most likely to get hit, he said. That "little guy" is most likely to be a dissenter expressing unorthodox views.[47]

Let us consider three organizations, each in its own way outside the mainstream of political thought in the United States, and each one audited by the IRS in recent years. Each group believes that it has been the victim of political harassment.

The North American Congress on Latin America

The North American Congress on Latin America (NACLA) conducts research and publishes a journal on Latin American affairs. Its stance is consistently critical of U.S. foreign policy. Only a few months before the IRS arrived on its doorstep, NACLA had been listed by the Heritage Foundation as a group that "could become an internal security problem." [48] The IRS audit, launched in March 1981, began inauspiciously for the group when the agent requested not only financial material but also all its board minutes, records, and publications.

The IRS agent recommended in September 1981 that its tax exemption be revoked because it failed to present a "full and fair exposition" of issues and thus was not truly educational. NACLA suspected that the recommendation to revoke was political. "There was no problem with our audit in a financial sense," said Janet Shenk of the group's staff. "The agent based his recommendation on the claim that our work was propaganda as opposed to education." [49] NACLA filed a Freedom of Information Act request for the IRS records of the investigation. Those records indeed showed that IRS agent D. Levine had been concerned with propaganda. He did not like an issue of their journal about the world auto industry, which, in his words said, "contains no propaganda passages except for concluding paragraphs of 3rd article: 'internationalism has served capital well, now it's labor's turn.' " He also took great exception to a comic book NACLA reprinted in 1979, called *The Incredible Rocky,* about the Rockefeller family. He sought to revoke the exemption because of the group's "partisan approach" and its criticism of Nelson Rockfeller as governor of New York and as vice-president.[50] Although Levine's recommendation was made after the *Big Mama Rag* case, Levine evidently did not consider the free speech implications of that decision.

In the summer issue of *Report on the Americas,* NACLA discussed the possible purpose behind the audit:

> The IRS was trying to grant exemptions to those who agreed with them and punish those who challenged, in a documented and educational fashion, the government's major policy lines. With their hit and run tactics, it was clear that the IRS was trying to intimidate dissident organizations. Once the news spread that NACLA or *Mother Jones* was threatened, other organizations, fearful of losing their exemption, would begin to tone down their criticism.[51]

NACLA appealed the denial of tax-exempt status and obtained legal assistance from the Center for Constitutional Rights. They won reinstatement of their status at the national level, but only after a year and a half. It was a long battle and a costly victory: The staff, lawyers, and accountants of an underfunded group had to devote hundreds of hours to a legal case because, in the words of the NACLA report, "one IRS agent didn't like our analysis of the Rockefellers."

The precedent was troubling for other, newer organizations. NACLA felt it was one of the dissident groups best equipped to handle an audit. Well supported with legal advice, and given donations by a readership developed over their sixteen years of existence, NACLA was far better able to defend itself than a fledgling operation that was unfamiliar with the bureaucracy and lacked connections and community respect. It could mobilize letters of support from university professors attesting to the scholarly excellence of their reports, use the Freedom of Information Act to obtain files, and appeal to public opinion. A weaker group might not be able to survive an audit, even though it had an equal right to express its views.

The Regional Young Adult Project

Rather than issuing publications critical of the government, the Regional Young Adult Project (RYAP) in San Francisco funds groups that work for social change. Many new private groups with a tax-exempt purpose, such as housing for the homeless, do not yet have their own tax-exempt status and funnel their donations through an established foundation that serves as an umbrella. The umbrella foundation, like RYAP, must supervise the group's expenditures to ensure that IRS rules are followed.

RYAP is housed in an upper floor of the Glide Church building in the Tenderloin District of San Francisco, sanctuary for the down-and-out. Its director, Herb Allen, is a middle-aged man who now smokes and worries more than he used to, afraid that his longtime role as godfather to social activists may be terminated by the Internal Revenue Service. Chairs and tables in his sparsely furnished office are piled high with binders of documents, responses, and protests to the IRS recommendation that RYAP's tax exemption be revoked. RYAP's situation differs in several ways from that of groups like NACLA whose publications were challenged: Not only might the groups under RYAP's umbrella go out of business if RYAP loses its exemption, but all the donors to RYAP-funded organizations could have their personal tax returns audited as well. The demise of this one group could carry others with it and, in addition, trouble a large percentage of the few wealthy individuals who support left and liberal causes in the United States.

Herb Allen is not bitter over what happened to the project he runs, but he is tired. The saga began when RYAP was audited in 1979 for the tax year 1977. "Things seemed to go routinely," Allen said in an interview in May 1983. "They had some questions which we answered in writing, and then we heard nothing. After a while we were told that another auditor was coming in since the first one hadn't done a complete job, so we were audited a second time for that same year. He also had a few questions, which we answered. Next, we were asked to sign an extension of time for them to audit, which we did, and we got a third auditor. One day this auditor, Mr. Cotter, left his files in our bookkeeper's office by mistake. Our bookkeeper couldn't resist—he looked. What he found was that the first two audits had been thorough. But in May 1982, we got a letter recommending that our tax-exempt status be revoked."

Allen continued his narrative. "We asked for our files, as we are entitled to do. IRS gave us all but thirty-seven documents. We asked that they give those to us, or not be allowed to use them in proceedings against us. We asked for this in August 1982, and still have had no answer. They are supposed to respond in one month. We filed our response to their recommendation in November; IRS was supposed to answer in thirty days, but we heard from them in March 1983, referring us to the Regional Appeals office."[52] Several months and $32,000 in legal fees later, RYAP was notified that it would not lose its tax-exempt status.

Allen notes ruefully that RYAP has been investigated by Social Security and the U.S. Postal Service as well as the IRS. He bemoaned the difficulties of explaining to bureaucrats what social change is all about. "The vocabulary of the left and of the IRS are totally different. Every word we use—*organize, political,*—those are red flag words to them. Our job is to educate people about issues, but they don't understand that at all, and they don't understand the law."

The IRS auditor's report on RYAP contained a twenty-five-page list of what he considered twenty-six infringements of regulations. RYAP's protest, filed by attorney Thomas Silk, contained rebuttals to each one. In every instance, the auditor cited expenditures of RYAP funds that were, in his view, inappropriate. Most of these involved the exercise of First Amendment rights. For example, $2,648 was spent to fund internships for minority journalism students with a socialist newspaper in San Francisco called *Common Sense.* The auditor noted that the paper "reflects the . . . belief that the present system in America exploits and oppresses the vast proportion of humanity," and advocates "an alternative to the capitalist media." RYAP's rebuttal explained that the money was spent for the legitimate purpose of job training, and asserted, "That the newspaper . . . expresses an unpopular view is irrelevant."

The auditor also took exception to a $200 grant to the San Francisco Poster Brigade, which, he noted, "offers an alternative perspective to the exploitive commercial advertising that seeks to perpetuate society based on consumerism." The rebuttal explained that RYAP spent the money for posters reading "Stop Banking on Apartheid," in support of a coalition (composed mainly of church groups) concerned about the denials of human rights in South Africa. The posters advocated withdrawing funds from banks that did business in that nation.

RYAP's appeal pointed out that charity and controversy can go hand in hand, quoting IRS regulations that state that advocacy of social change "with the intention of molding public opinion or creating public sentiment to an acceptance of its views does not preclude [an] organization" from a tax exemption. Social change, argued Herb Allen, is a legitimate, exempt activity, however much an IRS auditor may dislike the views expressed.

Mother Jones

Mother Jones is a muckraking monthly published in San Francisco by the Foundation for National Progress, a tax-exempt educational organization. In its eight years of publication, *Mother Jones* has won three National Magazine Awards, numerous other journalism prizes, and considerable notoriety by exposing corporate wrongdoing and governmental abuse of power. It also featured a cover story called "Investigating Reagan's Brain and Other Dark Regions on the Right." Among its best-known articles, an exposé of the Ford Pinto's exploding gas tanks and an examination of the way infant formula is marketed in underdeveloped nations.

The IRS began the audit of *Mother Jones* late in the Carter administration, but according to publisher Robin Wolaner, the audit became much more difficult after Reagan took office. Wolaner claimed that the IRS was out to get the magazine for its politics and outspoken criticism of the powers that be. The IRS insisted that politics had nothing to do with the matter, that the magazine was unrelated to the tax-exempt objectives of the Foundation for National Progress and owed $390,000 in back taxes. Wolaner retorted that the magazine has consistently lost $200,000 a year since its beginning, a sum that has had to be covered by donations and low-interest loans. According to Wolaner, the IRS has engaged in "voodoo accounting." "IRS allocated income to the magazine, but undercounted expenses attributable to the magazine so as to make it look more profitable. According to them, while the foundation lost money, the magazine made money. They assessed us back taxes of $750,000, which we bargained down to $390,000 at a meeting."

In her opinion, the IRS audit was politically motivated: "The IRS says that our foundation is exempt, and that *Mother Jones* is the primary activity of the foundation. We agree on these two things. But then they say that *Mother Jones* is a commercial venture, making an artificial separation of the magazine from the foundation. Tax law is clear: If your primary purpose is educational, you are exempt. We meet their criteria for exemption; the magazine is educational." In addition, she claimed, the IRS audited only the 1978 books, but based its case on three years: 1978, 1979, and 1980. The agency did not examine the books for the other two years. Finally, she argued that the IRS is a revenue-generating agency. Since *Mother Jones* never made any profits, there is no way the IRS can collect any revenue. "If they are not out to get money," she asked, "then what are they out to get? Their computations could only have been done with one thing in mind: to get us." [53]

Several major magazines are distributed in the same way as *Mother Jones—Ms., Smithsonian, Audubon, Natural History, Science 83, National Geographic, Oceans, Harper's,* and at least one of those takes strong political stands. But none has had the same kind of battle with the government as *Mother Jones* endured, a "struggle to the death," in the words of executive editor Deirdre English. The struggle has taken its toll: More than $120,000 went for legal expenses by the spring of 1983, as well as considerable staff, legal, and accounting time.

IRS spokesman Larry Wright consistently denied any political motivation for the audit. After explaining that federal law forbids him from commenting on individual cases without the approval of the auditee, Wright disclaimed any intention of trying to stop the magazine from publishing, or of singling out the dissident voice. "The IRS is not now nor has it ever been a political tool," he told the *Baltimore Evening Sun*.[54]

Publisher Wolaner acknowledged that the magazine's staff had made errors in dealing with the IRS. "First, we let them in and just gave them everything they wanted," she said. "We had nothing to hide. We now know that we should have required them to ask us in writing for the material they wanted." The audit began March 27, 1980; a year later, said Wolaner, on February 18, 1981, the auditor and her supervisor showed up at the magazine and said they wanted to revoke the foundation's exemption.[55] The foundation and the magazine filed a protest: In the spring of 1982, the IRS informed them that the foundation was indeed exempt, but the magazine was a commercial venture. In November 1982, the magazine, which until that time had denied that it was being singled out for persecution because of its politics, held a press conference, appealed for financial support, and accused the IRS of political harassment.

In an editorial in the January 1983 issue Executive Editor Deirdre English wrote, "Our success is *why* they want to stop us. Great choice: stay small and noninfluential and live. Become powerful and widely distributed, get ruled out of order by IRS, and go flying into oblivion." English promptly heard from some small, noninfluential groups like the

Advocado Press in Louisville, Kentucky, and La Semilla, a socialist cultural center in Sacramento, California, who also had been audited and felt somewhat aggrieved at her presentation. Angus Wright of La Semilla wrote,

> "I think it is important to keep in mind that what is being fought over here is a fundamental principle of free speech. In that light, an attack on one is an attack on all. No one should assume that one has to be big and influential to merit the ire of the Reagan administration—it is the poor and powerless who, after all, are the ones who are suffering most from this regime. The smallest grass roots organizations deserve a defense and need a sense of solidarity at least if not more than *Mother Jones*." [56]

After the publicity led to wide newspaper coverage and several editorials critical of the government, the magazine also heard from the IRS, which scheduled a hearing within two weeks, an "almost unheard of short time," according to Wolaner. "We spent a lot of money and effort preparing, but then, on the eve of the hearing, the IRS called and said it was skipping the regional hearing and going up to the national level. This case would set a precedent, they said, and they didn't want to decide it at the local level."

The magazine staff anxiously awaited the results, counting the psychological costs in the meantime. "As much as we continue to do what we have always done, we do think about it more; it's the old chilling effect," said Naomi Schalit, former program director at the Foundation for National Progress. "Our charitable activity has been in opposing abuses of power; it's ironic that we should be suffering such an abuse of power here." [57] The staff waited until October 1983, when the IRS ruled that the magazine was indeed tax exempt and nonprofit.

Not everyone involved in the battle on behalf of the magazine saw an orchestrated attempt by the Reagan administration behind the audit. Silk, an attorney for *Mother Jones* as well as for RYAP, took a different view. "I have no knowledge of whether the IRS audit was politically motivated," he said. "I'm not able to support the worst fears of the editorial staff about conspiracy and oppression. I think what's going on is more complicated and more pervasive." [58]

He offered a possible alternate motivation for the audit. "One thing to consider is the way a bureaucrat looks at a nonmajoritarian activity," he began. "Any decent midlevel bureaucrat will anticipate what he thinks his employer wants. The *Mother Jones* case is a little like the early fifties, when the Communist party in Manhattan was padlocked by Internal Revenue, unknown to the District of Columbia office. If the national office had prereviewed the case, that would never have happened."

Whatever the motivation behind the audit, a conflict remains between the IRS regulations and the First Amendment. This was made clear in congressional hearings held in May 1983 by Congressman Doug Barnard, Jr., chair of the Subcommittee on Commerce, Consumer, and Monetary Affairs. Congressman Barnard questioned IRS spokesman S. Allen Winborne about regulations governing tax-exempt publications. He asked when and how a magazine published by an exempt organization might lose its exempt status. Winborne replied that lack of educational methodology might be one cause. He explained, "For instance, if a magazine takes a controversial position, and insists on espousing that position but does not in any way use an educational methodology, such as presenting enough information so that a reasonable person could make a reasonable decision about the position that is being espoused, if the magazine in short is relying exclusively on emotion, on hatred, on bigotry, on things of that sort, then that could possibly call into question the exemption of that magazine."

"How do you get around the IRS being a censor of information?" Barnard continued.

"We hope we are not censors. We hope we are not telling them what they can espouse. We just hope we are saying if you do it, do it in an educational way. . . . I might add that maybe we are [censors]. There is at least one court, the Circuit Court for the District of Columbia, which said that our regulations were in violation of the Constitution of the United States. That question is now open. It is back in court in another case. Frankly, at this point in time we are not 100 percent perfect." [59]

Mother Jones editor English, by contrast, thinks the IRS standards are perfect, but in a different sense:

> The legislation separating tax exempt from commercial magazines works perfectly to stop a comprehensive political analysis and critique. If your publication is for profit, you can criticize the government but you can't take on the corporations or you'll lose your advertisers. If you are nonprofit, you can criticize the corporations, but you can't criticize the government, or you might lose your tax exemption.[60]

CANADIAN FILMS

"Stand up for the First Amendment: Expose yourself to an evening of DANGEROUS PROPAGANDA," read the invitation. The Northern California ACLU and *Mother Jones* magazine sponsored a showing of three Canadian films the Justice Department had declared propaganda.

Labeling the films propaganda led to an uproar, and undoubtedly the controversy vastly increased the audience for films that otherwise might have had limited appeal. Two were about acid rain, films suitable for elementary school students; the third was the Oscar-winning "If You Love This Planet," a speech by Dr. Helen Caldicott, a physician who is a one-woman antinuclear movement. Predictably, the acid rain films depicted the death of lakes, the spread of pollution, and other ill effects of U.S. pollution on Canadian lakes and land. The films urged that action be taken before the effects of acid rain become irreversible. The antinuclear film carried a message also: Dr. Caldicott urged her listeners to give priority in their lives to ending the threat of atomic war, and aimed her message especially at mothers. "Bring your baby and march in Washington," she said. "If you haven't got a baby, borrow one." She suggested letting hundreds of naked toddlers loose on the floor of the Congress as part of a mass campaign to preserve the planet. The film was punctuated with old film clips—some from the Department of Defense minimizing the dangers of nuclear weapons, some exhibiting the ghastly scars deforming the survivors of Hiroshima, and some showing President Reagan playing the part of an eager air force officer in World War II.

To an administration devoted to freeing industry from regulation and to increasing spending on atomic weapons, these films were presumably unwelcome. And since they had been produced by the National Film Board of Canada, they could be placed under the purview of the Foreign Agents Registration Act (FARA). FARA requires material produced abroad and intended to influence American political opinion to be labeled propaganda, registered with the Justice Department, and designated as material of which the United States government does not necessarily approve. In the past six years, forty-seven films and eight public television programs have been so labeled.

On a May evening in 1983, five hundred people gathered in San Francisco's huge Palace of Fine Arts theater, a massive relic of the 1915 Panama Exposition, to protest the government's action. Wine and cheese were served; speakers from the ACLU, the Justice Department, and *Mother Jones* magazine debated. The Justice Department's representative—U.S. Attorney Joseph Russoniello—supplied the historical background. FARA was enacted in 1938 in response to German propaganda "of the subversive type," he said, to protect an unwary public. Amendments in 1942 and 1966 increased the requirements that material from foreign sources intended to influence U.S. public opinion be labeled propaganda. In response to charges of government censorship, Russoniello claimed that the FARA regulations actually *increased* the amount of information made available to the public by making the viewer aware that "some one may be trying to influence you." Russoniello concluded that no injury had been done by the rule and the whole affair was "a tempest in a tea pot."

Quite the opposite interpretation was taken by ACLU Legal Director Burt Neuborne, who spoke next. He noted that many film distributors would have to report to the Justice Department about which theaters had booked the films and the size of the audience. "The government has no business keeping such information," he charged. In addition, the government, by labeling the films propaganda, seriously denigrated their messages and diminished the impact they might have on the public. Neuborne attributed the incident to "the cyclical recurrence of a fear of foreign ideas" on the part of our government. The refusal to admit the widow of slain Chilean President Salvador Allende to give a speech at Stanford as "not in the best interest of the United States," the attempt to halt tourism to Cuba, and the attempt to impound publications from Cuba and North Vietnam similarly manifested what Neuborne called "this administration's particular sensitivity to foreign ideas." He declared, "We can tell for ourselves what ideas are propaganda; we don't need Big Brother to tell us." He continued, "This statute is a horror; it's ambiguous, and so bad that it caused Eisenstein's great film *Potemkin* to be labeled propaganda. Any law which does that has got to be bad. . . . The government must get out of the business of registering ideas."

Neuborne announced to loud applause that just the day before, during pretrial maneuvering, a federal judge in Sacramento had found the categorization of the films as political propaganda to be unconstitutional. Issuing a temporary order forbidding the labeling of the films, Judge Raul Ramirez agreed that the government's action unfairly stigmatized the films and identified the distributors as pushers of distorted information on behalf of a foreign government. This, he found, violated the protections of the First Amendment. In the legal brief filed to defend the labeling, the government had asserted its right to stigmatize as propaganda foreign speech that might contain ideas incompatible with current policy. In warning about "doctrines alien to our democratic form of government," the government brief sounded both xenophobic and silly, as well as anxious to discredit criticism of administration policies.

California State Senator Barry Keene, who filed the suit against the Justice Department's labeling, contended that he wished to show these films to his fellow legislators in order to dramatize the issues of pollution and disarmament.[61] He protested the parts of the Foreign Agents Registration Act that would characterize him as a disseminator of foreign propaganda. He should be able to discuss public affairs like acid rain and disarmament free from government intervention, licensing, or stigmatizing, he argued, and he objected to having his name reported to the federal government as an exhibitor of propaganda, a report that might at some later time be made public and come back to haunt him. Finally, Keene pointed out that copies of the official Soviet newspaper *Izvestia* circulate in the United States, unlabeled. Why, he asked, should Canadian documentaries be considered more dangerous than that?

The business of registering foreign ideas and their disseminators may seem attractive to an administration eager to suppress informed discussion and dissent. But it seems an incongruous policy for a government that spends more than $500 million each year to broadcast its own propaganda around the world. Besides the Voice of America, which has been criticized for changing from a news station to a propaganda outlet under the Reagan administration, our government beams its messages through Radio Free Europe and Radio Liberty behind the Iron Curtain and has persuaded a recalcitrant Congress to authorize millions more for Radio Marti to do the same to Cuba.

Illogic permeated the government's argument on behalf of its right to label as propaganda these messages of which it disapproved. The Justice Department argued in the case of these three films that if Senator Keene really wished, he could snip off the labels that had been attached. Judge Ramirez then noted wryly that it made little sense to require the labels if they could be removed before the "unsuspecting public" could be "forewarned."

Of all the attempts to discredit dissent in the early 1980s, this one was probably the silliest.

PACIFICA: SUPPRESSION FROM THE PRIVATE SECTOR

The suppression of dissent most often is carried out by government. But as *Nation* editor Victor Navasky pointed out, government actions also set a tone for the private sector. If the tone is tolerant, private groups and individuals are more likely to be tolerant. If it is intolerant, then intolerance by private groups and individuals may be exacerbated, and dissenters may find themselves under attack from that quarter as well.

A new kind of private organization that developed in the early 1980s has become active in the suppression of dissent: the right-wing legal foundation. Modeled on the public interest law firm pioneered by Ralph Nader, these legal foundations are motivated by a procorporate, free enterprise ideology rather than the prounderdog, consumerist ideology that drives Nader's raiders. Funded by corporations and rich individuals, the right-wing legal foundations have taken on test cases in order to set important precedents. Working for the Reaganite goals of deregulating industry and strengthening corporations at the expense of the environment, workers, and consumers, the legal foundations spend their massive resources on lawsuits that hamper, for example, rent control, antinuclear activists, labor unions, and affirmative action.

Legal foundations affiliated with the National Legal Center for the Public Interest, in Washington, D.C., spread across the country. Some of the affiliates are the Mid-Atlantic Legal Foundation in Philadelphia, Mountain States (once headed by former Interior Secretary James Watt) in Denver, Southeastern in Atlanta, Great Plains in Kansas City, and Mid-American in Chicago. Other conservative legal foundations of the same ilk are the Pacific Legal Foundation in Sacramento, California, and the American and Capital Legal Foundations in Washington, D.C.

These firms, tax-exempt and claiming to function "in the public interest," are flourishing at the same time as the publicly funded Legal Services Corporation, established to provide legal services to the poor, is being gutted by the Reagan administration.

Among the targets of these well-funded foundations are certain free speech rights. Besides pressing a lawsuit against the antinuclear Abalone Alliance, Pacific Legal Foundation filed suit to prevent the United Farm Workers from picketing the homes of growers. It (unsuccessfully) supported the giant Pruneyard shopping center in San Jose in opposing the right of political groups to hand out leaflets on shopping center property. In a notable effort by a private group to suppress dissent, the American Legal Foundation filed a petition before the Federal Communications Commission in September 1981 to deny the license renewal of radio station WPFW in Washington, D.C.[62] A small, listener-sponsored affiliate of the left-liberal Pacifica Foundation, WPFW is managed by a predominantly black staff and addresses itself far more than commercial stations to social problems and issues affecting the poor.

In October 1980, the ultraright Accuracy in Media (AIM) had attacked the Pacifica network in its bimonthly *A.I.M. Report*, and the attack had been picked up by the widely read *National Enquirer*. The *Enquirer* article, called "Anti-American Radio Stations get $2.5 Million of Your Tax $," quoted Reed Irvine, head of Accuracy In Media, blasting the station "for broadcasting filth, racist material, and programs that encourage violence."[63] Irvine charged that the stations "have laced the nation with a web of shame, offending Americans with anti-American, anti-Christian and anti-Semitic propaganda."[64] Both *A.I.M. Report* and the *Enquirer* made much of the $2.5 million in public funding received by the network between 1970 and 1981, and the *Enquirer* accused the stations of hiding "behind the U.S. Constitution's guarantee of free speech" while "viciously biting the hand that feeds them."[65]

The same kinds of allegations formed the basis for the American

Legal Foundation's license challenge: The station broadcast exclusively a "leftist political philosophy," failing to present fairly "controversial issues of public importance," claimed the ALF. Among the issues singled out for comment were Central American policy, race, and nuclear war. On each score, the ALF found WPFW reporting scandalously biased.

Curiously, the foundation condemned a WPFW statement that the station was presenting "an alternative look at Central America." The legal foundation took as evidence of unfairness an announcer's saying to the listeners, "You can get the other side in the *Washington Post*, the *Star*, on television, etc. The point of view we are presenting is not one you have ready access to." The legal foundation apparently objected that the station did not echo the opinions of other media. The foundation claimed that the staff of WPFW sees the station not as a broadcaster but rather "as an organ for radical social and political change"—plainly, in the legal foundation's view, a bad thing to be.

The station's humor, as well as the use of dirty words, was cited as a basis for the license denial. The ALF brief appeared to frown on an announcer's warning to listeners preceding a comedy show: "If you're of a sensitive nature," said the announcer, "We advise you at this time to go over to your stereo . . . and get a large ax handle and come down right through the middle of it. Therefore, you won't hear the shit we're talking." The monologue that followed, by a Hispanic comedian playing a black Mickey Mouse, concerned his visit to Snow White, "for some loving." But Mickey was dismayed to discover, upon removing his clothes, that he "didn't have no dick," because "the motherfucker [cartoonist] didn't draw one on." ALF was not amused.

The ALF disapproved, as well, of a broadcaster on the station saying that President Reagan "has a Hitler-like mentality" and of Bella Abzug calling the Moral Majority immoral. According to FCC rules, alleged the brief, WPFW ought to have contacted the president and the Moral Majority to inform them that personal attacks had been leveled against them, and that they had the right to reply.

Again and again throughout the seventy-page brief, the ALF cited statements with which it disagreed as the basis for removing the station from the air. The ALF also found inadequate the ascertainment process used by the station. *Ascertainment* refers to a requirement by the FCC that the station interview listeners and community members to discover what issues they find worthy of discussion on the air. WPFW failed in this, said ALF, since they interviewed urban residents to the near exclusion of suburban, and did not interview leaders of "traditionally oriented" groups and recognized civic organizations. WPFW did interview a number of black professors from Howard University, and in fact has more genuine ties with its community than do most commercial stations. The station has also received an award from the mayor of Washington for its service. But those ties were not with the community considered appropriate by the ALF.

The brief also cited a few minor violations of FCC regulations: not having sufficient documents available for public inspection (although the station had explained the deficiency to the FCC); having a broadcaster plug his own nightclub show (WPFA fired that broadcaster); and using the station's newspaper to ask listeners to lobby against funding cuts for public broadcasting (since the newspaper was not funded by federal money, such use, according to the station, is legitimate).

WPFW, at a cost of $13,000, filed a response to the ALF petition. The station asserted its First Amendment rights to free speech and claimed that the ALF had not presented any valid objections to its practices. It had quoted spokesmen and officials from the Reagan administration in its reporting on Central America, nuclear arms, and racism, as well as pillars of the right wing such as Senator East and Jerry Falwell. It cited the many broadcasting awards the station and Pacifica have won, as well as endorsements by university professors and the National Black Media Coalition. Finally, the station complained about having to respond to "a politically motivated petition to deny," which placed a great strain on what is essentially a "shoestring operation."

The ALF, which devotes itself to media issues, normally opposes the very FCC procedures it employed in challenging Pacifica by a petition to deny its license renewal. As an advocate of deregulation, ALF seeks to get the government out of the airwaves. In fact, ALF devotes much of its energy to opposing petitions to deny that have been filed by the National Black Media Coalition (NBMC). NBMC, also based in Washington, surveys the hiring practices of radio and television stations, and when they find stations that are not in compliance with Equal Employment Opportunity Commission guidelines, they oppose license renewals. NBMC's objective is to increase the number of minorities hired; because broadcasters require licensing by the federal government, they are subject to EEOC regulation, and NBMC seeks to force compliance. David Honig, research director at NBMC, calls NBMC a "strong free speech organization." He does not wish to abridge First Amendment rights, he says, but stations must comply with applicable regulations, and his group will use FCC procedures to see that they do.

Yet NBMC filed a petition to deny a station's license in May 1983 with the intent of keeping certain material off the airwaves. Station KTTL in Dodge City, Kansas, broadcasts antiblack, anti-Jewish messages. A mom and pop station run by Nellie and Charles Babbs, the station has, according to the *New York Times,* suggested to listeners that they take down the names and addresses of local Jews, go to their homes, and kill them.[66] Honig said that the Babbses have every right to get on a soapbox and say just the same thing they say on the airwaves about blacks and Jews—except for the incitement to violence. Their right to defame groups of people on the station, he says, is not as clear, since the airwaves are subject to regulation.

According to Honig, NBMC asked the ALF to join in the challenge to KTTL's license. The legal group refused; as attorney William Kehoe explained, they did not wish to engage in a pattern of filing petitions to deny, a process they find objectionable. Yet in a 1981 interview, ALF chairman Daniel Popeo said that his group "would not rule out" future challenges to all Pacifica radio stations.

The FCC took more than two years to decide whether to dismiss the challenge to WPFW or to schedule a hearing on it. Changes in the FCC leadership accounted in part for the delay, but there was also perhaps a reluctance to decide the politically touchy issue. Pacifica president Peter Franck said that if the station had to prepare for a hearing, legal costs would exceed $200,000.

Franck also expressed suspicion of the simultaneous attacks from newspapers and the ALF, and two highly unusual surprise FCC inspections of their Houston and Los Angeles stations. He saw these attacks in the print media and the license challenge as part of a concerted attempt by the right to hurt independent media. "The right is not content just to use the media to put over its point of view. . . . They are also trying to shape the rest of the media to their will," he said.[67]

The FCC denied the ALF petition November 30, 1983, ruling that the foundation had not proved its case, and granted WPFW a renewed license on the condition that the station keep careful records of its broadcasting about controversial issues.

Despite its alleged aversion to government regulation of the air waves, ALF filed other complaints with the FCC. Earlier in 1983, ALF asked the commission to revoke the licenses of all stations owned and operated by the Columbia Broadcasting System (CBS) because, they alleged, two CBS programs allegedly violated the commission's fairness doctrine. It is curious to note that, in both cases, attorney Dan Burt, president of the Capital Legal Foundation, represents the persons who filed libel suits against the very same CBS programs. Burt represents General William Westmoreland, who claimed that the network broadcast inaccurate and defamatory material in its documentary "The Uncounted Enemy: A Vietnam Deception." Burt also represented Dr. Carl Galloway, who sued on account of a "60 Minutes" segment called "It's No Accident," which implicated him in alleged insurance fraud.

Dr. Galloway lost his suit; as of early 1984, General Westmoreland's has yet to be heard.

The sister legal foundations attacked the same programs on two fronts: before the FCC and in the courts. If this is a concerted strategy to punish CBS, and if it is an indication of more to come, broadcasters may find themselves hamstrung by the tactics of the conservative legal groups.

As 1984 dawned, the miserable world depicted in George Orwell's novel *1984* had not come to pass. Big Brother was not watching in every home, and thought control remained in the realm of fantasy where it belongs. But the expression of dissent had become riskier under the administration of Ronald Reagan. High officials including the president himself tarred administration critics with accusations of disloyalty. Scientists at work in federal agencies faced the possibility of demotion or dismissal for voicing factual conclusions that ran contrary to the president's desire for less regulation of industry. Government procedures were administered in ways that made trouble for groups that criticized Reagan administration policies.

Laws that were designed to assure diversity and the expression of many viewpoints, like IRS rules giving tax advantages and lower postal rates to educational and nonprofit organizations, were used against those who expressed certain viewpoints. Those who exercised their right to dissent in the early eighties faced an increased chance that they might suffer reprisals either from the government or from the private sector.

6

Conclusion

"They that can give up essential liberty to obtain a little temporary safety deserve neither liberty nor safety."
—*Benjamin Franklin*

Despite the best intentions of America's founders, civil liberties did not appear fully developed after the British had been driven from our soil. In two hundred years of uneven progress free speech, a free press, and the public's right to know evolved to the point where the United States allowed freedom of speech up until incitement to violence, the right to distribute leaflets and to picket, the least regulated press in the world, and a Freedom of Information Act.

During those two centuries, hundreds of thousands of Americans have suffered because they were denied their First Amendment rights: They were thrown in jail because they criticized the president or U.S. involvement in a particular war, deported for holding unpopular political beliefs, beaten for picketing an employer, fired for failing to sign a loyalty oath. Our progress toward the ideals set down during the American Revolution has been slow, but, in general, state and local laws inhibiting free speech have been gradually overturned.

Free speech reached an apogee in the 1960s and 1970s, decades that saw wild and weird publications distributed widely, venomous criticism of public officials, and a whole counterculture breaking the rules of polite expression. During the same period, in large measure as a result of First Amendment rights exercised by the people, basic democratic rights were extended to racial minorities, women organized to combat sex discrimination, and the United States halted the war in Vietnam. The press flourished to the point where reporters became almost as famous as entertainers, and the media distinguished themselves with first-rate investigative reporting.

But if current trends in First Amendment rights continue, the 1960s and 1970s may turn out to be aberrant periods in our history. Given the Reagan administration's clampdown on government information and its battery of orders restricting the access of the press and public disclosure, the success of book banners in schools and libraries, the increase in libel and slander actions, and the hostile attitude toward dissenters and the press, the First Amendment may once again be in for a long siege. In addition, if the economy continues to go downhill, if the global standoff of the superpowers intensifies, and if leftist revolutions erupt in neighboring nations, the resulting climate would likely encourage more intolerance, censorship, fear of new or foreign ideas, and other attitudes incompatible with free expression and open government.

Nature itself may be on the side of the censors. The population of the United States, demographics tell us, is growing older all the time. Older people tend to be more conservative in their religious and political views, and since there will be more of them, they will have more political clout. Thus, the prospects are that the fundamentalist conservative ideology will grow more influential and there will be less diversity in schools, books, films, and other kinds of expression. Politicians responsive to the elderly may enact a "Christian" moral code into law. This prediction, put forth by People for the American Way, contradicts that of some observers who feel that the television evangelists of the fundamentalist right have peaked and are no longer a growing force in the American political scene.

Should the intolerant gain power, children in schools would learn a narrow, pseudopatriotic version of American history; novels by writers such as Kurt Vonnegut and J. D. Salinger would be tucked under mattresses instead of being on display in libraries, information about birth control and abortion could be outlawed, novels and books advocating homosexuality might be banned, and criticism of the free enterprise system might join evolution as a vanishing idea.

If the trends set in motion by the Reagan administration continue, our America may change even more. Those who oppose nuclear war may hesitate to join SANE or a local antiwar group for fear that FBI infiltrators are reporting the group's activities to authorities, and are sowing the seeds of factional strife within the peace movement. Fearing also to be labeled "dupes of the KGB," sympathizers with the group's objectives may withhold their money and their membership, because they don't want to be considered a security risk.

The same possibility holds true for those wishing to oppose U.S. policy in Central America, except they would fear CIA, rather than FBI, actions to disrupt their work. If the Reagan administration continues to deny visas to foreigners whose views it dislikes, and if travel restrictions like those to Cuba persist, the United States may become an ideological fortress forbidding the entry of those with supposedly subversive ideas and forbidding U.S. citizens to visit nations where leftist governments hold sway. Should the U.S. supported regime in El Salvador fall to the leftist rebels, Americans might well not be allowed to visit or trade with that nation. Those who have supported the rebels, like the Committee in Solidarity with El Salvador, might find their names on subversive lists.

Let us go further. If the Reagan-backed attempts to cut back on the Freedom of Information Act should succeed, researchers and reporters will not be able to uncover government duplicity or even to discover how government policy is being made. And if more and more information is classified, a helpless public will be forced to rely on official press releases for an impression of what its government is doing. Should the tendency to restrict contacts between press and officials continue, along with polygraph tests and punishments for leakers, informed debate over government policy will dwindle. An administration protected from scrutiny can become more and more removed from its people, and less and less accountable for its actions.

If corporate America decides to increase the number of libel actions against its critics, or merely threatens such actions, the consumer movement spearheaded years ago by Ralph Nader and his associates could be crippled. Consumer publications, drained by the expense of legal actions, could go bankrupt even if the lawsuits failed. Blizzards of libel suits could disrupt the media and again, even if they fail, create such a terrorized atmosphere that hard-hitting reporting could become endangered. If numbers of organizations adopted the Synanon "sue them" policy, the media could be intimidated and refrain from covering their activities.

One of the things that has made America great is diversity. The revolutionary principle that ideas should be free to compete and rub up against one another has permitted in our nation an extraordinary range of media, organizations, religions, political candidates, life styles, and value systems. Even though the reality has not matched the promise—our history is filled with examples of intolerance and bigotry—the ideal is worth fighting for. Another principle that has made America great, though it too has not been fully realized, is democracy—the sovereignty of the people. This ideal requires an informed electorate and a government accountable to the electorate: Without information, it can't succeed.

Both ideals—diversity and accountable government—are under attack. The attacks do not stem from a particular conspiracy; the CIA doesn't huddle with Parents of New York United and Mobil Oil to see how the First Amendment can be cut back. But the fact that separate groups whose interests are best served by limiting free expression and the public's right to know have gained political strength in recent years makes for a powerful, if inadvertent, convergence.

Let us turn for the moment from what could happen to what is happening. The senior White House correspondent for *U.S. News and World Report,* Sara Fritz, spoke in June 1983 to a gathering of journalists. She warned them about the Reagan administration's concerted actions to shut down the flow of information. "I've had it up to my keister with the Reagan attacks on the press," she complained to the audience. "And the press has been intimidated into not fighting back." She listed the administration's measures: the lie detector tests for federal employees suspected of leaking information, the cutback in statistical information, the attempts to gut the FOIA, the closing of Government Printing Office bookstores, the unleashing of the FBI and the CIA.

After two and one-half years covering the administration, she concluded that its much-touted war on leakers had little to do with national security. In fact, she said, the chief architect of the leak-plugging campaign, former National Security Adviser William Clark, was well known as "one of the biggest leakers in the administration." "I can't help thinking that one thing Ronald Reagan wants to do is to make sure that no one writes a book on U.S. policy in Central America," she said.

Fritz admitted that the press made mistakes. Reagan's hair shows no hint of orange coloring, as the press has suggested, she said; in fact, it is rapidly turning gray. But journalistic inaccuracies hardly excuse or account for the administration's bent for secrecy. What enables the secrecy measures to be implemented, she continued, is the "attitude that the press is the enemy of the people." The president dislikes facts, she said, and his statements often require correction. If the press does not have access to factual information, then it cannot embarrass the president by correcting him. And if the press is intimidated from performing its function as critic of the government, democracy itself is jeopardized.

So it is not only the press that suffers from administration actions, Fritz concluded, as she urged reporters to fight back: "I think [the president] is tearing down the accountability of government, and that affects not just the press, but all of us."

The strength of the United States has been its openness, its willingness to look toward the future, its (now somewhat shaken) faith in progress. As a nation, we are committed to diversity and democracy. We have signed accords favoring the free exchange of ideas between nations. But it appears that as individuals and as a nation, we are suffering an attack of insecurity. Feeling beleaguered, we react with anger toward ideas we don't like and with suspicion toward those who differ from us. Parents trying to raise their children with strict moral codes attempt to censor the notions they find obnoxious rather than teach the young how to evaluate and reject those notions themselves. Administration officials, rather than publicly put forward their Central American policies and attitudes toward disarmament and the reasons for them, act in secret, labeling their critics advocates of a weaker America.

Many people are worried—about retribution from the government for honest speech, about covert action, about censorship, about the national security bureaucracy policing political activity, about the press. The convergence of forces hostile to free expression, free speech, and the public's right to know may be short-lived and its effects only temporary. But if that is not the case, the United States may become a very different place in which to live.

Notes

Bibliography

Index

Notes

INTRODUCTION

1. *Griswold v. Connecticut,* 381 U.S. 479 (1965).
2. Letter from James Madison to W. T. Barry, August 4, 1822, in *The Complete Madison* (Padover edition 1953), p. 337.
3. *Editor and Publisher,* February 27, 1982, p. 11 (remarks prepared for keynote address at 54th annual Georgia Press Institute in Athens, Ga., February 18).
4. Charles L. Heatherly, ed., *Mandate for Leadership: Policy Management in a Conservative Administration* (Washington, D.C.: The Heritage Foundation, 1981), p. 940.
5. Letter to Col. Edward Carrington, January 16, 1787, in Adrienne Koch and William Peden, eds., *The Life and Selected Writings of Thomas Jefferson* (New York: Modern Library, 1944), p. 411.
6. From the film "Liberty and Life: For All Who Believe," produced by People for the American Way, a project of Citizens for Constitutional Concerns, Inc., Washington, D.C., 1982.
7. Ibid.

CHAPTER 1. HISTORY

1. Zechariah Chafee, Jr., *Free Speech in the United States* (Cambridge, Mass.: 1964), p. 128.
2. Edwin S. Newman, *Civil Liberties and Civil Rights* (Dobbs Ferry, N.Y.: Oceana Publications, 1964), p. ii.
3. In 1922, for example, the U.S. Supreme Court denied citizenship to Takao Ozawa, who had been born in Japan but lived for twenty years in the U.S. The government opposed Ozawa's application, arguing before the court that "the men who settled this country were white men from Europe . . . it was to men of their own kind that they held out the opportunity for citizenship in the new nation," *The Ozawa Case,* 260 U.S. 178 (1922).
4. Milton R. Konvitz, "The Flower and the Thorn," in Alan Reitman, ed., *The Pulse of Freedom: American Liberties, 1920–1970s* (New York: Norton, 1975), p. 219.
5. Irving Brant, *The Bill of Rights: Its Origins and Meaning* (New York: New American Library, 1967), p. 224.
6. Nat Hentoff, *The First Freedom* (New York: Delacorte Press, 1980), p. 82.
7. Ibid., p. 91.
8. Brant, *The Bill of Rights,* p. 344.
9. Hentoff, *The First Freedom,* p. 129.

10. Ibid., p. 190.
11. Milton R. Konvitz, *Fundamental Liberties of a Free People* (Ithaca, N.Y.: Cornell University Press, 1957), p. 302.
12. Jerold S. Auerbach, "The Depression Decade," in Reitman, *The Pulse of Freedom,* p. 67.
13. Chafee, *Free Speech in the United States,* p. 446.
14. Ibid., p. 116.
15. Hentoff, *The First Freedom,* p. 140.
16. Franklyn S. Haiman, *Speech and Law in a Free Society* (Chicago: University of Chicago Press, 1981), p. 275.
17. Chafee, *Free Speech in the United States,* p. 490.
18. Konvitz, *Fundamental Liberties of a Free People,* p. 233.
19. Ibid., p. 116.
20. Ann Fagan Ginger, *The Law, the Supreme Court, and the People's Rights* (Woodbury, N.Y.: Barron's, 1977), p. 178.
21. *Griswold v. Connecticut,* 381 US. 479 (1965).
22. *Red Lion Broadcasting Co. v. Federal Communications Commission,* 395 U.S. 367 (1969).
23. Haiman, *Speech and Law in a Free Society,* p. 275.
24. Newman, *Civil Liberties,* sixth edition (Dobbs Ferry, N.Y.: Oceana Publications, 1979), p. 31.

CHAPTER 2. THE FEDERAL GOVERNMENT AS CENSOR

1. *New York Times,* July 31, 1980.
2. John H. F. Shattuck, "Tilting at the Surveillance Apparatus," *The Civil Liberties Review,* Summer 1974, p. 72. See also *U.S. v. Krogh,* 366 F. Supp. 1255 (D.D.C. 1973).
3. *TV Guide,* March 20, 1982.
4. Charles Peters, "What Has Happened to the American Public?" in Arnold J. Meltsner, ed., *Politics and the Oval Office: Towards Presidential Governance* (San Francisco: Institute for Contemporary Studies, 1981), p. 28.
5. *Washington Post,* January 24, 1982.
6. Michael Getler, "Administration Attempting to Stem Information Flow to a Trickle," *Washington Post,* June 6, 1981.
7. Ibid.
8. *Oakland Tribune,* May 4, 1981.
9. *New York Times,* March 17, 1982.
10. *Washington Post,* March 15, 1982.
11. James Goodale and Lawrence Martin, "Will They Classify Even the Alphabet?" *New York Times,* April 11, 1982.
12. *Washington Post,* March 19, 1982.
13. Ralph McGehee, *Deadly Deceits: My 25 Years in the CIA* (New York: Sheridan Square Publications, 1983), p. 196.
14. Ibid., p. 203.
15. U.S. Congress, House Committee on Government Operations, *Report: Security Classification Policy and Executive Order 12356,* 97th Congress, Second Session, 1982, p. 36; *Washington Post,* April 3, 1982.
16. *Washington Post,* August 10, 1982.
17. *New York Times,* January 14, 1983.
18. *Wall Street Journal,* April 29, 1983.

19. Report of the Interdepartmental on Unauthorized Disclosures of Classified Information, Department of Justice, March 31, 1982, pp. A-4, C-11.
20. *New York Times,* May 2, 1983.
21. Statement of Mark H. Lynch on behalf of the ACLU before the House Judiciary Subcommittee on Civil and Constitutional Rights and the Post Office and Civil Service Subcommittee on Civil Service on the Presidential Directive Requiring Prepublication Review, April 21, 1983, p. 3.
22. *New York Times,* October 20, 1983.
23. *Congressional Record,* March 24, 1983, p. S4054.
24. *The Quill,* March 1984, p. 9.
25. *Columbia Journalism Review,* March/April 1983, p. 24.
26. 5 U.S.C. 301.
27. Note to author.
28. John Anthony Scott, Address to the Annual Meeting of the American Historical Association, December 28, 1979, p. 1.
29. "A Citizen's Guide on How To Use the Freedom of Information Act and the Privacy Act in Requesting Government Documents." House Report No. 95–793, November 2, 1977. *Thirteenth Report* by the Committee on Government Operations, p. 2.
30. Scott, p. 2.
31. U.S. Congress, Senate Committee on the Judiciary, *Hearings: Freedom of Information Act,* Subcommittee on the Constitution, 97th Congress, First Session, 1982, vol. 1, p. 638.
32. Ibid., p. 578.
33. Ibid., pp. 971–972.
34. Ibid., pp. 545–546.
35. Ibid., p. 496.
36. Ibid., pp. 139–140.
37. James Mann, "Closing the Files on an Open Government," *Working Papers,* May 1982.
38. Note from Don Edwards to author.
39. *Village Voice,* May 11, 1982.
40. Interview with author.
41. *New York Times,* April 10, 1982.
42. Philip Kurland, Letter of September 25, 1980. *Congressional Record,* March 1, 1982, p. S1234; *The Nation,* March 14, 1981, p. 301.
43. Herman Schwartz, *The Nation,* July 3, 1982, p. 12.
44. *The Nation,* March 20, 1982, p. 324.
45. John Stockwell, *In These Times,* June 30–July 13, 1982, p. 17. "Walter Karp, "New Cloaks for the CIA," *Village Voice,* November 11, 1981.
46. Angus Mackenzie, "Darker Cloaks and Longer Daggers," *The Progressive,* June 1982.
47. Media Alliance Panel, September 21, 1982.
48. *Snepp v. U.S.,* 444 US. 507 (1980).
49. John Shattuck, "The Sorcerer's Apprentice: Civil Liberties and National Security a Decade after Watergate," typescript, Washington, D.C., October 1982, p. 30.
50. *Congressional Record,* April 22, 1980, p. E1920.
51. Ibid., p. E1921.
52. *New York Times,* June 11, 1982.
53. *Washington Star,* February 5, 1980.

54. *News Media and the Law,* February-March 1982.
55. Victor Navasky, *New York Times,* November 10, 1982.
56. Morton S. Halperin, *National Security and Civil Liberties: A Benchmark Report* (Washington, D.C.: Center for National Studies, 1981), p. 40.
57. Vannevar Bush, *Science, The Endless Frontier* (Washington, D.C.: National Science Foundation, 1980), pp. 11, 22. This work was first published in 1945.
58. *New York Times,* March 30, 1982.
59. Ibid.
60. U.S. Congress, Senate, Select Committee on Small Business, Subcommittee on Monopoly and Anticompetitive Activities, *Hearings: Government Patent Policies: Institutional Patent Agreements,* 95th Congress, Second Session, 1978, Part I, pp. 771–772.
61. U.S. Congress, House, Committee on Government Operations, *Report: The Government's Classification of Private Ideas,* 96th Congress, Second Session, 1980, p. 24.
62. *Science,* January 22, 1982, p. 383.
63. *United States v. Endler Industries,* 579 F2d 516 (9th Cir. 1978).
64. U.S. Department of Justice, Office of Legal Counsel. Memorandum for William B. Robinson, Office of Munitions Control, Department of State. Re: Constitutionality of the Proposed Revision of the Technical Data Provisions of the International Traffic in Arms Regulations. Undated and unpublished document.
65. John Walsh, "DoD Funds More Research in Universities," *Science,* May 29, 1981.
66. *Science,* January 8, 1982.
67. Ibid.
68. *San Francisco Chronicle,* December 22, 1982.
69. Christopher Paine, "Admiral Inman's Tidal Wave," *Bulletin of the Atomic Scientists,* March 1982, pp. 3–6.
70. *New York Times,* March 18, 1982.
71. Paine, p. 6.
72. Interview with author.
73. *Newsweek,* February 12, 1983.
74. Jim Sibbison, "Censorship at the New EPA," *The Nation,* September 11, 1982.
75. *Congressional Record,* August 20, 1982, pp. S11111, S11114.
76. *Washington Post,* November 9, 1982.
77. *Zemel v. Rusk* 381 U.S. 1 (1965).
78. *New York Times,* July 15, 1980.
79. Angel Rama, "Catch 28," *Index on Censorship,* April 1983, p. 9.
80. *Haig v. Agee,* 453 U.S. 280 (1981).
81. U.S. Congress, House Subcommittee on Census and Population, Committee on Post Office and Civil Service, *Hearings,* "Impact of Budget Cuts on Federal Statistical Programs," 97th Congress, Second Session, March 16, 1982.
82. U.S. Congress, *Hearings,* "Impact of Budget Cuts," p. 19.
83. *New York Times,* December 4, 1982
84. *Oakland Tribune,* February 5, 1982.
85. *Hearings,* "Impact of Budget Cuts," p. 111.
86. Schiller, Anita R. and Herbert I., "Who Can Own What America Knows?" *The Nation,* April 17, 1982.

87. Interview with author.
88. Interview with author.

CHAPTER 3. CENSORSHIP IN SCHOOLS, LIBRARIES, AND BUSINESS

1. The story of *Ms.* magazine and Contra Costa County is based on interviews with Carolyne Benning and Ernest Wutzke and a very brief talk with Mrs. Marlys Tash. Other librarians, as well as minutes of meetings and newspaper accounts, provided further information.
2. Interviews with Jean Dickinson, Carolyne Benning, and school board member Sherry Sterrett.
3. The story of the June 26 meeting is based on interviews with Sherry Sterrett, Dennis McCormac, and Zoia Horn, as well as minutes of meetings and newspaper accounts.
4. *Contra Costa Times,* July 31, 1980.
5. Interview with author.
6. For an excellent history of school censorship, see Jack Nelson and Gene Roberts, *The Censors and the Schools* (Boston: Little, Brown, 1963). Much of what follows has been taken from that source.
7. Ibid., p. 129.
8. Press release from National Council of Teachers of English in Convention at Washington, D.C., November 20, 1982.
9. Barbara Parker, "Target: Public Schools," *The Graduate Woman,* September/October 1981. Washington, D.C.: American Association of University Women, p. 11; "Censors vs. Reality," editorial in the *Los Angeles Times,* February 22, 1982.
10. Association of American Publishers, American Library Association, Association for Supervision and Curriculum Development, *Limiting What Students Shall Read,* Washington, D.C., 1981. See "Findings," pp. 9–13.
11. Ibid., p. 11.
12. Ibid., p. 12.
13. Letter from Gene Friese, Director of Learning Resources at Highline School District, Seattle, Washington, to Washington ACLU.
14. William Trombley, "Educators Fear Rising Tide of Textbook Censorship," *Los Angeles Times,* February 14, 1982.
15. "Life and Liberty: For All Who Believe," film produced by People for the American Way, Washington, D.C., 1982.
16. *Brooklyn Tablet,* April 25, 1981.
17. "Censorship News," No. 9, March 1982. Published by the National Coalition vs. Censorship.
18. Morton Hunt, "Self-Appointed Censors: The New Threat to Our Schools," *Families,* February 1982.
19. Frances FitzGerald, "A Disciplined, Charging Army," *The New Yorker,* May 18, 1981.
20. Moral Majority fund-raising letter, January 1, 1981.
21. Jerry Falwell, "Liberals Guilty of Book Censorship," *Moral Majority Report,* March 1983.
22. "Citizens' Bill of Rights About Schools and Libraries," *The Phyllis Schlafly Report,* February 1983.
23. Barbara Morris, "Schools' End Best for U.S.," *National Educator,* July 1977, p. 1.

24. Barbara Parker, "IMPACT, bell, book and candle," *San Francisco Examiner,* October 14, 1982, and James Kinsella, "Book banning on the rise," *California Lawyer,* February 1983.
25. *Handbook Number One, Humanism* (Longview, Texas: Educational Research Analysts, June 1981).
26. *As Texas Goes, So Goes the Nation: A Report on Textbook Selection in Texas,* Appendix D (Washington, D.C.: People for the American Way, 1983).
27. Ibid., Appendix C.
28. Hunt, p. 32.
29. *The Franklin Journal* (Indiana), August 4, 1981.
30. Barbara Parker, "Target: Public Schools," *The Graduate Woman,* September/October 1981. Washington, D.C.: American Association of University Women.
31. Alex Heard, "Attention to Evolution in Textbooks Decreasing, Study Says," *Education Week,* October 20, 1982.
32. *New York Times,* June 24, 1982.
33. Barbara Parker, "They Censor Their Own Books," *Washington Post,* August 28, 1982.
34. *Los Angeles Times,* February 14, 1982.
35. *As Texas Goes, So Goes the Nation: A Report on Textbook Selection in Texas,* Appendix F (Washington, D.C.: People for the American Way), 1983.
36. Gerald Skoog, "The Coverage of Evolution in High School Biology Textbooks Published in the 1980s," *Science Education,* April 1984, p. 121.
37. *As Texas Goes, So Goes the Nation,* Appendix F.
38. Marvin Perry, "Banning a Textbook," *New York Times,* May 31, 1981.
39. Julia Malone, "Creationists' New Doubt Seen in Biology Texts," *Christian Science Monitor,* December 10, 1981, p. 70.
40. Charles Wynn and Arthur Wiggins, *Natural Sciences: Bridging the Gap* (Minneapolis: Burgess Publishing Company, 1981), p. 129.
41. Nat Hentoff, "Is Any Book Worth the Humiliation of Our Kids?" *Village Voice,* May 17, 1982.
42. *Sipapu* (newspaper for librarians), vol. 13, no. 2 (Winters, California), 1983.
43. Dena Kleiman, "Influential Couple Sanitizes Books for Anti-Americanism," *New York Times,* July 14, 1981.
44. Nat Hentoff, "Huck Finn Better Get Out of Town by Sundown," *Village Voice,* May 4, 1982.
45. William A. Stanmeyer, "Obscene Evils vs. Obscure Truths: Some Notes on First Principles," *Capital University Law Review* (1978), p. 647.
46. Valerie Miner, "Fantasies and Nightmares," *Jump Cut* (December 1984), p. 48.
47. Helen E. Longino, "Pornography, Oppression, and Freedom: A Closer Look," in Laura Lederer, ed., *Take Back the Night: Women on Pornography* (New York: Morrow, 1980).
48. Ibid., p. 51.
49. Stanmeyer, pp. 664, 673.
50. *Village Voice,* August 17, 1982.
51. Aryeh Neier, "Expurgating the First Amendment," *The Nation,* June 21, 1980.

52. California State Department of Education, *Standards for Evaluation of Instructional Materials with Respect to Social Content,* Sacramento, California, 1982, p. 50.
53. Ibid., p. 11.
54. Texas Textbook Proclamation, no. 58, section 1.5(2), 1.5(4), 1.9, 1.9(1), 1982.
55. *New York Times,* August 3, 1983.
56. Letter from Raymon L. Bymun, Texas Commissioner of Education, to Robert D. Fitzgerald of Allyn and Bacon, February 11, 1983.
57. Gene I. Maeroff, "Texas Textbook Choices Prompt Wide Concern," *New York Times,* August 15, 1982.
58. Texas Education Agency, 1983 *Textbook Adoption Changes and Corrections Requested of Publishers, Health Education,* grades 4–8, pp. 9, 10.
59. Texas Education Agency, 1982 *Textbook Adoption Changes and Corrections Requested of Publishers,* p. 35.
60. *Tinker v. Des Moines Independent Community School District,* 393 U.S. 503 (1969).
61. *President's Council, District 25 v. Community School Board No. 25 (New York City),* 409 U.S. 998 (1972).
62. *Minarcini v. Strongsville (Ohio) City School District,* 541 F2d 577 (6th Cir. 1976).
63. *Right to Read Defense Committee v. School Committee of the City of Chelsea,* 454 F. Supp. 703 (D. Mass. 1978).
64. *Bicknell v. Vergennes Union High School Board,* 475 F. Supp. 615 (D. Ut. 1979); 638 F2d 438 (2d. Cir 1980).
65. *Loewen v. Turnipseed,* 488 F. Supp 1138 (N.D. Miss. 1980).
66. *Board of Education, Island Trees Union Free School District No. 26 et al., v. Pico, et al.,* 454 U.S. 891, 73 L Ed. 2d 435, pp. 449, 450.
67. Jim Mann, "Court to Decide if School Boards May Ban Books," *Los Angeles Times,* October 14, 1981.
68. *Board of Education v. Pico,* 73 L. Ed. 2d, pp. 449–450.
69. Ibid., p. 464.
70. Interview with author.
71. *Time,* August 23, 1982.
72. Press Conference, Austin, Texas, July 30, 1982.
73. *Time,* August 23, 1982.
74. Interview with author.
75. Ibid.
76. Interview with author.
77. The story of Paul Maccabee, Kool, and the *Twin Cities Reader* is based on articles in the *Twin Cities Reader,* April 8, 1982; the *Minnesota Daily,* April 13, 1982; and the *Wall Street Journal,* November 22, 1982, and an interview with Dr. Paul Magnus on June 1, 1982.
78. Elizabeth M. Whelan, Margaret J. Sheridan, Kathleen A. Meister, Beverly A. Mosher, "Analysis of Coverage of Tobacco Hazards in Women's Magazines," *Journal of Public Health Policy,* March 1981, p. 35. The story of *Death in the West* is based on interviews with Dr. Paul Magnus, Dr. Stanton Glantz, and KRON news director Mike Fehring, and on Adam Hochschild, "Shoot-Out in Marlboro Country," *Mother Jones,* January 1979.
79. *Wall Street Journal,* November 22, 1982.
80. Whelan et al.

81. Ibid.
82. Robert Sherrill, "The Book That Du Pont Hated," *The Nation,* February 14, 1981.
83. Ibid., p. 174.
84. Gerard Colby Zilg, *Du Pont: Behind the Nylon Curtain* (Englewood Cliffs, N.J.: Prentice-Hall, 1974), p. 311.
85. Sherrill p. 174.
86. Ibid., p. 174.
87. Ibid., p. 175.
88. Ibid., pp. 175–176.
89. *Gerard Colby Zilg v. Prentice-Hall, Inc. and E. I. Du Pont De Nemours & Co., Inc.,* Southern District Court of New York, Docket No. 78-CIV0130-CLB.
90. *Gerard Colby Zilg v. Prentice-Hall, Inc. and E. I. Du Pont De Nemours & Co., Inc.,* N.S. Court of Appeals, 2d Cir. No. 620, Docket Nos. 82-7335, 88-7425.

CHAPTER 4. LIBEL

1. *New York Times v. Sullivan,* 376 U.S. 254 (1964).
2. *Washington Post,* November 30, 1977.
3. Anthony Lewis, "New York Times v. Sullivan Reconsidered: Time to Return to the Central Meaning of the First Amendment," *Columbia Law Review,* 83 (1983), p. 619.
4. James C. Goodale, "Tavoulareas and the *Washington Post:* Getting Even with the Press," typescript, 1982, p. 17.
5. *Hutchinson v. Proxmire,* 443 U.S. 111 (1979).
6. *Time, Inc. v. Firestone,* 424 U.S. 448 (1976).
7. *Herbert v. Lando,* 441 U.S. 153 (1979).
8. Lyle Denniston, "When the Press Cops a Plea," *Washington Journalism Review,* April 1982, p. 54.
9. *Libel Defense Resource Center Bulletin,* "Defamation Trials and Damage Awards," August 15, 1982, p. 3.
10. *Hutchinson v. Proxmire,* 120, n. 9.
11. "Summary Judgment in Libel Litigation: Assessing the Impact of *Hutchinson v. Proxmire,*" *Libel Defense Resource Center Bulletin,* No. 4 (Part 2), October 15, 1982, p. 3.
12. Joseph R. Tybor, "The Libel War Escalates," *National Law Journal,* April 21, 1980.
13. *New York Times,* January 14, 1983.
14. The National News Council, "UPI against Synanon Foundation, Inc." Filed November 21, 1979, p. 1.
15. *Los Angeles Times,* July 3, 1982.
16. National News Council Report, "United Press International against Synanon Foundation, Inc.," November 21, 1979, p. 16.
17. Ibid., p. 18.
18. Ibid.
19. Ibid., p. 19.
20. Ibid., p. 29.
21. Interview with author.
22. *Newsweek,* November 20, 1978.

23. James C. Goodale, "Tavoulareas and the *Washington Post*—Getting Even with the Press," typescript sent to author, p. 16.
24. *Business Week,* June 14, 1982.
25. Denniston, p. 54.
26. Goodale, p. 9.
27. *New York Times,* November 4, 1982.
28. Ibid.
29. Lewis, p. 613.
30. Memorandum from Ira Glasser to ACLU Board of Directors on revision of libel policy, October 7, 1982, p. 3.
31. Thomas I. Emerson, *The System of Freedom of Expression* (New York: Vintage Books, 1971), p. 530.
32. From ACLU Policy on Libel #6, passed October 1982 and January 1983.
33. Goodale, pp. 21–22.
34. Interview with author.
35. *Phillips v. Freed et al.* No. 81–1407; *Phillips v. Hill & Co. Publishers, Inc., et al.* Civil Action No. 81–2578. U.S. District Court for the District of Columbia Civil Division. Complaint *Death in Washington.*
36. Circuit Court of Montgomery County, Maryland. Law No. 57691.
37. Interview with author.
38. Interview with author.
39. *Publishers Weekly,* June 17, 1983.
40. *Bindrim v. Doubleday and Company, Inc.,* 444 U.S. 984 (1979).
41. *Los Angeles Times,* January 2, 1978.
42. William Safire, "My Way," *New York Times,* October 13, 1983.
43. Interview with author.
44. *William D. Nugent and Galleon Properties, Inc. v. Pat Haworth, Does One Through Fifty,* Superior Court, County of Santa Cruz, No. 74598.
45. Superior Court of San Francisco No. 745–811. Filed November 1978.
46. *Telford L. Smith v. Tim Jenkins,* Superior Court of California, County of Santa Cruz, No. 66556.
47. Interview with author.
48. Interview with author.
49. Raymond Greunich interview with author.
50. *Okun v. Superior Court,* 29 Cal. 3d 442 (1981).
51. Interview with author.
52. Ibid.
53. *Webb v. Fury,* 282 S.E. 2nd (1981).
54. Interview with author.
55. *Webb v. Fury.*
56. *Haddad v. Ernest Newman et al.,* Monterey Superior Court, No. 10819. Filed November 20, 1980.
57. Interview with author.
58. *John Sununu v. Clamshell Alliance,* New Hampshire Supreme Court. Docket 81–188.
59. *Long Island Lighting Co. v. Shad Alliance,* No. 80–17, 792. New York Superior Court. Filed September 18, 1980.
60. Interview with author.
61. Gordon J. Johnson, "The Case Against LILCO" in *Bill of Rights Journal,* published in New York by the National Emergency Civil Rights Committee, December 1982.

62. *County of San Luis Obispo, Consumer Alert, et al. v. Abalone Alliance, Greenpeace Foundation et al.,* Superior Court of California, County of San Luis Obispo, Docket No. 55664.
63. Interview with author.
64. *Levin and Mathis v. Ana and Ramon Serrano,* Docket No. 784097, Superior Court of California, City and County of San Francisco.
65. "Police Sue to Silence Detractors," *National Law Journal,* June 9, 1980.
66. Serrano interview with author.
67. Interview with author.
68. Interview with author.
69. Interview with author.
70. The cases are *Levin and Mathis v. Ana and Ramon Serrano* (already cited); *Falzon v. Schell,* Superior Court of San Francisco, No. 785792; *Holly C. Pera and Corbett Dickey v. Bay Area Reporter et al.,* Superior Court, City and County of San Francisco, No. 782616; and *San Francisco Police Association v. NAACP and Bayview-Hunters Point Foundation,* Superior Court of San Francisco, No. 745-811.
71. Interview with author.

CHAPTER 5. SUPPRESSION OF DISSENT

1. Interview with author.
2. " 'The Terrorist Threat' as an Excuse for Curtailing Civil Liberties," a talk given by Kathy Engel before the National Network of Grantmakers, September 23, 1981, p. 2.
3. Samuel T. Francis, "Leftists Mount Attack on Investigatory Panel," *Human Events,* July 17, 1981, p. 12.
4. Victor Navasky, "The New Boys on Terrorism," *San Francisco Chronicle,* February 14, 1981.
5. Jeff Kisseloff, "Welcome to Hard Times," *Rights,* April-June 1981, p. 5.
6. U.S. Congress, Senate, Committee on the Judiciary, Subcommittee on Security and Terrorism, *Hearings: The Domestic Security Investigation Guidelines,* 97th Congress, Second Session, 1982, p. 12.
7. Ibid., p. 3.
8. Ibid., p. 36.
9. Ibid., p. 80.
10. Remarks by Senator Jeremiah Denton before the Senate Subcommittee on Security and Terrorism, March 25, 1983.
11. U.S. Congress, Senate, *Hearings: The Domestic Security Investigation Guidelines,* p. 207.
12. Frank Donner, "But Will They Come," *The Nation,* November 6, 1982.
13. Ellen Ray and William Preston, *Our Right to Know* (New York: Fund for Open Information and Accountability, 1983).
14. *Congressional Record,* September 29, 1982, p. S12509.
15. Ira Glasser, Letter to the Editor, *Washington Post,* October 9, 1982.
16. *Organizing Notes,* November-December 1982, p. 3. The periodical is published by the Campaign for Political Rights, Washington, D.C.
17. Nat Hentoff, "The Passionate Congressman and the Wayward Press," *Village Voice,* December 14, 1982.
18. Ronald Reagan, Oval Office Press Conference, December 10, 1982.
19. *Organizing Notes,* January-February 1983, p. 8.

20. Jay Peterzell, "Reagan, Denton and the Freeze," *First Principles* (Washington, D.C.: Center for National Security Studies, November-December 1982).
21. *Congressional Record,* September 29, 1982, S12509.
22. U.S. Congress, House, Select Committee on Intelligence, *Hearings,* July 14, 1982, quoted in *Village Voice,* December 21, 1982.
23. *Village Voice,* December 21, 1982.
24. Michael Ratner, "Reagan to Unleash FBI and CIA," in *No More Witch Hunts: Tools for Resistance: A Manual for Protecting Civil Liberties in the 80's,* published by Fund for Open Information and Accountability, Inc., New York, 1981, p. 6.
25. Quoted by David Sobel, "FBI Given Broader 'Domestic Security' Powers," *Organizing Notes,* April-May 1983, p. 3.
26. *Halkin v. Helms,* 690 F 2d 977 (1982).
27. *Gardels v. C.I.A.,* CADC, 689 F 2d 1100 (1982).
28. *Jabara v. Webster,* CA Mich, 691 F 2d 272 (1982).
29. David Burnham, *The Rise of the Computer State* (New York: Random House, 1982), p. 133.
30. *Blitz v. Donovan,* 538 F Supp 1119 (1982).
31. Letter from Dr. Bailus Walker to Dr. Peter Infante.
32. Letter of April 21, 1982, from Joel R. Bender, M.D., Medical Committee Chairman, The Formaldehyde Institute, to Mary Martha McNamara.
33. Letter of June 2, 1981, from S. John Byington of Rogers, Hoge and Hills, Washington, D.C., to Mark Cowan of OSHA.
34. U.S. Congress, House, "Proposed Firing of Dr. Peter Infante by OSHA: A Case Study in Science and Regulation," Hearing before the Subcommittee on Investigations and Oversight of the Committee on Science and Technology, U.S. House of Representatives, 97th Congress, 1st Session, July 16, 1981.
35. Ibid., pp. 69, 78–80.
36. Seth Rosenfeld interview with David Vladeck.
37. Richard Viguerie, "We Must End Federal Aid to the Left," *Conservative Digest,* April 1982.
38. *Wall Street Journal,* January 26, 1983.
39. Richard Goldstein, "No Politics Please, We're Funded," *Village Voice,* February 15, 1983.
40. "Stockman Walks Away from It," *San Francisco Chronicle,* March 14, 1983.
41. *San Francisco Chronicle,* March 11, 1983.
42. *Columbia Journalism Review,* November-December 1981, p. 31.
43. *Big Mama Rag, Inc. v. United States,* 494 F. Supp 473 (District Court, District of Columbia, 1979). Reversed and Remanded: 671 F 2d 1030 (Court of Appeals, District of Columbia, 1980).
44. *National Alliance v. U.S.,* 81-1 USTC 9464. Reversed and Remanded: 710 F 2d 868, District of Columbia Circuit Court, 1983.
45. Francis J. Flaherty, "A Tax on Dissidents?" *The Progressive,* June 1983.
46. Ibid.
47. Interview with author.
48. Charles Heatherley, ed., *Mandate for Leadership* (Washington, D.C.: Heritage Foundation, 1981), p. 935.
49. Interview with author.
50. Steve Volk, "NACLA vs. the IRS, A Taxing Victory," *NACLA Report on the Americas,* July-August 1982, p. 4.
51. Ibid., p. 41.

52. Interview with author.
53. Interview with author.
54. *Baltimore Evening Sun,* November 26, 1982.
55. Interview with author.
56. Letter from Angus Wright to Deirdre English, December 17, 1982.
57. Interview with author.
58. Interview with author.
59. Transcript, U.S. Congress, House, Committee on Government Operations, Subcommittee on Commerce, Consumer and Monetary Affairs, *Hearing: IRS Oversight of Tax-Exempt Foundations,* 98th Congress, First Session, May 11, 1983, pp. 211–212.
60. Interview with author.
61. *Keene v. Smith and Clarkson,* U.S. District Court for the Eastern District of California, CIVS-83-287, p. 19.
62. American Legal Foundation, Petition to Deny License Renewal to Pacifica Foundation's WPFW, submitted to Federal Communications Commission, September 1, 1981, File 3 BRH-810601 VX.
63. *National Enquirer,* January 27, 1981.
64. *A.I.M. Report,* October 11, 1980.
65. *National Enquirer,* January 27, 1981.
66. *New York Times,* May 18, 1983.
67. Interview with author.

Bibliography

BOOKS AND ARTICLES

"ACLU vs. the First Amendment." *National Review,* December 14, 1979.

American Library Association. Conference on Intellectual Freedom, Washington, D.C. 1965. *Freedom of Inquiry; Supporting the Library Bill of Rights.* Proceedings. Chicago. ALA, 1965.

American Library Association, Office for Intellectual Freedom. *Censorship Litigation and the Schools.* 1981.

Anastaplo, George. *The Constitutionalist: Notes on the First Amendment.* Dallas: Southern Methodist University Press, 1971.

Bayley, Edwin R. *Joe McCarthy and the Press.* Madison: University of Wisconsin Press, 1981.

Belfrage, Cedric. *The American Inquisition, 1945–1960.* Indianapolis: Bobbs-Merrill, 1973.

Bell, Daniel, ed. *The Radical Right.* Garden City, N.Y.: Doubleday, 1963.

Berns, Walter Fred. *The First Amendment and the Future of American Democracy.* New York: Basic Books, 1976.

Brant, Irving. *The Bill of Rights: Its Origins and Meaning.* New York: New American Library, Inc., 1967.

Caughey, John W. *In Clear and Present Danger: The Crucial State of Our Freedoms.* Chicago: University of Chicago Press, 1958.

Center Magazine, March-April, 1979.

Chafee, Zechariah, Jr. *Free Speech in the United States.* Cambridge, Mass.: Harvard University Press, 1964.

Commager, Henry Steele. *Freedom, Loyalty and Dissent.* New York: Oxford University Press, 1954.

Commager, Henry Steele; Carr, Robert K.; Chafee, Jr., Zechariah; Gellhorn, Walter; Bok, Curtis; and Baxter III, James P. *Civil Liberties under Attack.* Freeport, N.Y.: Books for Libraries Press, 1951. Reprinted 1968 by arrangement with Univ. of Pennsylvania Press.

Cowan, Paul; Egleson, Nick; and Hentoff, Nat. *State Secrets.* New York: Holt, Rinehart & Winston, 1974.

Cox, Archibald. *Freedom of Expression.* Cambridge, Mass.: Harvard University Press, 1981.

Donner, Frank J. *The Age of Surveillance: The Aims and Methods of America's Political Intelligence System.* New York: Vintage Books, 1981.

Dorsen, Norman. *The Rights of Americans: What They Are and What They Should Be.* New York: Pantheon Press, 1970.

Emerson, Thomas I. *Toward a General Theory of the First Amendment*. New York: Random House, 1966.
Emerson, Thomas I.; Haber, David; and Dorsen, Norman. *Political and Civil Rights in the United States*. Boston: Little, Brown, 1976.
Feuerlicht, Roberta S. *Joe McCarthy and McCarthyism: The Hate That Haunts America*. New York: McGraw-Hill, 1972.
Ginger, Ann Fagan. *The Law, the Supreme Court, and the People's Rights*. Woodbury, N.Y.: Barron's, 1977.
Goodale, James C. "Tavoulareas and the Washington Post: Getting Even with the Press." Typescript, New York, 1982.
Griffith, Robert. *The Politics of Fear: Joseph R. McCarthy and the Senate*. Lexington: University Press of Kentucky, 1970.
Haiman, Franklyn S. *Speech and Law in a Free Society*. Chicago: University of Chicago Press, 1981.
Halperin, Morton, and Hoffman, Daniel. *Top Secret: National Security and the Right to Know*. Washington, D.C.: New Republic Books, 1977.
Heatherly, Charles, ed. *Mandate for Leadership: Policy Management in a Conservative Administration*. Washington, D.C.: The Heritage Foundation, 1981.
Hentoff, Nat. *The First Freedom*. New York: Delacorte Press, 1980.
Hudon, Edward G. *Freedom of Speech and Press in America*. Washington, D.C.: Public Affairs Press, 1963.
Jaffe, Susan. "Legal Showdown at Shoreham." *The Nation,* March 21, 1981.
Kamper, Paul G. *Civil Liberties and the Constitution*. Ann Arbor: University of Michigan Press, 1962.
Konvitz, Milton R. *First Amendment Freedoms: Selected Cases on Freedom of Religion, Speech, Press, Assembly*. Ithaca, N.Y.: Cornell University Press, 1963.
———. *Fundamental Liberties of a Free People*. Ithaca, N.Y.: Cornell University Press, 1957.
Kupferberg, Seth. "Libel Fever." *Columbia Journalism Review*. Sept.-Oct. 1981.
Lewis, Anthony. "New York Times v. Sullivan Reconsidered: Time to Return to the Central Meaning of the First Amendment." *Columbia Law Review,* 83 (1983): 619.
Lipset, Seymour M., and Raab, Earl. *The Politics of Unreason*. New York: Harper and Row, 1970.
Mackenzie, Angus. "When Auditors Turn Editors." *Columbia Journalism Review,* Nov.-Dec. 1981.
McGraw, Onalee. "Censorship and the Public Schools: Who Decides What Students Will Read." *American Education,* December 1982.
McGuigan, Patrick B., and Rader, Randall R., eds. *A Blueprint for Judicial Reform*. Washington, D.C.: Free Congress Research and Education Foundation, 1981.
McWilliams, Carey. *Witch Hunt: The Revival of Heresy*. Boston: Little, Brown, 1950.
Marnell, William H. *The Right to Know*. New York: Seabury Press, 1973.
Meiklejohn, Alexander. *Free Speech and Its Relation to Self-Government*. New York: Harper & Bros., 1948.
Meltsner, Arnold J., ed. *Politics and the Oval Office: Towards Presidential Governance*. San Francisco, Calif.: Institute for Contemporary Studies, 1981.
National Academy of Science. *Scientific Communication and National Security*. Washington, D.C.: National Academy Press, 1982
National Education Association. *Kanawha County, West Virginia: A Textbook*

Study in Cultural Conflict. Washington, D.C.: National Education Association, 1975.
Neier, Aryeh. "Expurgating the First Amendment." *The Nation,* June 21, 1980.
Nelson, Jack, and Roberts, Gene. *The Censors and the Schools*. Boston: Little, Brown, 1963.
Newman, Edwin S. *Civil Liberty and Civil Rights*. Dobbs Ferry, N.Y.: Oceana Publications, 1964 and 1979.
Parker, Barbara. "Target: Public Schools." *The Graduate Woman,* Sept.-Oct. 1981.
Reitman, Alan, ed. *The Pulse of Freedom: American Liberties, 1920–1970s*. New York: W. W. Norton, 1975.
Roche, John P. *The Quest for the Dream: The Development of Civil Rights and Human Relations in Modern America*. New York: Macmillan, 1963.
Root, E. Merrill. *Brainwashing in the High Schools*. New York: Devin-Adair, 1958.
———. *Collectivism on the Campus*. New York: Devin-Adair, 1954.
Rovere, Richard H. *Senator Joe McCarthy*. New York: Harcourt Brace and World, 1959.
Schwartz, Bernard. *Rights of the Person*. New York: Macmillan, 1968.
Sherrill, Robert. "The Book That Du Pont Hated." *The Nation,* February 14, 1981.
Spinrad, William. *Civil Liberties*. Chicago: Quadrangle Books, 1970.
Stanmeyer, William A. "Obscene Evils v. Obscure Truths: Some Notes on First Principles." *Capital University Law Review,* 7 (1978): 647.
Wynn, Charles, and Arthur Wiggins. *Natural Sciences: Bridging the Gap*. Minneapolis: Burgess Publishing Company, 1981.
Zilg, Gerard Colby. *Du Pont: Behind the Nylon Curtain*. Englewood Cliffs, New Jersey: Prentice-Hall, 1974.

GOVERNMENT PUBLICATIONS

U.S. Congress. House. Committee on Government Operations. Subcommittee on Government Information and Individual Rights. *Hearings: Executive Order on Security Classification*. 97th Congress, Second Session, 1982.
———. House. Committee on Government Operations. Subcommittee on Government Information and Individual Rights. *Hearings: Freedom of Information Act Oversight*. 97th Congress, First Session, 1981.
———. House. Committee on Government Operations. *Hearings: Executive Order on Security Classification*. 97th Congress, Second Session, 1982.
———. House. Committee on Government Operations. *Report: Security Classification Policy and Executive Order 12356*. 97th Congress, Second Session, 1982.
———. House. Committee on Government Operations. *Report: The Government's Classification of Private Ideas*. 96th Congress, Second Session, 1980.
———. House. Committee on Government Operations. *Hearings: The Government's Classification of Private Ideas*. 96th Congress, Second Session, 1980.
U.S. Congress. Senate. Committee on the Judiciary. Subcommittee on the Constitution. *Hearings: Freedom of Information Act*. 97th Congress, First Session, 1981.
———. Senate. Committee on the Judiciary. Subcommittee on Security and Terrorism. *Hearings: The Role of Cuba in International Terrorism and Subversion*. 97th Congress, Second Session, 1982.

Department of Defense. *Handbook for Writing Security Classification Guidance.* (DoD 5200.1-H.) October 1980.

———. *Report of the Defense Science Task Force on University Responsiveness to National Security Requirements.* January 1982.

General Services Administration, Information Security Oversight Office. *Report.* 1980–81.

Interagency Classification Review Committee. *Progress Report: To Strike a Balance.* 1977.

Index

Eve Pell has written scores of news and feature articles for *The Nation, New West, In These Times, Politicks, The San Francisco Examiner,* and many other publications. Pell is editor of *Maximum Security,* a book of letters by convicts who describe conditions in California's toughest prisons, and coauthor of *To Serve the Devil,* a two-volume history of ethnic groups in the United States.